D1188568

OTHER BOOKS BY *Patrick Granfield*

Theologians at Work
  (New York: Macmillan, 1967).

Kyriakon—Festschrift Johannes Quasten,
  2 vols., edited with Josef A. Jungmann
  (Münster: Aschendorff, 1970).

ECCLESIAL CYBERNETICS

ECCLESIAL CYBERNETICS

A Study of Democracy in the Church

PATRICK GRANFIELD

The Macmillan Company • New York, New York

Collier-Macmillan Publishers • London

To My Father and Mother

The Macmillan Company
866 Third Avenue, New York, N.Y. 10022
Collier-Macmillan Canada Ltd., Toronto, Ontario

Library of Congress Catalog Card Numbers 72-87158

FIRST PRINTING

PRINTED IN THE UNITED STATES OF AMERICA

Contents

Preface

MANKIND TODAY is experiencing a hectic period of transition. The twentieth century is the middle ground on the road to a radically new way of life. Christians are keenly aware of this transitional phase. Vatican II spoke of "a new age in human history." Other formulations were more specific: John Courtney Murray referred to "postmodernity"; Kenneth Boulding, to "post-civilization"; and Bishop Robinson, to "post-Christianity." This transition, for many Christians who are facing a changing Church in a changing world, is in the phrase of Alvin Toffler, an experience of "future shock."

Religious change parallels the changes in the rest of society. A fundamental change in both areas has been the unprecedented increase in communication. People are able to learn more about one another and the world at large than ever before. So significant is the increase in information that cybernetics, the science of communication and control, has been developed to enable man to understand the all-pervasive role of information. Norbert Wiener marks the beginning of the Second Industrial Revolution with the production of the computer; and, most properly, he calls this time of intensified informational exchange "the Cybernetic Age."

Even for the Church, the problems of a cybernetic age need cybernetic solutions. It is for this reason that I have called this book *Ecclesial Cybernetics*. I first used the term "ecclesial cybernetics" in an article which appeared in *Theological Studies* in December 1968. I believed then, and I have become more convinced in subsequent years, that an understanding of the problem of communication and control in the Church is basic to its future maintenance and development. The thesis of the book is that the Church needs cybernetic reform through democratization. The inspiration for this position is twofold: first, the contemporary democratic experience with its stress on participation in decision-making and on the co-responsibility of all citizens for the common good; and second, the vision of the Church suggested by Vatican II with its principles of liberty and collegiality and its recognition of the charismatic role of all members of the Body of Christ. This book asks the question: Can some form of participatory democracy, if cybernetically sound and theologically justified, be used to help the Church through this period of crisis to a new age of Christian consciousness and community?

Ecclesial Cybernetics answers this question tentatively, but positively. Part One is an analysis of the Church in terms of its cybernetic elements and its organizational unity. Part Two illustrates how this organizational unit has operated in four crucial controversies: slavery, birth control, ecumenism, and priestly celibacy. Part Three examines the historical precedents and theological justifications for a greater, although possibly limited, participation by clergy and laity in ecclesial decision-making. Lastly, Part Four, looking to the future, assesses the need, the problem areas, and the techniques of democratization in the Church.

The *New English Bible* is the main source of the scriptural quotations used throughout the book.

Finally, I express my gratitude to the many persons who helped me at various stages of the book. A special word of thanks goes to my brother, David, for his constructive ideas, editorial skills, and constant encouragement. My thanks also to Professors John Quasten, Charles E. Curran, and Peter J.

Kearney of The Catholic University of America for reading parts of the manuscript and contributing many useful suggestions; to Professor James A. Coriden of the University for his help on some canonical matters; to Rev. Joseph T. Merkt, graduate student at the University, for his valuable research assistance; to Miss Carolyn Lee and Mr. David Gilson of the library staff at the University for their help; to Mrs. Edward Malloy for carefully typing the manuscript; and to all others who have helped in innumerable ways.

PATRICK GRANFIELD

Washington, D. C.
November 1, 1972

PART ONE

A Cybernetic Analysis
of the Church

WHEN ST. PAUL CALLED "the power of governing" a special gift of the Spirit for the building up of the Church[1] and when Plato, centuries earlier, referred to the arts of the statesman in civil society,[2] both used cognates of the popular modern term *cybernetics*. The basic Greek word, *kubernetes*, means "steersman." The Latin *gubernator* derives from the Greek and leads to the English word "governor." The use of the term *ecclesial cybernetics* to describe Church government would not seem strange to St. Paul. In fact, he might not be surprised to learn that the recently developed science of cybernetics is today essential for a thorough understanding of the modern Church.

The French scientist André Ampère coined the word cybernetics, but it was Norbert Wiener who gave it its current meaning.[3] Focusing on the role of the steersman, he defined cybernetics as the study of the regulation of goal-oriented

---

[1] I *Cor.* 12:28.

[2] Plato, *Republic*, VI, 488 d, and *Euthydemus*, 291, c, d. Pindar (*Pythian Odes*, 5,164) was perhaps the first to use what became traditional among the Greeks—the deity as the one who steers or rules the universe.

[3] *Cybernetics* (New York: John Wiley, 1949), p. 19.

I

behavior. In a seminal paper, Wiener, Rosenblueth, and Bigelow used the term *servomechanism* for machines with "intrinsic purposeful behavior"[4] and limited the term cybernetics to the transmission of messages directing the comportment of a mechanism. But the concept expanded swiftly. Wiener later wrote: "It is the purpose of cybernetics to develop a language and techniques that will enable us to attack the problem of control and communication in general, but also to find the proper repertory of ideas and techniques to classify their particular manifestations under certain concepts."[5] Through the pioneering efforts of those just mentioned, as well as others like Claude E. Shannon, Warren Weaver, W. Ross Ashby, and John von Neumann, cybernetics made immense progress. Soon it moved from strict technology to biology and the social sciences. David Easton and Karl W. Deutsch have skillfully applied cybernetics to political life.[6] A cybernetic analysis of the Church, therefore, is a normal and predictable development, and a necessary one as well, if the Church is to manifest in its operation the fullness of prudence which Aquinas calls the proper virtue of the ruler.

[4] A. Rosenblueth, N. Wiener, and J. Bigelow, "Behavior, Purpose and Teleology," *Philosophy of Science*, 10 (1943), 18–24.

[5] *The Human Use of Human Beings* (New York: Doubleday Anchor Books, 1954), p. 17. W. J. Horvath and A. Rapoport define cybernetics as "the theory of complex interlocking 'chains of causation,' from which goal-seeking and self-controlling forms of behavior emerge" ("Thoughts on Organization Theory and a Review of Two Conferences," *General Systems*, 4[1959],90).

[6] Easton, *A Framework for Political Analysis* (New York: Prentice-Hall, 1965) and *A Systems Analysis of Political Life* (New York: John Wiley, 1965); Deutsch, *The Nerves of Government* (New York: Free Press of Glencoe, 1963). Also see K. E. Boulding, *The Image* (Ann Arbor: University of Michigan Press, 1956); M. A. Kaplan, *System and Process in International Politics* (New York: John Wiley, 1957); C. R. Dechert, ed., *The Social Impact of Cybernetics* (Notre Dame, Ind.: University of Notre Dame Press, 1965); J. Singh, *Great Ideas in Information Theory, Language and Cybernetics* (New York: Dover, 1966); J. C. Charlesworth, ed., *Contemporary Political Analysis* (New York: The Free Press, 1967); F. J. Crosson and K. M. Sayre, eds., *Philosophy and Cybernetics* (Notre Dame, Ind.: University of Notre Dame Press, 1967); W. Buckley, ed., *Modern Systems Research for the Behavioral Scientist* (Chicago: Aldine, 1968); and G. A. Almond and G. B. Powell, *Comparative Politics: A Developmental Approach* (Boston: Little, Brown and Company, 1966).

Philosophically, cybernetics with its relativistic inspiration may not be in full harmony with Catholic doctrine. In the first decades of this century, a new conception of the universe was formed, a probabilistic, contingent world-view, replacing the rigid determinism of Newtonian physics largely through the influence of Gibbs in England and Bolzmann in Germany,[7] The shift was from concern over what would always happen to concern over what would happen with the greatest probability. The principle of contingency, based on the concept of organic incompleteness, laid the foundation for the flowering of the cybernetic age.

Whatever the cosmological theories involved, however, social and political life are peculiarly susceptible to cybernetic analysis. The Church is no exception. For we are concerned here with the probabilities of interaction, claim and decision. This is functional ecclesiology with an emphasis on communication and control, information, and power. The Church is, indeed, a very proper object for cybernetic analysis.[8]

The purpose of this first part is a presentation of the fundamentals of ecclesial cybernetics. To accomplish this goal, we focus on two areas: systems analysis and the Church. First, we examine the basic elements of cybernetics with reference to that open system which is the Church; then we examine the organizational unity of the Church in both its universal and local structures with reference to systems analysis.

---

[7] Cf. Wiener, *The Human Use of Human Beings*, pp. 7–12.

[8] Little work has been done on the relationship between theology and cybernetics. See: P. Granfield, "Ecclesial Cybernetics: Communication in the Church," *Theological Studies*, 29(1968), 662–678; M. V. Orna, *Cybernetics, Society and the Church* (Dayton, Ohio: Pflaum Press, 1969); H.-D. Bastian, *Theologie der Frage* (Munich: Chr. Kaiser Verlag, 1969), pp. 180–195; W. W. Everett, *Body-Thinking in Ecclesiology and Cybernetics*, a 1970 unpublished Ph.D. dissertation from Harvard University; and B. F. Donahue, "Political Ecclesiology," *Theological Studies*, 33 (1972), 294–306.

1

The Cybernetic
Elements

THE VARIOUS ELEMENTS forming a cybernetic unity focus on information transmission for the purpose of communication and control. In its main outlines, the subject matter of cybernetics is fairly simple. There are four main divisions: first, the unit of communication and control called the system; second, the environment with which the system interacts; third, the negative entropy that moves the system toward information and order; and fourth, the information-conversion process, with its input, output, and feedback, by means of which the system achieves the goals of negative entropy. Furthermore, we will consider each one of these elements with a view to understanding its ecclesial dimensions.

I. *The Cybernetic System*

The description of cybernetics as system analysis or system theory reveals the central point of this study of communication and control—the system. Broadly speaking, the system is an organized complex of interacting elements. The atom, the plant, the human being, the body politic, and the Church are just the more obvious examples of the ubiquitous system.

Whether the system involved is an Apollo missile or the solar system, certain common elements emerge. First, the system is a whole, a unit, an undivided oneness. Second, it has a multiplicity of interdependent parts—interrelating or interacting. Third, its parts are bound together by communication which organizes them into a unity. Fourth, the system is distinct from its environment, the world of systems that surrounds it. Communication, then, welds multiplicity into a unity distinct from other unities. In brief, the system is a whole composed of interdependent parts held together by communication and distinct from an environment made up of other systems.

Systems, for the sake of functional precision, are classified in terms of their relationship to their environment, as closed systems and open systems.

A *closed system* is static because it is isolated from its environment. There is no informational exchange between the two. Closed systems receive no input from outside, nor do they make any output. Since they are actually existing they are necessarily related to other systems, but their interaction is minimal if it is present at all. For example, a rock can be affected by its surroundings, but it has no adaptive capabilities to deal with these same surroundings. A completely closed system, as far as its surroundings are concerned, is inert. Internally, it has either achieved equilibrium or tends toward it inexorably.

An *open system*, on the other hand, is dynamic, because it is in constant interaction with its environment. The information exchange is unending: the reception of inputs and the production of outputs. There is a dependence of the system on its environment. Therefore, for a system to be separated from its environment may mean the destruction of the system—the fish-out-of-water effect. Depending on its adaptive capabilities and a beneficial environment, the open system can avoid equilibrium indefinitely.

A political system, such as the Church, is an open system composed of living beings, themselves open systems, who are organized through communication. There is interplay both between the whole system and the environment and between the parts and their own particular environment, which is composed of the other parts and the external ecosystem. A political system, using the term in the broad sense, is more than a collection of individuals; rather it is a structure made up of roles. The roles are the part of the individual's activities involved in the social or political process. The structure is formed by the sets of roles which are related to one another. The structure then comprises the regularly observable activities which make up the system.

The Church is an open system. Its parts, through their role activity, form the ecclesial structure. Before cybernetic analysis, these facts were described in terms of office (role) and institution (structure): the members of the Church have their various offices or duties; that is, activities incumbent upon them. Broadly speaking, they are divided into laymen and clerics. Moreover, some clerics have governing roles: they are the hierarchy. A tight network of communication and control on both the natural and supernatural levels forms the members into an institution that is called the Body of Christ. The Church exists in the world but is concerned pre-eminently with a totally different aspect of its environment, a divine Ecosystem, "the Other"; that is, the immanent and transcendent God.

Many forms are used to describe the open system which is the Church. Since the Church is a mystery, no form is completely satisfactory. Some theologians follow a long tradition, recognized in Vatican II, and use society as a model for the Church.[1] Accordingly, the Church can be compared with other open systems, a decided methodological advantage provided its uniqueness is recognized. Some, like Möhler[2] and Khomiakov,[3] object to this usage as encouraging a mechanical view of the Church which obscures its spiritual function. They emphasize the input from the divine Ecosystem and refer to the Church as a redeemed and sanctified organism, the Body of Christ. Others emphasize the spiritual aspect but on a somewhat lower level.

---

[1] *Constitution on the Church*, Art. 8. Translations of the texts of Vatican II are taken from *The Documents of Vatican II*, ed. W. M. Abbott (New York: Association Press, 1966).

[2] J. A. Möhler, *Die Einheit in der Kirche* (Tübingen: H. Laupp, 1825).

[3] Cf. A. Gratieux, *A. S. Khomiakov et le mouvement slavophile* (Paris: Editions du Cerf, 1939).

They see the Church as a movement oriented toward the world in order to transform its environment.[4] The Church does share all of these functions. It is an organization (a human society), an organism (the Body of Christ), and a movement (a missionary force). But always and everywhere, the Church is unique. Nevertheless, despite its uniqueness, it is an open system subject to cybernetic analysis. In fact, an analysis of its cybernetic elements manifests clearly its special nature.

Traditionally, the Church has been given many names: the New Covenant, the *Ekklesia*, the People of God, the Kingdom of God, the Congregation of Believers, and the Mystical Body of Christ.[5] When we use the term *Church*, we refer to the Catholic Church as a unique historical and sacramental manifestation of the Church of Christ on earth. The Catholic Church is an assembly, the eschatologically redeemed community that professes belief in the Lordship of Jesus Christ, that ratifies its faith by sacramental baptism, and that is joined together by a threefold unity: a unity of creed (an affirmation of essential doctrines); a unity of code (an acknowledgment of common moral precepts as well as papal and collegial authority); and a unity of cult (a participation in a sevenfold sacramental system). This triple bonding presupposes the operation of grace, a supernatural input from God to man whereby man is able to act on a spiritual level and even to participate existentially in the nature of God. It is this divine input that is ultimately responsible for the bonds of communication which link the members one to another and make them parts of this open system which is the Church. The unity of code, creed, and cult reflects the power of God working in His People.

---

[4] Cf. G. Baum, *The Credibility of the Church Today* (New York: Herder and Herder, 1968) and T. Westow, *The Agony of the Cross* (London: Sheed and Ward, 1968).

[5] The following studies on ecclesiology are recommended: H. Küng, *The Church* (New York: Sheed and Ward, 1968); L. Cerfaux, *The Church in the Theology of St. Paul* (New York: Herder and Herder, 1963); R. Schnackenburg, *The Church in the New Testament* (New York: Herder and Herder, 1965); P. S. Minear, *Images of the Church in the New Testament* (Philadelphia: Westminster, 1960); and R. Latourelle, *Christ and the Church: Signs of Salvation* (Staten Island, N. Y.: Alba, 1972).

II. *The Environment*

From the point of view of any system, the world can be divided into two parts; the system itself and all that is not the system—that is, its environment.

The question of environment is important for cybernetic analysis only when open systems are involved. The closed system does not interact with its environment. There are no inputs or outputs. The closed system acts as if its environment did not exist. An open system, on the other hand, implies interaction. It does not, like a closed system, move inexorably to a state of equilibrium. In fact, the final state of an open system is not limited by its initial components or their concentrations. It can rise above its beginnings, because it receives something from outside itself, from its environment.

This environmental interaction enables the open system to realize two related goals: homeostasis and evolution. Homeostasis is the ability of the system to regulate itself so that it achieves a steady state despite the changes inside and outside it. Evolution is the ability of the system to improve itself, to achieve quantitative and qualitative changes transcending its original datum. The two functions are anti-entropic. The one preserves the system: the other perfects it. Both are modalities of the open system's environmental interaction. Without an adequate environment, the system cannot realize either homeostasis or evolution but is put into total subjection to the laws of entropy.

Moreover, it is possible to speak of internal and external environment. For within the system, one part is related to all the other parts as to its environment as well as to all that is outside the system.

Even this distinction is an oversimplification, because the same people belong to many different systems. They have multiple roles. A man may be a citizen, the head of a family, a medical doctor, as well as a deacon. Through a number of particular sets of activities, he functions as part of various systems—the state, the family, the medical profession, and the Church. Obviously, then, these systems cannot be spatially isolated one from the other. They all meet in the same person. What, then, is this thing called environment? How can we say, for instance, that the state forms part of the environment of the Church, when both depend on the role activities of the same person? When the Bible warns the Christian against the world, it in some way warns the Christian against himself.

The environment, therefore, includes all that is outside the system, considering the system precisely as a structure of roles rather than a structure of persons. The whole person is part of the system because of his role activities: but everything else that is in him is part of the system's environment. Thus the whole person is a member of the Church, but he fulfills that special activity in a cultural, economic, social, and even individual context which forms a part of the system's total environment.

This interpenetration of systems which is based on the multiplicity of roles possible to an individual person shows us the full dimensions of the concept of total environment and keeps us from the fallacy of analogizing geographically. In other words, the line of demarkation between the Church and the state is not like the boundary between the United States and Mexico. Nor can the Church in the world be compared to an Indian reservation. It is not, except accidentally, a semipolitical enclave. The members of the Church and the state, or the Church and the world, can be the very same people. The point of distinction is their role activities, not their personal individuality. Environment, then, is a function of this specificity.

Traditionally, the Church has thought of its environment as manifesting two aspects: the divine and the human, God and the world, the powers of good and the powers of evil. Christ was the prince of peace, Satan was the prince of this world. Christians have internalized, at least as far as their thinking is concerned, the harsh indictment made by St. John:

> Do not set your hearts on the godless world or anything in it. Anyone who loves the world is a stranger to the Father's love. Everything the world affords, all that panders to the appetites, or entices the eyes, all the glamour of its life, springs not from the Father but from the godless world. (I *John* 2:15–16).

Despite the enduring influence of the Johannine condemnation, his attitude to the world was not entirely negative. Early in his Gospel, John states: "God loved the world so much that he gave his only Son" (*John* 3:16). Very briefly, for St. John "the world" could refer to all creation, the earth, mankind, or those in opposition to God. In all of these senses, the world is part of the environment of the Church.

According to Paul VI, "The Church is not separated from the world but lives in it."[6] There is no Church apart from men. The Church exists in the world. It is part of the social process, a kind of human interaction. This interaction is not only a physical necessity, it is a spiritual duty. Christ commanded his apostles: "Teach you all nations" (*Matt.* 28:19). Mindful of this missionary role, Vatican II speaks of the Church as a kind of sacrament, "the sign and instrument . . . of the unity of the whole human race."[7] It is a sign because Christ, its Head, came to unite all men to one another by uniting them to God. It is an instrument because, through Christ, it is the means by which this unity is achieved. The Church is an open system. The Gospel is a message of good tidings to the whole human family, not just a privileged few. God is redemptively present throughout the world. The Church mediates His grace to mankind.

The total environment of the Church can lead us to union with God. As Teilhard de Chardin wrote: "In the name of our faith, we have the right and the duty to become passionate about the things of the earth."[8] Through the coming of Christ, St. Paul tells us, "there is a new world" (II *Cor.* 5:17). But for this, the Church must be open to the world. It must reject the tradition, which H. Richard Niebuhr termed "exclusive Christianity," that "uncompromisingly affirms the sole authority of Christ over the Christian and resolutely rejects culture's claims to loyalty."[9] The Church must walk a narrow path between isolationism and secularism. The Church cannot allow itself to be estranged from the world, nor can it allow its involvement with the world to

---

[6] *Ecclesiam Suam, Acta Apostolicae Sedis,* 56 (1964), 627.

[7] *Constitution on the Church,* Art. 1.

[8] *The Divine Milieu* (New York: Harper and Row, 1960), p. 69.

[9] *Christ and Culture* (New York: Harper, 1956), p. 45. The relationship between the Church and its cultural environment is skillfully discussed by A. Mirgeler, *Mutations of Western Christianity* (New York: Herder and Herder, 1964).

cause it to lose its own identity. The interaction with the environment of this open system which is the Church can at times prove injurious to the Church. Nevertheless it is the will of Christ and a social necessity that this interaction should occur. For, after all, as Bishop Robinson has observed—thereby formulating the central tenet of secularization theology—"The house of God is not the Church but the world."[10]

In this broader perspective, the concept of an ecosystem proves helpful. The Church can be considered as part of that larger system which is the world. Primarily, it consists of human interaction; that is, men seeking values in an arena of limited resources. This arena is the biosphere, the geophysical foundation, that combination of the earth's land crust, waters, and atmosphere in which men live. Within this ecosystem the Church, composed of men, interacts with its environment. As part of a larger ecosystem, the Church experiences interdependence. Its members interact with other men, the members of other human systems. Competing claims result in conflicts resolved eventually by some kind of decision-making process. Because men live in a world of limited resources, their competition for power and material wealth prevents isolationism even as it limits personal liberty.

Although the Church may form the Communion of Saints, it is still part of the community of man. Significant social, cultural, political, scientific, religious, and moral changes in the larger society necessarily affect the life of the Church. It cannot successfully immunize itself against, or isolate itself from, these influences. So close is the interaction between the Church and its environment that the solution of any one problem depends on the recognition of the function of several environmental factors.

In the past theologians have shown little interest in this ecological perspective. William Kuhns argues that traditional theologians erred by using a triangular model to deal with the categories of sin, guilt, love, faith, and hope. These major issues were examined in terms of man's threefold relationship—to God, to his fellow man, and to himself. Kuhns urges that this model be replaced by a quadrangular construct which would add the

[10] *The New Reformation* (Philadelphia: Westminster, 1965), p. 92.

total environment to any analysis of basic Christian problems.[11]

Today a growing number of theologians, especially those dealing with moral or social problems, have incorporated this environmental dimension into their methodology. For example, the urban society, with the mobility, anonymity, crowding, and poverty which technological development has helped create, has had a radical influence on sexual morality, sex roles, family life, economics, and culture. The moral theologian cannot discuss the ethical obligations of modern man without a deep awareness of these environmental influences.

The present vocation crisis in the Church exemplifies the environmental complexity of most ecclesial problems. Why are priests and nuns leaving the service of the Church? Why is the rate of new vocations decreasing? Many reasons are given. Certainly the breakdown of the family and the emphasis on sexual fulfillment is important. On a different level, the anti-authoritarianism of the young, their desire to do their thing without control by the establishment, may be just as important. The tremendous progress in technology in the last few decades has made traditional, historically grounded institutions look outmoded and irrelevant. The reasons can be multiplied, but they add up to the tremendous impact of the environment on the Church.

Nor is the vocational problem a self-contained unit. Personnel loss from the teaching orders and institutions has drastically limited Catholic education. The shortage of teachers coupled with spiraling operational expenses—a by-product of environmental inflation—has forced many schools to close. In 1971, some eight hundred parochial elementary and secondary schools ceased to operate. Between 1961 and 1971 enrollment in Catholic elementary and secondary schools dropped by 17 percent, with a decrease of over a million students. All this in a time of rapid population growth in the nation at large. The decrease in the number of schools most probably will affect the number of future vocations, since traditionally the majority of vocations came from Catholic schools.

In brief, then, a cybernetic analysis of the Church must give great importance to its environmental context, for the "People of

---

[11] *Environmental Man* (New York: Harper and Row, 1969).

God," as the Church calls itself, are obviously and ineradicably part of the family of man.

III. *Negative Entropy*

Systems are units of negative entropy. They reflect order rather than disorder, information rather than noise. A closed system, insulated from its environment, moves inexorably toward entropy. Open systems, on the other hand, interact with their environment, thereby fulfilling their goals of maintenance and development and avoiding that disorganizational death called entropy. Open systems, like the Church, are characterized by this negative entropy, the possibility of ordered achievement. To understand the life of the Church, we consider first positive entropy, and then the forces of negative entropy which enable this open system to persevere and flourish. Christ spoke of positive and negative entropy: "The thief comes only to steal, to kill, to destroy; I have come that men may have life, and may have it in all fullness" (*John* 10:10). In fact, Christ spoke specifically of victory over the forces of entropy: "On this rock I will build my church, and the forces of death shall never overpower it" (*Matt.* 16:18).

What is this entropy that threatens cybernetic systems? Entropy is the tendency to the most probable condition of things, a random state of statistical uniformity of energy. Entropy, formulated in the Second Law of Thermodynamics, reaches its maximum when the system becomes totally undetermined and undifferentiated. It is the very antithesis of order and organization. In the stages of entropy leading to this terminal state, there is a steady decrease in energy output, integration, and development. The flow of information is gradually reduced. Information and entropy are related in inverse proportions: the more information in the system, the less entropy; the more entropy, the less information. The aging body illustrates this information breakdown in all its systems, such as the muscular, genital, nervous, and vascular. Not just individuals but the whole universe is moving toward a stable equilibrium in accordance with the law of entropy. No system, open or closed, is freed from the dominion of this law. The only countervailing force is the input from the environment. Entropy within a system is a function of its environment. The open system has a fundamental dependence on the quantity and duration of the informational flow from outside. When that flow is cut off, the system becomes closed. A random state of disorder is its inevitable fate. If, however, we postulate a permanent inflow, the system has theoretical immortality, an indefinite postponement of static equilibrium.

Entropy operates in social systems as, in Kenneth Boulding's words, "the principle of diminishing potential."[12] Political units, institutions, societies, and private clubs move from creative energy to stagnation. Churches and religious groups manifest this same tendency. As open systems, they have hope of permanence; but the realization of this goal depends on their own powers and resources as well as their environmental interaction. They seek to counteract entropy in two ways: maintenance and development. The first of these functions is called homeostasis. It is the self-regulation by which the system achieves within itself an ordered harmony. For example, the body keeps its temperature and the acid content of the stomach fairly constant despite the changes from outside. All open systems need this ability to adapt, to adjust, to self-regulate. Secondly, the system must be able to operate in order to fulfill its goals. This developmental or evolutionary function aims at greater order and information. It uses the flow of information from the environment to achieve a higher synthesis. Through homeostasis and evolution, the system is able to preserve itself and to perfect itself. It realizes the twin goals of maintenance and development which can be summed up in the term negative entropy.

To understand a system dynamically, it is necessary to consider in more detail both its anti-entropic functions—maintenance and development—and the goals to which they are oriented. This analysis is especially pertinent in ecclesial matters because of the Church's unique function and goals. We will discuss first the anti-entropic functions and then the anti-entropic goals.

[12] *The Meaning of the Twentieth Century* (New York: Harper and Row, 1965), p. 138.

A. ANTI-ENTROPIC FUNCTIONS

Anti-entropic functions counteract entropy through adaptive mechanisms enabling the system to regulate itself and renew itself in an environmental context. A social system is called stable if it can continue to operate under constant conditions: it is called ultrastable, if it can do so under changing conditions. Ultrastability or morphogenesis is the characteristic of the successful adaptive system. Ultrastable systems adjust to a fluctuating environment. They resolve to their own advantage the tension between stability and change. All open systems must adapt or perish. Evolutionary biology gives us many examples of this negative entropy. But on the social level, we see it also in the dramatic rise and fall of the great empires as well as in the trend toward planned diversification of the mammoth business corporations.

The Church's relation to entropy, however, is different from that of all other social systems. The badge of its uniqueness is indefectibility. This faith-affirmation signifies that the Church will remain in existence without ever being destroyed by the forces of evil and error. Christ spoke of the rocklike stability of the Church (*Matt.* 16:18) and promised to be with it until the end of time (*Matt.* 28:18-20). This guarantee of indefectibility is grounded on the intimate union of Christ with his Church.[13]

Nevertheless the Church must contend with the forces of entropy. It has not yet reached the state of terminal perfection. Indefectibility refers to the Church's ability to endure until the end of time: it does not imply freedom from a hostile environment.[14] As an incarnational Church it must manifest its ultrastability by adapting to fluctuating change. For nearly two millennia it has survived in spite of bitter and prolonged persecution, changing cultural, political, economic, and social patterns, and internal dissensions of major proportions. Traditional

---

[13] St. Augustine described the Church's indefectibility in the following way: "The Church will falter when her foundation falters. But how can Christ falter? As long as Christ does not falter, neither shall the Church" (*Enarr. in Ps.* 103,2,5 [*Corpus Christianorum, Series Latina*, 40, 1493-94]).

[14] The entropic condition of the Church, its social pathology, is discussed by Baum in *The Credibility of the Church Today*, pp. 55-101.

Catholic theology has referred to this ecclesial ultrastability as a "social miracle." Vatican I saw the Church's "unshaken stability" as part of a "great and perpetual motive of credibility and an irrefutable proof of its own divine mission."[15] It is not enough for the Church to overcome the evils of displacement and confusion, it must grow in holiness and in the life of the Spirit. Vatican II acknowledges the need for constant renewal. In the *Constitution on the Church*, it contrasts Christ and the Church: "While Christ, 'holy, innocent, undefiled' knew nothing of sin, the Church, embracing sinners in her bosom, is at the same time holy and always in need of being purified."[16] This same principle is stated in the *Decree on Ecumenism*: "Christ summons the Church, as she goes on her pilgrim way, to that continual reformation of which she always has need, insofar as she is an institution of men here on earth."[17] The Council has thus officially sanctioned the traditional theological axiom: *Ecclesia semper reformanda.* It should be noted, however, that this is not simply a call to maintenance of the status quo in the face of evils from within and without. Rather it is a recognition of the vocation of holiness to which the whole Church is called, to "be brought into a unity in Christ" (*Eph.* 1:10).

The Church, situated in an entropic universe, has many ways to achieve both homeostasis and evolution. First of all, there are the strictly spiritual means, prayer, the sacraments, and good works, all of which acknowledge God as an all-powerful and all-loving Father. The Church has confidence that it will receive, as long as it requires it, the necessary power to fulfill the promises of Christ. The Church is ever open to the divine input it needs. Secondly, there are the various social techniques, especially recruitment, education, and reform. Let us consider these three functions briefly.

First, there must be a constant flow of new members to provide for new growth as well as for the replacing of the activities of incompetent, defecting, or dying members. The major

---

[15] *Enchiridion Symbolorum. Definitionum et declarationum de rebus fidei et morum*, ed. H. Denzinger, rev. A. Schönmetzer (Freiburg: Herder, 1967³⁴), 3013. Hereafter cited as Denzinger-Schönmetzer.

[16] Art. 8.

[17] Art. 6.

source of new membership comes from within the system and consists of the offspring of members. The other source is the conversion of those outside the system.

Second, there is the training of members, new and old, for their special role activities on all levels of the life of the system. This educational operation is a constant preoccupation of Catholicism in both its schools and its churches. Persons are prepared for a full and fruitful membership by training in creed, code, and cult. They learn the beliefs and practices they have in common as well as the special activities pertaining to their differing roles.

Third, there is the retraining of members for role activity more in harmony with the goals of the system. Members must ever learn to be more faithful to the revelation of Christ and more attuned to the exigencies of the present. This purifying and updating of role activity affects the hierarchy as well as the rest of the faithful. Reform is a constant concern, because changes in the Church take place very slowly. This fact has caused John L. McKenzie to wonder whether present renewal efforts "may not produce by the year 2000, a Church which will be exactly suited to the needs of 1890."[18] One notes that the ecumenical movement did not begin until 400 years after the Reformation and that only recently have we seen the re-emergence of collegiality, the vernacular liturgy, and a married diaconate.

None of these anti-entropic functions, necessary though they may be, are ends in themselves. They are directed toward the realization of a highly integrated value structure. This preferred event, looking at the goals as a unit, must be studied if we are to understand the dynamism of the Church's negative entropy.

B. ANTI-ENTROPIC GOALS

Anti-entropic goals give the system a positive direction. They point to information and order and away from noise and chaos.

---

[18] In his debate with Charles Davis in Chicago, Illinois, June 30, 1968. A tape recording of the debate is available from Argus Communications, Chicago, Illinois.

These value choices determine the nature of the interaction between the various elements of the system and between the system and its environment.

Anti-entropic goals characterize the Church whose founder promised life to the world. He explained, "As the Father has life-giving power in himself, so has the Son by the Father's gift" (*John* 5:26). But life manifests order of the highest degree. It is the most anti-entropic of all anti-entropic things. The ecclesial system instituted by Christ is a thrust at the very heart of entropy, since it promises eternal life.

The ultimate goal of the Church is the glorification of God and the sanctification of man. No person is excluded. As St. Paul wrote: "Such prayer is right and approved by God our Saviour, whose will it is that all men should find salvation and come to know the truth" (I *Tim.* 2:3–4).

The Church, however, exists in time and space. A cybernetic analysis of the Church focuses on this existential manifestation. Nevertheless, even the activities of this phase are specified by the ultimate aims of the Church. We are speaking here of the incarnational Church. At the Incarnation, God became man. The Church is the Body of this God-man, Jesus Christ, and now exists in a time-space continuum.

This incarnational Church has an eschatological orientation. It is this supratemporal aspect which helps distinguish it from the state. Christianity, Karl Rahner speaks of as "the religion of an infinite future."[19] While Christianity cannot conflict with progress, the ultimate truth that it represents always lies beyond the present. The Church, then, focuses on the permanent and eternal condition of man which can be fully realized only in the Kingdom. This is the final *kairos*—the end-time of salvation and judgment when God elevates the believers to union with him (I *Peter* 1:6).

The eschatological reality, however, cannot be separated from the temporal. The Church is a community of men and women existing in this world. To deny the temporal dimensions of the Church would be to distort its mission. The Church is not alienated from the world because of its insistence on the future

[19] *Theological Investigations* (Baltimore: Helicon, 1966), v, 153.

life.[20] In fact, as Karl Rahner points out, the experience of God is absolutely necessary for any integral humanism. The Church, according to Vatican II, exists to manifest Christ to men, since Christ is the "source and model of that renewed humanity."[21] Moreover, the Church "reveals to men the real truth about their condition and their total vocation."[22]

It is possible to distinguish three main missions of the Church whereby it realizes its goal of enabling men to share in the redemptive work of Christ. These missions are goal-oriented means of combatting entropy. In each one, the Church is sent by God to men for their sanctification and his glorification. The *kerygmatic* mission consists in the proclamation of the Word of God. It reveals the Kingdom of God already present and moving toward the *Parousia*. Here is the communication of divine truth, "sharper than a two-edged sword," which acts as input into those open systems called human beings, with the hope that a true information-conversion process will occur, resulting in salvation. The mission of the Church is to those both within and without the system, that they may turn to Christ on hearing his message preached. In the *Acts of the Apostles*, we hear of Paul's vision of Jesus, who said to him: "I send you to open their eyes and turn them from darkness to light, from the dominion of Satan to God, so that, by trust in me, they may obtain forgiveness of sins, and a place with those whom God has made his own" (*Acts* 26:18).

Second is the *diakonic* mission whereby the Church plays a role in making all things new according to Christ's liberating vision of integral humanity. In reconciling and healing, the Church serves mankind as a Suffering Servant, "to carry forward the work of Christ under the leadership of the befriending Spirit."[23] This mission implements the proclaiming of the Gospel. Together these two missions give both communication and control: the input is both word and work in the building up of the Kingdom.

---

[20] Vatican II agreed with this idea and taught that "a hope related to the end of time does not diminish the importance of intervening duties, but rather undergirds the acquittal of them with fresh incentives" (*Constitution on the Church in the Modern World*, Art. 21).

[21] *Decree on the Church's Missionary Activity*, Art. 8.

[22] *Ibid.*

[23] *Constitution on the Church in the Modern World*, Art. 3.

Third is the *koinoniac* mission. God inspires men to form and perfect that community of believers which is the Body of Christ. Vatican II states: "It is the function of the Church to make God the Father and His Incarnate Word present and in a sense visible."[24] This mission looks to the formation of the open system which is both the product and the protector of the revelation of God. God fashions this system which bears witness to its maker as a model for all the other communities of men.

The three missions focus on revelation, service, and community.[25] Through the Church, God achieves the goal of God's glory and man's salvation. Cybernetically, God does this through communication and control within an open system. Each mission fulfills one of these tasks. Together they help reveal that the Church is the Body of Christ. Bonhoeffer spoke of Christ as "the man for others."[26] The Church, then, becomes her true self, Bonhoeffer concludes, "only when she exists for humanity. . . . She must tell men, whatever their calling, what it means to live in Christ, to exist for others."[27] But we must remember that above all others, Christ placed His Father: "I always do what is acceptable to him" (*John* 8:29). So, too, love of the Father and obedience to His will, is ever the aim of that Church which is the Body of His Son.

IV. *The Conversion Process*

The cybernetic system is essentially an informational processing unit. Information includes both communication and control, not as separate things but as different aspects of the same thing. Information is whatever causes a change in another. To tell a man the time or to shoot him are both informational. Monads, impervious to all interaction, would not transmit infor-

---

[24] *Ibid.*, Art. 21. Cf. also: R. Caporale, "Christian Relevance and the Quest for Community," *Cross Currents*, 20 (1970), 29–37.

[25] The threefold mission of the Church is discussed in H. Cox, *The Secular City* (New York: Macmillan, 1965) and R. P. McBrien, *Do We Need the Church?* (New York: Harper and Row, 1969) and *Church: The Continuing Quest* (New York: Newman, 1970).

[26] *Letters and Papers from Prison* (New York: Macmillan, 1962), p. 233.

[27] *Ibid.*, p. 239.

mation. A monad would be a closed system which would not react with its environment, the outside world made up of other systems. Even a monad could, however, like open systems, experience an informational exchange in itself. Open systems, like the Church, transmit information within and without the system. These bits of information are, in modern systems-research, conceived of quantitatively: they can be measured, transmitted, stored, and retrieved. But the concept of information is not limited to the realm of quantified matter. Even as spiritual a reality as the grace of God can be viewed as information without risk of its being mathematicized. The interaction between the Creator and the creature does cause changes in the latter, changes which are characteristic of all cybernetic relationships; that is, they evidence communication and control.

The element of change reflects the dynamic quality of cybernetics. Cybernetic analysis deals not with static bits of information but with constant interaction. The conversion process is the center of this informational transmission. This conversion process has three basic elements: input, output, and feedback. Functionally, inputs are received by the system to be converted into outputs. Outputs, in turn, produce a further reaction in the system or its environment and determine through feedback the character of further inputs. The entire process involves communication, the transferral of units of information. In ecclesial cybernetics, the question is: How do these basic elements operate in that open and adaptive system which is the Church?

A. INPUT

An input is a unit of information that modifies the system in some way. Inputs flow within the system and act as determinants of behavior. Every open system, by definition, receives informational units from outside itself and from within. Thus communication may come from parts of the system, from subsystems, or from the system's local or total environment. Whatever their source, inputs affect the receiver and cause some kind of reaction. Since the Church is a kind of political system—admittedly a special kind—it is helpful to examine the two major kinds of political input, which are demands and supports.

1. DEMANDS

A demand, as defined by Easton, is "an expression of opinion that an authoritative allocation with regard to a particular subject matter should or should not be made by those responsible for doing so."[28] Demands are directed to the political elites. They are stressful messages that jar the status quo and create tension. In one form or another and with great variety, they are present in all political systems. Discontent, frustration, complaints, requests for power, recognition, or other values—all may be formulated as demands. Sometimes demands emerge from a context of emotional and unstructured aggression. At other times, they are the end-product of a closely reasoned effort. In all cases, demands cause a disturbance felt by the system. A stimulus-response-outcome pattern is established. The outcome, of course, may be negative or positive, depending on the quality of the demands and the responsiveness of the political system.

The Church has lived with demands throughout its existence. From the first-century circumcision controversy to the twentieth-century birth control controversy, demands have clamored for attention. The missionary apostolate, the ecumenical councils, the rise of the religious orders, the reform movements, and the development of doctrine are some of the responses that have been made to persistent demands by members of the Church. On the other hand, heresies, schisms, defections, and persecution are some of the negative reactions of petitioners whose demands were not acceded to by the Church.

Today a clear escalation of ecclesial demands can be noted in almost every area of the life of the Church. Four main categories appear: (1) demand for allocations of goods and services, such as hospitals, schools, Latin Masses, good church music, smaller and less expensive churches, and a better distribution of priests; (2) demands for the regulation of behavior, such as the approval of contraception, optional celibacy, right of remarriage after divorce, and the priestly ordination of women; (3) demands for participation in ecclesial decision-making, such as the right of

---

[28] *A Systems Analysis of Political Life* (New York: John Wiley, 1965), p. 38.

the laity to select pastors and bishops and the rights of the bishops in national hierarchies and in the synod of bishops; and (4) demands for communication and information, such as disclosure of parish and diocesan budgets, the abolition of secrecy in episcopal synods and councils, requests for clear statements of norms and policies, the right to confrontation of witnesses, and the right to legal due process.

To be effective instruments of change in any system, demands must be organized. An axiom of cybernetics states that it takes more messages to change a policy than to sustain or reinforce it. When demands flow randomly through the system without a specific focal point, they make little impact. When, however, a substantial volume of intense demands are focused on a particular issue, they can arouse a dormant or unconcerned system to take beneficial action. A successful demand depends primarily on the number and quality of the communication channels through which information can flow. As Mervyn L. Cadwallader notes: "The capacity for innovation cannot exceed the capacity for variety or available variety of information."[29] In other words, the greater the number and variety of input channels, the greater the possibility that the information will be recognized by the political elites.

The Church today urgently needs regularized input channels.[30] Although here we focus on demands, the channels serve equally well for supports. These channels of communication are essential to the success of the cybernetic process. Let us consider some of the more effective channels through which the members of the Church would be able to express their reaction to Church policies.

The first channel for communicating demands to ecclesial decision-makers is the *research center*. It aims at providing those in authority—bishops, pastors, religious superiors, and lay leaders—with reliable information on trends, opportunities, and projections as a basis for effective planning.

[29] "The Cybernetic Analysis of Change in Complex Social Organizations," in *Communication and Culture*, A. G. Smith, ed. (New York: Holt, Rinehart and Winston, 1966), p. 400.
[30] Cf. G. Wendel, "Political and Institutional Considerations for Future Policy Formation," *Liturgy*, 14 (1969), 2-5.

The research apostolate, encouraged by Vatican II, has developed rapidly in the last few years. In the United States, many such research units are in operation and are usually related to a university, religious order, diocese, or other church organization. For example, the Redemptorist Fathers have a data-processing service which, through the use of a computer, gives an 180-page report on the religious attitudes of the members of the parish with a "71-facet view of each practicing Catholic." Some research centers, however, are independent—for example, CARA (Center for Applied Research in the Apostolate), which began in 1965. This national organization for research and development has the following tasks: (1) to gather, correlate, and disseminate information from existing reports, surveys, and research projects in order to avoid duplication of efforts; (2) to undertake original data-gathering projects through surveys, questionnaires, and computer analysis; and (3) to make research data understandable to Church policy-makers.

Obviously, the modern electronic computer, the handmaiden of the cybernetic age, is an invaluable instrument of research and analysis. Technological skills now make possible a fuller assessment of what the teachings and practices of the Church mean in the lives of the faithful. In addition to information on the *consensus fidelium*, information on the *consensus theologorum* can be accurately gathered and disseminated.[31] Moreover, these two areas of information with intercreedal coverage

---

[31] The use of data-processing equipment to ascertain the *consensus theologorum* has been suggested by G. K. Malone, "Theological Consensus: The Present Dilemma," *American Ecclesiastical Review*, 154 (1966), 242–256. On the methods of retrieving, transmitting, and disseminating information in religious studies see G. MacRae, ed., *Scholarly Communication and Publication: Report of a Task Force* (Hanover, Pa.: Council on the Study of Religion, 1972). Cf. also F. Haarsma, "Consensus in the Church: Is an Empirical Inquiry Possible?", Vol. 71 *Concilium* (New York: Herder and Herder, 1972), 119–129. The legal profession has seriously studied the various uses of the computer. Many insights, which may be applied to theology, can be found in M. E. Caldwell, "Legislative Record Keeping in a Computer-Journal," *Harvard Journal of Legislation*, 5 (1967), 1–34, and C. S. Rhyne, "The Computer Will Speed a Law-Full World," *American Bar Association Journal*, 53 (1967), 420–424.

can afford a sound basis for ecumenical activities. The dimensions of these research tasks require the help of the computer, but with that help the research center proves to be an indispensable input channel.

The second channel is *publicity*. This comprises the communications media, the press, radio, television, and cinema. The printed word still plays the major role in conveying demands. In the United States, however, the 140 diocesan newspapers tend to be primarily supportive of the status quo rather than demanding. Nevertheless, the *National Catholic Reporter*, with its liberal views and anti-establishment policy, has been effective in catalyzing public opinion and influencing hierarchical action, often by the simple expedient of revealing the facts surrounding authoritative outputs. It has, according to Thomas F. O'Dea, "provided leadership for the crystallization of an articulate and intelligent Catholic opinion in the United States."[32] It should be noted that the burden of publicizing ecclesial relevancies is borne also by the secular press. Daily newspapers and national magazines, especially *Time* and *Newsweek*, with regular religion sections have such a wide readership and broad religious coverage that they are even more influential than the Catholic newspapers and magazines and have, in fact, contributed to the latter's drastic decline in circulation. But together, the secular and the Catholic communications media are an effective vehicle for articulating demands.

The third channel is *protest*. It is largely dependent on publicity but has its own special characteristics. Its increasing use in American Church affairs mirrors its prevalence in secular matters. Protests take several familiar forms: demonstrations, confrontations, picketing, sit-ins, financial boycotts, and signed petitions. The Roman Synod of 1971 experienced this current phenomenon. In fact, the Holy See, bishops, pastors, religious superiors, and the heads of Catholic universities and colleges are becoming accustomed to this kind of informational feedback. Letter-writing campaigns have not yet become as frequent a feature of Church controversy as of political conflicts. Congressmen and senators receive an average of 250 letters a day and

---

[32] *The Catholic Crisis* (Boston: Beacon Press, 1969), p. ix.

admittedly are influenced by them. Church leaders, however, are not elected officials. Letters may not be for them as coercive, but they should be as informative and, granting the good will of the ecclesial decision-makers, they are strong pressures for change. Protest, of whatever form, is a heightened demand that clamors for attention.

The fourth channel is the *official conference*. Two main types are important. The first is the episcopal conference, both national and international. Both of these officially sanctioned groups have helped decentralize Church authority. National conferences of bishops have been given new power from Rome to adjudicate special local problems, problems which would suffer from a universalized approach. But the universal Church, too, works through regular conferences. The synod of bishops was established by Paul VI in 1965 to deal specifically with problems affecting the whole Church. The synod has already met three times, in 1967, 1969, and 1971. Owing to its smaller membership, it has proved to be much more efficient than an ecumenical council and a very valuable instrument in these changing times. The second type of official conference is one in which there is lay participation as well as the participation of the nonepiscopal clergy. In 1969, the Council for the Laity was made a part of the Roman Curia. There are, besides this, a vast number of lay organizations, clerical groups, theological societies, priests, senates, parish councils, and religious and secular institutes. All of these, if properly organized and truly representative, exert considerable pressure on decision-making bodies.

Fifth is *election*. Here is the essence of representational government with the guarantee of effective communication of demands. This participation in decision-making inevitably makes the elected decision-makers more sensitive to their constituency and more accountable for their decisions. Election is certainly a prime channel for articulating demands, but it is not as yet an accepted procedure in the modern Church. The idea is a challenging one, however, since we are so committed to its civil counterpart, political democracy. This problem of ecclesial co-responsibility will be one of the major themes to be developed in this book. It is sufficient here to recognize election as a channel of demands.

2. SUPPORTS

Supports are the second kind of ˙ecclesial inputs. Whereas demands are negative, supports are positive. They provide for system continuity. With support and the cohesion it produces, a system is able to cope with the demands that are made. A political system requires at least minimal support for survival: sheer coercion will not compensate for lack of consent by the governed. The need for support is even more essential when the society is a voluntary one like the Church. If the members choose not to support the Church, the whole system breaks down.

In the Church, supports fall into four basic categories: (1) material contributions of resources; (2) obedience to doctrinal, moral, and disciplinary teachings; (3) participation in liturgical services and community projects; and (4) love and respect for authorities, rituals, traditions, symbols, and for the institution itself.

Ecclesial supports vary in intensity from the heroic witness of the martyr to the marginal allegiance of the nominal Catholic. The variation in intensity may also be a function of environmental input such as wars, natural calamities, and persecutions. Such misfortunes often strengthen support by engendering a deeper sense of community and religious values. However, support erodes when there is negative output from within the system, such as inept leadership, authoritative refusal of reasonable demands, or the suppression of legitimate dissent.

The extrinsic legitimacy of the Church is closely linked to support. Legitimacy is a function of support. Hence, to the extent that the members no longer share the values of the system, its legitimacy diminishes. As Seymour M. Lipset writes: "Legitimacy involves the capacity of the system to engender and maintain the belief that the existing political institutions are the most appropriate ones for the society."[33]

Many Catholics are currently experiencing a lessening of their belief in the institutional Church. Their feeling of anomie or alienation is characterized by their refusal to accept traditional ecclesial values. The complaints against the Church are numer-

---

[33] *Political Man* (New York: Doubleday Anchor Books, 1963), p. 64.

ous: paternalistic and clerical monopoly of Church leadership; insensitivity to personal needs; isolation from the real world of social injustice; outmoded doctrinal and disciplinary formulations, and inadequate societal structures. Some Catholics are so overcome by a sense of hopelessness over unfulfilled demands that they have left the Church. Others have ceased to be active members and have been content to be disinterested observers. Many others, however, have not withdrawn their support but have struggled to discover new sources of spiritual vitality and have worked for the gradual renewal of the Christian community.

Today the Church is in what Bishop Robinson calls "the overlap"—that transitional period bridging two world-views.[34] De Tocqueville's description of Europe in the mid-nineteenth century gives us a secular analog: "Epochs sometimes occur in the life of a nation when the old customs of a people are changed, public morality is destroyed, religious belief is shaken, and the spell of tradition is broken. In this situation the citizens have neither the instinctive patriotism of a monarchy nor the reflecting patriotism of a republic. They have stopped between the two in the midst of confusion and distress."[35] The pilgrim Church is in transition: it finds itself awkwardly balanced between the old and the new. A time of change is a time of frustration. Some demand that the old ways be restored: some demand that the new ways be imposed instantly. Many from both camps refuse full support when their demands are not met. The Church, therefore, must recognize this conflict and try to balance both the right to demand and the need for support. It must do so, in the words of Christ, "like a householder who can produce from his own store both the new and the old" (*Matt.* 13:52).

B. OUTPUT

An output is a bit of information emanating from the system and directed toward a subordinate part of the system or its environment. In a political system, outputs are the authoritative decisions of the governing subsystem. The response that the

---

[34] Robinson, *op. cit.*, pp. 78 ff.
[35] *Democracy in America* (New York: Knopf, 1945), I, 251–252.

political system makes to inputs, to information-conveying supports and demands, aims at stability, constructive adaptation, and development. These outputs change with the inputs and together reflect a transactional proportionality. In this dynamic and reciprocal flow of information, outputs appear from one point of view as terminal points, as reactions to a series of inputs; from another point of view, however, the outputs appear as starting points for a new series of interactions. Input and output, in short, are both parts of the same conversion process.

In the Church, as in other political systems, there are four main classes of output: (1) extractions: ordinary financial support, tithing, special collections, and personal services; (2) behavior regulations: laws, decrees, orders, and rules concerning both doctrinal and disciplinary matters; (3) distributions: spiritual, educational, and social benefits, as well as honorary awards and other forms of recognition; and (4) symbolic actions: communication of faith and morals, policies and values, and history and culture.[36]

Ecclesial authorities have responsibility for their outputs. It is true that their policy judgments can be implemented by sanction, but they should nevertheless be guided by the principle of human dignity enunciated by Vatican II that "the freedom of man be respected as far as possible, and curtailed only when and insofar as necessary."[37] Despite innumerable demands and fluctuating support, authoritative outputs must always be in harmony with that "perfect law of liberty" (*James* 1:25) which ordains all things to personal holiness, community good, and the divine glory.

On a more practical level, the authorities, in committing and directing resources, must carefully assess the informational input they receive; for not all demands, even those considered objectively worthwhile, can be immediately fulfilled. Here are three major problem areas: the compatibility of the demands with the goals of the system, the availability of resources, and the feasibility of implementation. Authorities, of course, are not limited

---

[36] Cf. G. A. Almond and G. B. Powell, *Comparative Politics: A Developmental Approach* (Boston: Little, Brown and Company, 1966), pp. 25-27.
[37] *Declaration on Religious Freedom*, Art. 7.

to the demands of the members. Because of their special information, experience, and expertise, the authorities themselves may initiate programs, reformulate objectives, and plan for future contingencies. Yet these outputs, too, are based on antecedent inputs.

The nature of the political system determines the production of outputs. In the Church, for example, major outputs originate in Rome. The administrative control of the Church is highly centralized. This consolidation of power has several advantages. The pope, as the focal point of ecclesial authority, has power not only within the system but over its environment. As the spokesman for millions of Catholics, he influences many outside the Church. The centralized government of the Church has traditionally been in a strong position to enforce regulations, control deviations, distribute goods and services, and initiate wide-scale reforms. On the other hand, centralization has its disadvantages. The Vatican, in the opinion of many observers, has become too vast, too remote, and too crowded with official machinery to be easily accessible or efficient. The legislative sluggishness of the Vatican, its delayed reaction to demands, and its bureaucratic involvements tend to impede any serious reform efforts. Since Vatican II, the Church has lagged in its move toward decentralization and subsidiarity. But some progress has been made; many administrative and juridical outputs formerly made by the Vatican are now handled by the local diocese or by the national or regional conferences. For example, a new set of norms for the resolution of marriage cases has been issued by the United States National Conference of Catholic Bishops. These norms have been approved by the Holy See on a provisional or experimental basis for a three-year period which began July 1, 1970. As a result of the improved procedure, matrimonial cases are now decided within a maximum time of eight months. Under the former practice, the time was two or three years.[38]

Important in the production of outputs is the manner in which authority is exercised. Ideally, it should be exercised *within* and *for* the community and not *over* it. Leaders fail seriously who use their power in an authoritarian or even paternalistic way.

---

[38] The norms are given in full in *The Jurist*, 30 (1970), 362–368.

Authority is necessary in a system in order to achieve a unity of effort where there is a complicated plurality of possible means. Authority, also, must compensate for the defects of some of the members or the organization. But, above all, its task is to aim at a realization of the common good. In the Church, authority must aim at that community of interest which is love of God and one's fellow man. Seen in this light, ecclesial authority is *diakonal* in a profound way: it is at the service of love. The leader in the Church must "proclaim the message, press it home on all occasions, convenient or inconvenient, use argument, reproof, and appeal, with all the patience that the work of teaching requires (II *Tim.* 4:2). Love-oriented decisions perform an anti-entropic function in the community. As Boulding remarks, in a cybernetic paraphrasing of Paul's words on charity: "Love, in the sense of the Greek *agape*, emerges as the most anti-entropic of all human relationships."[39]

C. FEEDBACK

Feedback is any bit of informational input that is returned to the system in reaction to antecedent output. This phenomenon is familiar in mechanical, biological, and neurological processes as well as in personal and societal ones. Feedback is important in political systems and can be positive or negative, consisting of supports or demands. The words *feedback loop* aptly describe this circular process which consists in a flow of information involving the system, its subordinate parts, its environment, and its outputs and inputs. Thus the authoritative outputs are communicated to other parts of the system or to the environment. The response is fed back to the system, which is able, on the basis of this new input, to formulate further outputs. The cycle repeats itself again and again. The feedback loop operates wherever there are open systems. Hence in the ecclesial arena, feedback is found on all levels: every individual and every group has its own feedback loop.

Information feedback, which enables a system to determine future plans on the basis of past results, has been called "the

---

[39] Boulding, *op. cit.*, p. 146.

dominant and most fertile intellectual innovation of our age."[40] The idea is not really new, just its systemization. The computer has made this response assessment amazingly accurate. A system is now able to insure its stability despite changing conditions and to modify or correct its behavior according to its successes or failures. Some amount of information feedback is necessary if a system is to develop and exhibit purposive behavior. Feedback provides authorities with two things: knowledge of the overall condition of the system and its environment; and knowledge about the impact (acceptance or rejection) of its decisions and actions. Without feedback, authorities must act with insufficient information. This lack weakens their control and lessens the chance of successful long-term planning.

In currect ecclesial language, feedback is sometimes called dialogue. When a Church leader is open and sensitive to feedback from the faithful, he is able to act in a more intelligent and productive way. Information feedback allows the Church to develop imaginative techniques to treat problems both old and new. By learning of the supportive attitudes of the members and the extent of the satisfaction or frustration of their demands, authorities can make wiser and more effective decisions. Enlightened by a knowledge of the state of the system and by a knowledge of the consequences of previous outputs, they are able to use the creative contributions of the faithful. The Church is then in a better position to renew itself. The popular phrase at Vatican II, *Ecclesia semper reformanda*—the Church must ever be reformed—implies feedback as a needed instrument of change. The Church is thereby enabled to develop new attitudes, new pastoral structures, and new doctrinal clarifications. It renews itself by returning to the original vigor of the Gospel message which has been distorted by sin and weakness. Feedback is an indispensable means for the restoration of all things in Christ.

[40] Easton, *A Systems Analysis of Political Life*, p. 367.

2

The Organizational Unity

THE CHURCH, as we have seen, functions cybernetically. Our next step is to analyze the organizational unity of this goal-oriented open system. In doing so, we limit our study to the Roman Catholic Church, although obvious similarities to other communions do exist.

Moreover, our focus is primarily that control system known as the hierarchy, the political elite of the ecclesial system. For, despite the liberating vision of Vatican II, the institutionalism of the Church, medieval in origin, is still operative. The clergy and the laity play a minimal role in its official governance. Yet there are some 500 million Catholics, 300 thousand priests, but only 3,000 bishops. Nevertheless it is the bishops under the leadership of the pope, the Bishop of Rome, who make all the major legislative, executive, and judicial decisions in the Church. The extent of the power of the hierarchy is even more impressive when one realizes that the bishops are not selected by their constituents, have no direct accountability to them, and usually remain in office several decades.

In a later chapter, we consider the historical and theological foundations of clerical and lay participation in ecclesial decision-making; but here we investigate Church government as it is today, almost exclusively hierarchical. We look first to the universal Church and then to the local Church.

I. *The Universal Church*

The present form of Church structure is the result of two thousand years of history, during which the Church spread throughout the world and developed into a highly centralized administrative organization.[1] There are four major organs of government: the Papacy, the College of Cardinals, the Roman Curia, and the College of Bishops. This division represents, in current order of importance, the structures that function in the Church today. It should be noted, however, that contemporary theology, applying the principles of Vatican II, would give greater emphasis to the College of Bishops. Unfortunately, the vision of the Council has only been partially implemented.

A. THE PAPACY

The pope is the most powerful ecclesial decision-maker. The traditional titles given to him indicate his pre-eminence. He is called the Vicar of Christ, the Supreme Pontiff, the Bishop of Rome, the Patriarch of the West, the Primate of Italy, the Archbishop and Metropolitan of the Roman Province, and the Sovereign of the State of Vatican City. The pope, according to dogmatic decrees of Vatican I, has several roles in the ecclesial system. He is the supreme teacher, who is infallible under certain conditions; the final judge in doctrinal and disciplinary matters; and the ultimate jurisdictional authority over each and every member of the Church, the bishops included. There is no individual or group in the Church who possesses authority superior to that of the pope. In the information-conversion process, the pope is the central figure and no appeal from his decision is possible. Al-

---

[1] The universal government of the Church is discussed in the following: H. Scharp, *Wie die Kirche regiert wird* (Frankfurt: J. Knecht, 1954); C. Falconi, *Il pentagono Vaticano* (Bari: Laterza, 1958); P. C. van Lierde, *The Holy See at Work* (New York: Hawthorn, 1962); P. Poupard, *Connaissance du Vatican* (Paris: Beauchesne, 1967); and C. Pichon, *Le Vatican, hier et aujourd'hui* (Paris: Fayard, 1968).

though morally the pope is expected to seek advice and consultation, there is no juridical norm that makes this imperative. Since he personally appoints cardinals, bishops, and important curial officials, his control over the recruitment of hierarchical members is guaranteed.

Another significant factor in the papal control over the ecclesial system is the lifelong tenure of the pope. Tradition supports this position, as the statement of Cardinal Suenens illustrates: "It is clear from the nature of the case that the need for an age limit does not apply to the Supreme Pontiff; the universal good of the Church demands that he remain in office for life."[2] There are, however, several ways in which the cessation of papal power can occur. The first and most obvious way is through death.[3] (The pope's health is usually a carefully guarded secret. Rome, conditioned by centuries of rumors and intrigues about likely successors to an ailing pope, is reluctant to reveal the extent of a pope's serious illness. Hence the Roman proverb: "The pope is not sick until he is dead.") A second way for a pope to lose his power would be for him to set a definite term of office. This has no historical precedent, but it is not in conflict with papal prerogatives.[4] A third way is resignation. It is based on the principle that since the pope freely accepted his ministry, he may freely abdicate it. The reasons for this may be physical or mental incapacity resulting in incompetence, or, on the other hand, pressures from the secular or ecclesiastical worlds that make it extremely difficult for the pope to exercise his office properly. The ultimate justification is that the good of the Church demands it.

[2] "Age Limit for Bishops," *Council Speeches of Vatican II*, ed. H. Küng, Y. Congar, and D. O'Hanlon (Glen Rock, N.J.: Paulist Press, 1964), p. 119.

[3] This death may be natural or violent. In the early centuries many popes died as martyrs. The last pope to die violently is said to be Lucius II, who was killed in 1145 while he was leading an assault on Rome with papal troops. Pope Paul VI escaped uninjured from an assassination attempt during his visit to Manila in November 1970.

[4] Concerning the theological and canonical arguments for a definite term of office for the pope and the bishops see: J. O'Donoghue, *Elections in the Church* (Baltimore: Helicon, 1967), pp. 167–168; L. Swidler and A. Swidler, eds., *Bishops and People* (Philadelphia: Westminster, 1970), pp. 22–37 and 54–70; and W. W. Bassett, "Subsidiarity, Order and Freedom in the Church," in *The Once and Future Church*, ed. J. A. Coriden (Staten Island, N. Y.: Alba House, 1971), 205–265.

The two most notable papal resignations were those of Celestine V, in 1294, who was later canonized, and Gregory XII, in 1415, who was the last pope to resign.[5]

The pope receives information about the state of the Church principally from the bishops and the Curia. Once aware of demands and supports, he must evaluate them and take action when necessary. His decisions may be communicated, publicly or secretly, either personally by him or through various channels such as the curial congregations, the bishops or the papal representatives. The pope's approval is required of all major decisions of the Curia and the acts of ecumenical, provincial, and diocesan synods. Besides regular general audiences, the pope occasionally addresses the whole Church by an encyclical letter. Other kinds of documents emanate from the Holy See and are classified according to their purpose, content, or audience. Some of the more common categories are: dogmatic bull, apostolic letter, apostolic constitution, decree, allocution, instruction, monitum, and rescript. These documents, except the ones which are confidential, generally appear in the official publication of the Holy See, the *Acta Apostolicae Sedis*.

B. THE COLLEGE OF CARDINALS

The Code of Canon Law describes the College of Cardinals as the principal advisors and assistants to the pope (Canon 230). In the past there were some lay cardinals. The most notable recent

[5] The circumstances surrounding the abdication of Gregory XII were complex. At the time there were three claimants to the papal office: Gregory XII of the Roman line, John XXIII of the Pisan line, and Benedict XIII of the Avignon line. There exists no magisterial pronouncement on which claimant was the legitimate pope. The present Code of Canon Law assumes the constitutionality of papal resignation. Thus, Canon 221 states that the validity of papal resignation does not depend on the consent of the cardinals or anyone else. On this question see W. Ullmann, "Medieval Views Concerning Papal Abdication," *Irish Ecclesiastical Record*, 71 (1949), 125–133; B. Tierney, *Foundations of the Conciliar Theory* (Cambridge: Cambridge University Press, 1955); J. M. Moynihan, *Papal Immunity and Liability in the Writings of the Medieval Canonists* (Rome: Gregorian University, 1961); H. Zimmermann, "Papstabsetzungen des Mittelalters," *Mitteilungen des Instituts für oesterreichische Geschichtsforschung*," 69 (1961), 1–84 and 241–291; 70 (1962), 60–110; and 72 (1964), 74–109; and H. Küng, *Structures of the Church* (New York: Thomas Nelson, 1964), pp. 249–319.

non-priest was Antonelli (d. 1876) who was Secretary of State under Pope Pius IX. The Code (Canon 232,1) decrees that cardinals must be at least priests, and Pope John XXIII ordered in 1962 that in the future all cardinals would also be bishops.[6] At present there are three categories in the College of Cardinals: Cardinal bishops, Cardinal priests, and Cardinal deacons. The bishops, with the exception of the patriarchs, and the deacons, are assigned to full-time service in Rome. The Cardinal priests have their own dioceses outside of Rome.

The cardinals form an elite corps within the Church. Because of their prestigious positions, they have easy access to the pope and may consult with him frequently on Church matters. The College of Cardinals has two special functions: to serve as a senate of advisors to the pope; and to act as electors of a new pope.[7] The senatorial role has been, in fact, minimal for centuries. Rarely do they meet in consistories to advise the pope. The establishment of the synod of bishops at Vatican II further weakened this function. The College, however, still elects the pope. In November 1970, Pope Paul decreed that all cardinals eighty years of age or older would be barred from participating in future papal elections.[8] The same decree added that at seventy-five all cardinals must voluntarily submit their resignation to the pope, who will decide each case personally, and that at eighty they are automatically retired from full curial service.

Many observers see this reform decree as heralding sweeping changes in the administrative machinery of the Church. At the time of the decree there were 127 cardinals. Forty-three were older than seventy-five and 25 were at least eighty years old. In the latter group, 11 were Italian. This raises the possibility that in the next papal election a non-Italian pope may be chosen. The

[6] *Acta Apostolicae Sedis,* 54 (1962), 256–258.

[7] The law governing the vacancy of the Holy See and the election of the pope can be found in: *Vacantis apostolicae sedis, Acta Apostolicae Sedis,* 38 (1945), 65–99, and *Summi Pontificis electio, ibid.,* 54 (1962), 632–640. During the past year there have been several unofficial reports from Rome that the Vatican is preparing new legislation concerning papal elections. This has not yet been published. It is thought by some that the electoral college may be expanded to include, besides the cardinals, some representatives of the national episcopal conferences.

[8] *Acta Apostolicae Sedis,* 62 (1970) 810–812.

last time this occurred was in 1522 when Adrian VI from Holland was elected.

The real power of the College of Cardinals is not in its corporate activities, but in the high-level positions that individual cardinals hold in the Roman Curia. We will now examine the curial structure.

C. THE ROMAN CURIA

The vastness of the Church with its large membership, its multiplicity of subsystems, apostolates, and institutions, makes it impossible for the pope alone to govern it personally. The Roman Curia is the administrative organ that helps the pope direct the worldwide government of the Church. It is similar to the Cabinet and the various departments, executive offices, and agencies of the United States Government which assist the President. The Curia is an information-processing unit within the ecclesial system. Its tasks are to keep abreast of the various aspects of Church life throughout the world; to receive and assess information concerning doctrinal, disciplinary, liturgical, educational and other areas of the apostolate; and to provide administrative judgments and programs. The Curia, therefore, is the ordinary channel for messages from the Church which are converted into appropriate outputs. It is not meant to be a power unto itself, but an instrument that should work for the good of the whole Church.

From its obscure beginnings in the fourth century, the Curia has developed into a centralized bureaucratic body with extensive power. Nevertheless the processes of entropy are at work. Several major reforms of the Curia have been necessary. In the sixteenth century, for example, it was plagued by nepotism, political pressure, greedy officials, and outrageous abuses of authority. Pope Sixtus V tried to correct these in 1588 by his Apostolic Constitution, *Immensa*. He set up fifteen commissions of cardinals to carry out Trent's program of ecclesiastical reform. It was he who first used the term "congregations" for the most important departments of Church government in Rome. His reorganization improved the Curia, but there was still an overlapping of jurisdiction, a proliferation of offices, and significant inefficiency. The Curia nevertheless operated for centuries under the general pattern outlined by Sixtus V, until its second major reform by Pope Pius X in 1908. When Pius X, known as "the second founder of the Roman Curia," became Pope there were thirty-seven departments and subdepartments in the Curia. In his Apostolic Constitution, *Sapienti consilio*,[9] in 1908, he reduced the number to nineteen and sought to separate the administrative functions from the juridical. He abolished some congregations and defined the competence of each department.

Many of the Fathers at Vatican II urged that the Curia again be reformed. Their complaints were many. They felt that it was too Italian and should be internationalized; that it should be more a servant than a master; that it should not interfere with papal power by claiming more authority than it rightfully has; and that it should avoid delays, secrecy, pettiness, and intrigue. The *Decree on the Bishops' Pastoral Office in the Church* enacted by the Council promised changes. A special commission to study curial reform was established by the Pope, and he personally involved himself in the work. Two important documents issued by the Pope detailed reform measures: the *motu proprio Pro comperto sane*, of August 6, 1967,[10] and the Apostolic Constitution *Regimini eccles...e universae*, of August 15, 1967.[11]

Pro comperto sane provided for a broader decision-making base. In order to make the Curia more representative, seven diocesan bishops are assigned to each congregation and participate in its plenary meetings. However, papal control over the appointment of these bishops continues. The pope selects them from a list of candidates submitted by the cardinal prefects of the congregations after they have consulted with national and regional episcopal conferences. In addition, the Congregation for Religious has three members chosen from the superior generals of religious orders or clerical congregations.

The Curia is not an independent organization but must work closely with other groups in the ecclesial system. It should do

---

[9] *Acta Sanctae Sedis*, 41 (1908), 425–440.

[10] *Acta Apostolicae Sedis*, 59 (1967), 881–884.

[11] *Ibid.*, 885–928. Cf. G. Zizola, "The Reformed Roman Curia," in J. A. Coriden, ed. *We, the People of God* (Huntington, Ind.: Our Sunday Visitor, 1968), pp. 49–77.

more than simply receive information from the world episcopate and adjudicate thorny issues. The Curia should foster the bishops' cooperation, seek their advice, and above all keep them informed. *Regimini ecclesiae universae* emphasized this collaboration and, in answer to a long-standing complaint, insisted, in Article 8, that: "Acknowledgments are to be sent to the bishops without delay for any document they may submit, and they are to be notified about departmental decrees that have special reference to their dioceses before these decrees are promulgated." In order to facilitate communication with the Curia, modern languages can be used, even though Latin remains the official language of the Church.

Two of the most anti-entropic provisions in the reorganization of the Curia in *Regimini ecclesiae universae* dealt with terms of office and operating procedures. In the first, the old practice of indefinite tenure was rejected. Now the heads and members of congregations, whether they be cardinals or bishops, and the consultors are appointed for a five-year term of office which can be extended by the pope alone. This new law has several advantages: it discourages careerism, protects against incompetent officials, and prevents the formation of a curial block which might tend to overextend its authority if allowed to remain in power too long. The success or failure of the recent curial reform depends, of course, on the pope's wise judgment. At the death of a pope, the heads of all the curial departments and offices, who are cardinals, must resign. The new pope is able to select his own advisors.

The second provision in the apostolic constitution concerned the more efficient operation of the Curia. Mutual cooperation rather than rivalry is the ideal. Where there are dovetailing competencies, it decreed that there should be frequent consultation among the heads of the departments at meetings presided over by the Secretary of State. A further step to insure collaboration was to make the heads of some departments members of others. For example, the presidents of the three secretariats are also members of the Congregation for the Evangelization of Nations; and the president of the Secretariat for Christian Unity is a member of the Congregation for the Eastern Churches.

The Curia is composed of several departmental subsystems:

the Secretariat of State with its Council for the Public Affairs of the Church (a kind of foreign ministry); ten congregations, three secretariats, three tribunals, six offices, and numerous commissions and councils. The principal curial departments are given in the schema on the opposite page.

Two elements in the Roman Curia deserve special attention from a cybernetic viewpoint: its membership and its informational flow. As regards the first, it is clear that the members of the Curia are not elected by the community or even by their peers, but directly appointed by the pope. Can we say, however, that the Curia is representative of the entire ecclesial system in that its membership is genuinely international?

For centuries there has been criticism that the Curia was exclusively Italian. Since Vatican II, however, the Curia has become more international. Fiorello Cavalli has analyzed the membership of the Curia from 1961 to 1970, and his study indicates dramatic changes.[12] In this period, the number of Italians in the Curia increased from 749 to 854, while the number of non-Italians increased from 573 to 1,406. This represents an increase of only 14 percent for Italians and 145 percent for non-Italians. Yet Cavalli points out that in 1970, Italy still supplied some 38 percent of curial workers. However, many of these were minor officials and clerks who are native Romans. This is understandable as long as Rome remains the center of Church government. The real indication of the increased international character of the Curia is the presence of non-Italians in the highly sensitive positions of Secretary of State and the prefects of the congregations. In 1961 the Secretary of State and 8 prefects of congregations were Italians. Today only 4 Italians head congregations and the present Secretary of State, Cardinal Villot, is from France.

---

[12] F. Cavalli, "Sviluppo dell'internationalizzazione nella Curia Romana," *La Civiltà Cattolica*, 2 (1970), 555–568. The international character of the College of Cardinals has also changed much in the last decade. At present there are 117 cardinals representing 42 nations. Of this number there are 72 Europeans, 14 Latin Americans, 13 North Americans, 9 Asians, 7 Africans, one Australian, and one New Zealander. There are now only 35 Italians, the lowest ratio the Italian hierarchy has had in the college for centuries.

POPE

Secretariat of State
(Council for the Public Affairs of the Church)

Congregations
Doctrine of the Faith*
Bishops
Oriental Churches
Discipline of the Sacraments
Clergy
Religious and Secular Institutes
Evangelization of Peoples
Causes of Saints
Divine Worship
Catholic Education

Councils
Laity

Secretariats
Christian Unity
Non-Christians
Non-Believers

Commissions
Justice and Peace
Biblical Studies
Revision of Vulgate
Revision of Code of Canon Law
Preparation of Oriental Code of
 Canon Law
Latin America
Social Communication
Sacred Archaeology
Interpretation of Decrees of Vatican
 II

Tribunals
Rota
Apostolic Signature
Penitentiary Apostolic

Offices
Apostolic Chancery
Economic Affairs of Holy See
Apostolic Chamber
Administration of Patrimony of Holy
 See
Prefecture of Apostolic Palace
Central Statistics

* There is a Theological Commission attached to this congregation. It was initially provided for in the *motu proprio, Integrae servandae,* of December 7, 1965. The statutes governing this body of consultors were issued on July 12, 1969. Their function is to assist the pope and the Congregation for the Doctrine of Faith in studying doctrinal questions. Its members, selected from outstanding theologians all over the world, are appointed by the pope on the advice of the Prefect of the Congregation, who has consulted the episcopal conferences. Their term is for five years. They met for the first time in October 1969.

43

A controversial area of curial membership is the insignificant number of women employed. In 1970, for example, there were only seventy women working in Vatican offices, and most of these held secretarial positions. There were, however, five who had staff positions in the Secretariat of State (two nuns and three laywomen); four nuns in the Congregation for Religious; and two nuns in the Council for Public Affairs. The attitude of the Holy See concerning women was reflected in the 1970 refusal to accredit Dr. Elizabeth Mueller as a counselor of the West German mission to the Vatican. The reason given was that since Dr. Mueller was single this would make social contact with Vatican officials difficult.[13]

The second cybernetic element in the Curia is information flow. We have already seen that inputs are directed to the Curia primarily from the bishops, who should participate in and be informed of decisions that affect them. There is another channel of information which is important in the Church's central government: the papal diplomatic corps. Under the control of the Council for the Public Affairs of the Church, the nuncios, pronuncios, and apostolic delegates form a sensitive link between Rome and the regional churches. The top-level positions in the diplomatic corps are usually occupied by Italians whose promotion is based on years of service. The diplomats act as a two-way communication channel. They inform Rome of the level of supports and demands in the local churches; receive reports from episcopal conferences and transmit them to Rome; and convey and interpret instructions from Rome to the local authorities. The diplomatic corps, in the mind of Pope Paul, has two principal functions: to enable the Holy See to work for peace through its delegates to various nations and to reinforce the bonds between the local churches and Rome.[14]

Minor curial outputs are usually approved by the heads of the departments, but all major decisions must be submitted to the pope. *Regimini ecclesiae universae* explicitated the relationship

---

[13] *NC News Service (Foreign)*, February 11, 1970.

[14] The duties of the papal legates are explained in the *motu proprio Sollicitudo omnium ecclesiarum, Acta Apostolicae Sedis,* 61 (1969), 473-484. Cf. J. Hennesey, "Papal Diplomacy and the Contemporary Church," in *The Once and Future Church,* pp. 179-204.

between the pope and the Curia, which it sees as an instrument assisting the pope in exercising his supreme power over the universal Church. The constitution, however, emphatically stated, in Article 136, the necessity of papal approval: "This solemn rule is to be held: that nothing serious and unusual is to be done before the department heads have informed the Supreme Pontiff." The Pope remains in close contact with the Curia. He receives reports regularly and meets frequently with major curial officials. The Secretary of State sees the Pope almost daily and other officials may request audiences with him or be summoned by him.

D. THE COLLEGE OF BISHOPS

The bishops of the world under the leadership of the pope form the episcopal college, which has responsibility for the universal Church. In the ninth chapter, we will examine the theological aspects of collegiality. Now, we will discuss the channels of communication that exist between the Vatican and the bishops: first the diocesan bishops; and second, the corporate episcopate.

As to the first, residential bishops are obliged to send written reports to the Holy See every five years (Canon 340). These and other regular reports sent to Rome describe in detail the spiritual and financial state of the diocese. They include statistical information on the number of baptisms, confirmations, ordinations, marriages, and converts. Diocesan bishops must also meet personally with the pope at set intervals. This *ad limina* visit is required every five years for European bishops and every ten years for others.

The second way the bishops communicate with the Vatican and with each other is through assemblies of different kinds. The most solemn of these is the ecumenical or general council, which includes all the bishops of the world. The ecumenical council is rarely convoked—they number no more than twenty-one throughout history. More common are three other types of councils: the provincial, the plenary, and the national. A provincial council, whose members are bishops of the several dioceses within a specific territory or province, are to be convoked every twenty years (Canon 283) by the metropolitan, the archbishop in charge of an ecclesiastical province. The plenary council is attended by residential bishops from several ecclesiastical provinces and is held with the permission of the pope, who appoints a legate to convene it and to preside over it (Canon 281). The national or regional council is attended by bishops from the same nation or region. These councils are decision-making bodies. They have the task of evaluating inputs and converting them into authoritative outputs. These decisions are designed to give positive pastoral direction, to increase the level of support, and to reply to demands, if not favorably at least reasonably. The acts of all these councils are sent to the Holy See for approval.

National episcopal conferences were especially urged by Vatican II. The Council saw them as appropriate ways to encourage collegial responsibility among the bishops. It was hoped that from them "there will emerge a holy union of energies in the service of the common good of the churches."[15] The decisions of episcopal conferences are deliberative in those matters which are prescribed by common law or determined by the Apostolic See. The bishops of the United States meet twice a year to discuss matters that affect the whole American Church. In the last few years, they considered such important matters as priestly celibacy, catechetical instruction, due process, poverty, war, racism, abortion, conscientious objection, and mixed marriages. Statements emanating from the conferences appear in the religious and secular press. While the present legislation limits carefully the authority of the episcopal conferences, it seems inevitable that in time they will assume greater autonomy.[16] The growing opposition to Roman bureaucratic control and the intensity and peculiarity of regional problems should hasten greater decentralization. This could also open the way to clerical and lay participation, if not on a deliberative level, at least on a consultative one.

---

[15] *Decree on the Bishops' Pastoral Office in the Church*, Art. 37.

[16] Cf. J. Hamer, "Les conferences épiscopales: exercise de la collegialité," *Nouvelle revue théologique*, 85 (1963), 966–969; P. Huizing, "The Structure of Episcopal Conferences," *The Jurist*, 28 (1968), 163–176; F. R. McManus, "The Scope of Authority of Episcopal Conferences," in *The Once and Future Church*, pp. 129–178; and R. W. Kutner, *The Development, Structure, and Competence of the Episcopal Conference* (Washington: Catholic University of America, 1972).

Besides the local, provincial, and national conferences, the Holy See has established an international episcopal conference, namely, the synod of bishops. It is one of the most significant structural developments to take place in the Church in centuries. The synod is an anti-entropic institution designed to combat stagnation and polarization in the ecclesial system by fostering communication among the members of the hierarchy. The idea of a consultative and representative assembly of bishops was suggested several times in the preparatory sessions of Vatican II, as well as in the conciliar debates. On September 14, 1965, Pope Paul announced, at the opening of the Fourth Session, that such a synod would be established. The next day it was formally instituted by the *motu proprio Apostolica sollicitudo*.[17] It is also described in Article 5 of the *Decree on the Bishops' Pastoral Office*:

Bishops from various parts of the world, chosen through ways and procedures established or to be established by the Roman Pontiff, will render especially helpful service to the supreme pastor of the Church in a council to be known by the proper name of Synod of Bishops. Since it will be acting in the name of the entire Catholic episcopate, it will at the same time demonstrate that all the bishops in hierarchical communion share in the responsibility for the universal Church.

The synod of bishops has several goals. First of all, it assists the pope in governing the universal Church by supplying him with information, advice, and support. Secondly, it is a valuable subsystem whereby representatives of the local churches can meet to resolve urgent problems and to make short-term and long-term plans. It is a vital element in the continual process of self-renewal. Thirdly, it is a public sign of the collegial responsibility of the bishops of the entire Church.

There are three kinds of synodal meetings. The *general assembly* is the largest and comprises curial cardinals, patriarchs and some archbishops from the Eastern Catholic churches, delegates from national episcopal conferences, and ten representatives from religious orders of men. The general assembly met in 1967 and 1971 with about two hundred members in attendance. The *extraordinary assembly* is a smaller body which is con-

---

[17] *Acta Apostolicae Sedis*, 57 (1965), 775–780.

vened to deal with problems requiring immediate discussion. The only delegates are the curial cardinals, the presidents of the national episcopal conferences, patriarchs and archbishops of the Eastern Catholic churches, and three elected clerical representatives of religious communities. About a hundred and fifty members attended the 1969 synod. The *special assembly*, which has not yet met, deals with problems in a particular geographic area. The representatives are chosen from that area. Curial cardinals are selected if their congregation has competency in the matter to be discussed.

The synod of bishops, representing the worldwide episcopate, is an integral part of the administration of the universal Church. It is a legislative, problem-solving body, but it remains essentially a consultative organ. The pope is not juridically bound to accept its decisions. According to the original legislation establishing the synod, the rights of the pope were clearly enunciated. It is the pope's privilege to convoke a synod whenever and wherever he wishes; to appoint a permanent secretary; to ratify the election of the delegates; to select as many as one-third of the delegates himself; to preside over the discussions; and to give final approval of any decisions reached.

Many of the bishops at the 1969 Synod suggested that the synod become more of a parliamentary and deliberative assembly. Serious reservations were expressed about the almost absolute papal control over the synod, and demands were made to modify this by increasing episcopal representation in the functioning of the synod. The Pope finally accepted three major recommendations made by the delegates which reflect greater shared responsibility: that the synod be called regularly at least every two years; that the permanent Synod Secretariat, a key structure in practical collegiality, be expanded to include bishops from all parts of the world; and that the bishops be allowed to contribute to the formulation of the agenda. These provisions will undoubtedly affect the development of the synod. As a juridical institution it is still in its formative stage. We can expect further refinements in time. The following questions should be considered, since the synod deals with issues that concern the entire ecclesial system: Should there not be adequate representation from the two other principal segments in the Church, the clergy and the laity? Should the College of Cardinals be reorganized to act as a permanent "senate of advisors" to the pope and hold frequent consistories? and Should the synod in the future be given the responsibility of electing a pope?

II. *The Local Church*

The universal ecclesial system is divided into geographic units called dioceses, which in turn are divided into parishes. These local communities are not simply administrative segments of the larger Church but specific actualizations of the entire mystery of the Body of Christ which is one. Called together and sustained by the Spirit, the local churches share in the common apostolic faith of the universal Church, but preserve their own unique character. In a word, they are communities of faith—each proclaiming and representing the saving mission of Christ. As communities, organization is an essential element of their existence. Structures are necessary if goals are to be achieved. Our concern here is with the organizational structure of the diocesan Church from a cybernetic viewpoint. Using the principles of communication and control, we will analyze the following elements: the bishop, the diocesan curia, synods and councils, the laity and clergy, and finally a diocesan example.

A. THE BISHOP

The bishop is the leader of the local ecclesial system. He has pastoral responsibility for each of the faithful under his care. Although not selected by the community, he is their spiritual father. Through his episcopal consecration, the bishop has the duty to promote holiness and unity within the community and to oversee its activities. Traditionally, the bishop's office is seen as one of service, *diakonia*. Consequently, whether he is celebrating the Eucharist, proclaiming the word of God, ordaining and confirming, or counseling and administering, he should act as a servant of his people. The bishop governs the diocese in the name of Christ, and not simply as a representative of the pope.

The bishop is the chief decision-maker in the diocese. Vatican II states clearly that the bishops, as successors of the Apostles, "automatically enjoy in the dioceses entrusted to them all the ordinary, proper, and immediate authority required for the exercise of their pastoral office."[18] The Council adds that the prerogatives of the pope remain intact. In exercising this pastoral authority, the bishop may produce several types of output to meet demands made by the people or required by circumstances. He has to provide for proper teaching and preaching; build new churches, schools, or hospitals; ordain new priests; see that each part of the diocese has sufficient spiritual care, and, on occasion, adjudicate disputes. In all things the bishop must work for the good of his people and encourage their own spiritual growth. As part of his teaching office, further outputs may appear in the form of pastoral letters, instructions, or decrees on doctrinal and disciplinary matters. These should only be issued after proper consultation with the clergy and laity of his diocese.

B. THE DIOCESAN CURIA

To assist the bishop in governing the diocese there is a permanent staff of collaborators and several offices which together form the diocesan curia. Although individual members of the community may contact the bishop personally, their demands are usually communicated to him through curial channels. The curia may be divided into three sections: administrative, judicial, and archival. The administrative officials, priests appointed by the bishop, who confers regularly with them, are: the vicar-general, diocesan consultors, pastor-consultors, synodal examiners, vicars forane, and the vicar of religious. The vicar-general holds the most important post in the Curia. He is the bishop's *alter ego* and is directly concerned with ordinary administrative detail. Vatican II, in a step toward decentralization, urged that when the government of a diocese requires it, the bishop should appoint, in addition to the above-mentioned officials, one or more episcopal vicars.[19] They are given charge of a part of the

---

[18] *Decree on the Bishops' Pastoral Office in the Church*, Art. 8. Other Roman documents discussed episcopal rights and duties: *Pastorale munus, Acta Apostolicae Sedis,* 56 (1964), 5–12; *De episcoporum muneribus, ibid.,* 58 (1966), 467–472; and *Ecclesiae sanctae, ibid.,* 58 (1966), 757–782.

[19] *Decree on the Bishops' Pastoral Office in the Church*, Art. 27.

diocese, of a special apostolate, or of a particular rite. Priests as well as auxiliary bishops may hold this position, which entrusts them with the same authority the law gives to the vicar-general. In Liverpool, for example, the episcopal vicars are bishops, but in Detroit they are priests.

The judicial officers of the diocesan tribunal also exercise control functions. As a duly established ecclesiastical court, they work primarily with marriage cases, but they are competent to deal also with contentious and criminal cases. The main officers of the tribunal are the officialis, promoter of justice, defender of the bond, synodal judges, and auditors. The bishop appoints them. To insure adequate replacement of qualified canonists in the diocese, he may urge some of his priests to pursue advanced study in Canon Law.

The archival section of the diocesan curia is, according to the Code, an information-tabulating office. The chancellor, vice-chancellor, and notaries have the responsibility of keeping the archives of the diocese, arranging them in chronological order and indexing them. The archivists, therefore, process information and keep an accurate control of all communications coming in and going out of the chancery. In actual practice, however, these duties are usually done by secretarial help. In most dioceses the chancellor is much more than an archivist. He is usually a very influential person in the diocese, a personal confidant of the bishop, and has charge of several important administrative areas.

Besides the diocesan staff, there are also other offices or committees which assist the bishop in his pastoral concern for the community. In large dioceses these may number as many as thirty or forty. For example, there are usually commissions dealing with pastoral, liturgical, ecumenical, and building problems; offices for education, finance, charities, and cemeteries; organizations of men, women, and youth; and, finally, groups dealing with specific apostolates. Their membership is composed of both clergy and laity. Working together under the authority of the bishop, they should be allowed to make creative plans, discover and evaluate new solutions, and call upon the community for support. Such offices can contribute dynamic input to the self-renewing character of the ecclesial system.

C. THE SYNODS AND COUNCILS

The present legislation of the Church also provides for several advisory systems on the diocesan level. The most formal of these is the diocesan synod (Canon 356), which is to be held every ten years and presided over by the bishop. The Code restricts membership in this synod to clergy and male religious. Since Vatican II, however, diocesan synods have included representatives from the laity and women's religious groups. Vatican II urged that two other groups be formed in the diocese as permanent consultative bodies: the priests' senate and the diocesan pastoral council. The priests' senate, found in most dioceses of the United States, is, according to mandate, to "give effective assistance to the bishop in his government of the diocese."[20] The diocesan pastoral council, composed of representatives from the clergy, religious, and laity, is given the duty "to investigate and to weigh matters which bear on pastoral activity, and to formulate practical conclusions regarding them."[21] About eighty dioceses in the United States have pastoral councils, and others are in the process of forming them.

Another organization, the parish council, has become com-

---

[20] *Decree on the Ministry and Life of Priests*, Art. 7. Also see *Decree on the Bishops' Pastoral Office in the Church*, Art. 27 and, *Ecclesiae sanctae*, I, 15.

[21] *Decree on the Bishops' Pastoral Office in the Church*, Art. 27 Also see *Decree on the Apostolate of the Laity*, Art. 26; *Ecclesiae sanctae*, I, 16; and R. Pagé, *The Diocesan Pastoral Council* (Paramus, N.J.: Newman, 1970). In spite of the Conciliar and post-Conciliar emphasis on priests' senates and pastoral councils and synods, it is disconcerting that the 1971 revised draft of the *Lex Fundamentalis Ecclesiae* makes no mention of them. The *Lex*, intended to provide a constitution for the Church, was prepared by the Commission for the Revision of Canon Law. It was severely criticized by theologians and canonists. The main reason was that it advocated an outdated ecclesiology and failed to incorporate the principles of collegiality and co-responsibility. The *Lex* is now undergoing further revision. Cf. The Canon Law Society of America, "A General Analysis of the Proposed Schema of the *Lex Fundamentalis*," *The Jurist*, 31 (1971), 342–362; "A Critique of the Revised Schema of the *Lex Fundamentalis*," in *Proceedings of the Canon Law Society of America, 1971 Convention*, pp. 65–77; and *Notes for a Critical Analysis of the Schema of the Lex Ecclesiae Fundamentalis* (Bologna: Istituto per le scienze religiose, 1971).

monplace in American dioceses since Vatican II.[22] There are thousands of parish councils throughout the United States, and a conservative estimate suggests that over half a million people are involved. Their task has been broadly defined as assisting the pastor and his priests in the life of the parish.

In theory, the diocesan pastoral councils and the parish councils are claimed to be practical manifestations of subsidiarity and co-responsibility. In practice, this is rarely the case. Ideally, they should be organs of communication and control, channels of constructive input, and centers of dynamic planning within the diocese. They often fall short of these goals. The reasons for this failure are many. The councils are still in the process of defining their roles, and the newness of collaborative effort is baffling to many. In some dioceses, council members are elected by the people; in others, the bishop or pastors appoint them. The former tend to be more active. Some bishops and priests see the councils as encroaching on clerical preserves and hence refuse to cooperate. When they do, they are disappointed that willing workers are difficult to find, that few younger members take part, that attendance is often poor, and that internal controversies take up an inordinate amount of time. The laity complain that the councils possess no real power and are only feeble efforts at shared responsibility, since the clerical members tend to dominate. Blame undoubtedly falls on both parties. One thing that has to be clarified is the relationship between the councils and existing diocesan structures. Another is the precise authority that the councils possess. At present their authority is too often determined solely according to the discretion of the pastor. If these questions can be settled and clergy and laity put aside their suspicion and apathy, the councils can be valuable instruments in the diocese.

There is another organization in the United States which, though not strictly speaking diocesan, is certainly related to the activities of the local Church. It is the United States Catholic Conference (USCC), which is the operational or service arm of

---

[22] Cf. *Decree on the Apostolate of the Laity*, Art. 10 and 26, and *Constitution on the Church*, Art. 37. Cf. also B. Lyons, *Parish Councils: Renewing the Christian Community* (Techny, Ill.: Divine Word Publications, 1967) and D. P. O'Neill, *The Sharing Community: Parish Councils and Their Meaning* (Dayton, Ohio: Pflaum, 1968).

the National Conference of Catholic Bishops (NCCB). The USCC, with headquarters in Washington, D.C., is a kind of communications center which disseminates information and implements the programs of the American hierarchy. It has major departments dealing with education, communication, social development, health services, and international affairs. Of special interest for the laity is the National Council of Catholic Laity (NCCL), which was established in 1971 as a coalition of the former National Council of Catholic Men and the National Council of Catholic Women. The NCCL is composed of diocesan-level Catholic organizations that represent about twenty-five million American Catholics. It could become an effective voice for the laity in America and represent a serious step toward functional co-responsibility. Hierarchical support, however, will be indispensable for this goal to be attained.

A further effort to coordinate national diocesan efforts is the emergence, in many countries, of the national pastoral council. Unlike the national episcopal conference, it includes a proportionate representation from all levels of Church membership. The purpose of such a council is to strengthen interdiocesan communication and to use collected information as a basis for constructive problem-solving and planning. Holland held the first national pastoral council in 1966, and other nations are preparing for them. In the United States, the National Conference of Catholic Bishops, in February 1970, commissioned its Advisory Council to undertake a feasibility study of a national council. Membership in the Advisory Council was representative. Ten persons, from different parts of the country, were selected from the following groups: bishops, diocesan priests, religious, lay women, and lay men. At their meeting in September 1971, they reported that a national council should be held, but not before 1976. The Advisory panel suggested that in order to make the council "optimally effective," the American clergy and laity needed a thorough education in the theoretical and practical dimensions of shared responsibility as it applies to the local, regional, and national Church.

A post-Conciliar phenomenon in the American Church has been the establishment of dozens of unofficial organizations. Most are independent lobbying or pressure groups formed around specific demands. These groups, involving clergy, religious, and laity, are frequently irritants to the hierarchic control system and make wide use of the communications media to publicize their demands. Their different platforms represent a polarity in the American Church and also indicate a loss of confidence in Church leadership. For example, the National Association for Pastoral Renewal (1966), the Society of Priests for a Free Ministry (1968), and the National Federation of Priests' Councils (1968) advocate, among other things, optional celibacy for priests. The National Association of Laity (1967) is a liberal organization, while the National Federation of Laymen (1968) and the Catholics United for the Faith (1968) are conservative. American religious women have also established several groups: the National Black Sisters' Conference (1968), the National Coalition of American Nuns (1969), the Association of Contemplative Sisters (1969), and the National Assembly of Women Religious (1970). The two main organizations of Black Catholics are: the National Office for Black Catholics (1968) and the National Black Lay Caucus (1968).

D. THE CLERGY AND THE LAITY

In the local ecclesial system, the diocesan clergy are leaders of the smaller subsystem, the parish. They are the main channels of communication between the bishop and the people. On the one hand, the ordained ministers collaborate with the bishop in proclaiming the word of God, celebrating the sacramental mysteries, and teaching the People of God the true meaning of the Christian revelation. The priests, as the final official link in the output process, have the additional duty to transmit and explain to their community the doctrinal and disciplinary norms that come from the bishop. On the other hand, the priests are usually the first to receive input from the laity. Expressions of support and demand are ordinarily initially directed to the parish priests. The type of feedback they receive is predominantly in the form of demands: requests, complaints, questions. If the priest is sensitive to the needs of his parishioners, he will carefully assess the demands and take positive steps to restore support. The pastor, although he is the principal decision-maker in the parish, should make important judgments only in consultation with his priests and parish council. Many delicate issues may be handled more equitably in an atmosphere of co-responsibility. The operative criterion in all parochial action is the spiritual welfare of the people. Or, as Vatican II reminded us: "The parish exists solely for the good of souls."[23]

Members of religious orders form another significant part of the local Church. They are a subsystem that contributes valuable input to the spiritual life of a diocese. Religious, both men and women, have given heroic service to the Church in the United States. The Church owes much to the educational and charitable apostolates of the active congregations, but no less to the prayer and example of the contemplative orders.

Finally, there is the laity, the core of the Christian community. They do not belong to the ordained ministry, nor do they take religious vows. They are persons living in the world who have committed themselves to Christ and try to manifest this conviction in their daily lives. Numerically, the laity comprise the largest segment in the Church, and hierarchic outputs are directed mainly to them. Without them, there is no Church. But for centuries their role has been described only in terms of dependence and support. The official Church calls them to holiness, loyalty, and obedience and urges them to maintain the community through generous financial help. Furthermore, the married laity are expected to bring up their families in a genuine Christian environment and encourage their children to accept God's call to a priestly or religious life. What has been lacking is the participation of mature Christians in the decision-making of the Church. Cast in a subordinate position, the laity have had a minimal voice in Church administration. A rich source of talent and energy has been neglected. The laity are capable of contributing more than support—however indispensable this may be—to the ecclesial system. Vatican II has helped correct this imbalance by proposing the ideals of shared responsibility and collaboration. In practice, however, these are barely beginning to develop. The clerical image still endures and lay participation remains minimal.

---

[23] *Decree on the Bishops' Pastoral Office in the Church*, Art. 31.

E. THE DETROIT EXPERIENCE

Several dioceses have attempted to reorganize their structures in order to facilitate communication and to broaden the decision-making base. One of the most successful programs has been developed by the archdiocese of Detroit, which has a million and a half Catholics, 350 parishes, 1,500 diocesan and religious priests, 150 brothers, and 4,600 nuns. The goal was to increase shared pastoral responsibility in this large urban diocese. After three years of preparation, during which some eighty thousand people participated and some sixty-five thousand proposals were made, a diocesan synod was held in 1969.[24] Its principal recommendation was the establishment of the vicariate system. The diocese was divided into twenty-five vicariates and one pro-vicariate for the campus ministry. Each vicariate comprises about a dozen parishes and is presided over by an episcopal vicar, a priest elected for a three-year term by the laity, religious, and clergy. The task of the vicar is to organize the parishes so that they meet together regularly to exchange ideas, attack common problems, and collectively work together to develop a genuine Christian assembly. The vicariate council, made up of representatives of groups within the vicariate, meet frequently to coordinate the work of the entire vicariate.

One major casualty in the Detroit plan was the chancery. It was suppressed. Instead of having nearly forty offices, there are now six service departments: Christian worship, Christian service, education, communication, research and planning, and administrative services. There is also a tribunal for the entire diocese and three delegates—for clergy, laity, and religious.

The purpose of the Detroit model is to give everyone a voice in the life of the archdiocese. By the strengthening and unifying of individual parish activities, duplicated efforts are avoided. The increased number of effective channels of internal communication help develop a sense of community. The bishop becomes less remote from his people, since the episcopal vicars, who meet with him biweekly, inform him of the levels of support and demands.

[24] The history, statutes, and commentary of the Detroit synod are described in Synod/69, published by the Archdiocese of Detroit.

Where it would be difficult to assemble 350 pastors, the bishop can easily meet with the 25 vicars for coordinating and planning sessions. Bureaucratic delay has been reduced, and the laity are able to enter into a productive relationship with other members of the diocese, both clerical and lay.

The Detroit experience has been a fruitful one. Although still in the process of improvement, it has become a precedent for change and a model for imitation that has influenced the Church both here and abroad. Moreover, from a cybernetic point of view, it should be noted that this diocesan reorganization was the fruit of widespread participation by all members of the community. It was not an imposition by authoritative output but an evolution based on communicative interaction.

CONCLUSION

Having examined both the elements of cybernetics and the organization of the Church, we can make two general conclusions:

First, the Church is clearly susceptible of cybernetic analysis. For it is an open system with channels of communication and control interacting with an environment both human and divine. Its conversion process makes use of the feedback loop in successfully resisting the forces of entropy. Moreover, the concept of the Church as an information-processing unit provides a deeper understanding of its theology as well as its role in the complex world of today.

Second, this cybernetic analysis of the Church indicates an imbalance in its role structure. Authoritative outputs are almost solely within the exclusive competence of the hierarchy, with little significant participation by the lower clergy or the laity. Although inputs are received from the nonhierarchical members of the system, these channels are inefficient and in need of reorganization. Since Vatican II a beginning, at least, has been made in this direction. Nevertheless it is safe to say that in the modern Church there is little democratization.

These conclusions will be even stronger when, in the next part, we consider four crucial instances of cybernetic interaction in the Church.

PART TWO

*Four Examples of
Cybernetic Analysis*

YBERNETICALLY, every development in the Church, whether doctrinal or disciplinary, is a response to input received from the members or the environment. The Magisterium or collegial authority in the Church functions as an information-processing unit. We consider here the interaction between inputs (supports and demands) and outputs (authoritative decisions and actions).

The crucial instances of cybernetic interaction which we have selected are of special relevance for the American Church. Not only do they concern areas of historical and current interest, but they focus on that precious value which is "the liberty of the sons of God."

Moreover, each one of the instances illustrates a different theological problem area for decision-makers. Two are doctrinal; two disciplinary. The slavery question involves the fundamental human right of personal freedom which was finally declared by the consensus of the universal Church to be a necessary part of the natural law and the Gospel message. The birth control debate centers on the doctrinal aspects of the individual right of conscience in an area of moral ambiguity. The ecumenical

movement includes disciplinary norms as well as doctrinal principles as it determines the freedom of Christians to worship
together. Lastly, the controversy over priestly celibacy deals
with an essentially disciplinary matter, the freedom of all members of the Church to marry.

3

The Slavery Question

BY THE END OF the eighteenth century, slavery was well established in the American colonies. During the next fifty years it had a phenomenal growth. There were many reasons for this development: slaves were in abundant supply and relatively inexpensive to purchase; plantation owners considered them a good investment, since their maintenance was minimal in comparison to the years of work they and their offspring gave; and, finally, the flourishing cotton economy of the South was dependent upon this form of cheap labor. At the same time, however, there were serious moral questions raised both about the very existence of slavery and about the grave injustices done to slaves in the United States. In our cybernetic analysis of this question, we wish to examine the role played by American Catholics in the movement that lead to the Emancipation Proclamation in 1863. Did the Catholic hierarchy, clergy, and laity contribute significantly to the abolition of slavery?

I. *Output*

Several popes explicitly condemned the slave trade. Pope Paul III (1534–1549) excommunicated anyone who would capture and enslave the natives of Latin America.[1] Similar denunciations were made by Urban VIII (1623–1644)[2] and Benedict XIV (1740–1758).[3] A letter of Gregory XVI to the bishops of Brazil was frequently quoted during the American struggle for abolition. The Pope admonished all believers in Christ that "no one henceforth may dare unjustly to molest Indians, Negroes, or other men of this sort; or to despoil them of their goods; or to reduce them to slavery . . . or to exercise that inhuman trade by which Negroes, as if they were not men, but mere animals . . . are bought, sold, and doomed sometimes to the most severe and exhausting labors. . . ."[4]

The declaration of Gregory XVI was used by the abolitionist forces to enlist the aid of Catholics, but without success. This failure may be attributed to the interpretation given it by some members of the Catholic hierarchy. Bishop John England of Charleston, for example, argued that the Pope was speaking out against only the slave trade and the inhuman treatment given to slaves. The Bishop did not think that the Pope's words applied to "domestic slavery" as it was practiced in the United States.[5] The abolition of slavery, he felt, was a political issue and not a moral one. While he considered the introduction of slavery into a country as a moral evil, when asked whether he was "friendly to the existence or continuation of slavery," he replied: "I am not, but I see the impossibility of now abolishing it here. When it can and ought to be abolished, is a question for the legislature and not for me."[6]

---

[1] Denzinger-Schönmetzer, 1495.

[2] *Bullarium diplomatum et privilegiorum sanctorum romanorum pontificum*, XIV (1868), 712.

[3] *Bullarium Benedicti XIV*, I (1841), 123.

[4] Denzinger-Schönmetzer, 2746.

[5] *Works*, ed. S. G. Messmer (Cleveland: A. H. Clark, 1908), 5:187.

[6] *Ibid.*, 5:311.

Other bishops more or less agreed with Bishop England's assessment. Many episcopal statements, however, recommended manumission; urged better conditions for the slaves; exhorted slave owners to treat their charges kindly and justly; and sought proper religious and sacramental care of the slaves. Yet one looks in vain for an explicit condemnation of slavery as immoral.

The same reluctance is found in the outputs of the episcopal councils held before the emancipation. At the First Plenary Council of Baltimore in 1852, when the country was already deep into the slavery crisis, the bishops did not discuss the question at all. Few people today would agree with the observation made by historian Peter Guilday concerning this omission: "Perhaps the outstanding proof of the wisdom of our prelates lies in their silence over the slavery question, then dividing political parties, ... the hierarchy rejected the apparent demand for such a decision and refused to break with the traditional policy of the Church which excluded rigorously all discussions on political debate."[7] That this attitude prevailed among the hierarchy is clear from the pastoral letter of the Third Provincial Council of Cincinnati in 1861. The bishops expressed their concern over the Civil War that had just begun, but they took no stand on slavery. "The spirit of the Catholic Church is eminently conservative," the prelates wrote, and hence, "they do not think it their province to enter into the political arena."[8]

In short, we can say that the American Catholic hierarchy failed to provide any positive leadership in regard to the question of slavery. The bishops left it up to individuals to respond to the problem in terms of their own conscience and in harmony with local customs. John Tracy Ellis gives the reason for this stance: "Official Catholic doctrine held that slavery, thought of theoretically and apart from specific abuses to human dignity, was not opposed to the divine or natural law."[9]

---

[7] *A History of the Councils of Baltimore* (New York: Macmillan, 1932), pp. 183–184.

[8] *Acta et secreta quatuor conciliorum provincialium Cincinnatensium* (Cincinnati: Benziger, 1886), p. 145.

[9] *American Catholicism* (Chicago: University of Chicago Press, 1956), p. 87.

II. *Input*

The major feedback in the form of demands came, not from
Catholics, but from Protestants. The Quakers especially were
early leaders in the movement to abolish slavery. Even in post-
Revolutionary times, Protestants formed antislavery societies in
most of the states and urged the government to abolish the slave
trade and to grant immediate freedom to the slaves. By the end
of the eighteenth century this movement waned, but it revived
with vigor in the 1820s and '30s. Northern Protestants founded
dozens of abolitionist societies, wrote pamphlets and books
against slavery, and used every political and propaganda expedient to galvanize their fellow citizens to force the government to
act. Bishop Martin John Spalding accused the New England
Protestant ministers of causing the Civil War, because their
demands for abolition created a government crisis in 1860–
1861.[10] Some Protestants agreed with this assessment. So intense
was the feeling between Northern and Southern Protestant
churches that the Baptists, Methodists, and Presbyterians separated into different communions.

American Catholicism presented another picture.[11] In colonial
America and later, many Catholics in both the North and the
South owned slaves. This included some members of the hierarchy, priests, and religious orders such as the Jesuits, Capuchins,
and Ursuline nuns. The Jesuits, however, were ordered by their
General in 1836 to free their slaves. By and large, American
Catholics followed the practice of the region in which they lived.
They did not participate significantly in the abolitionist movement. Since they felt that the slavery issue was a political and
not a moral question, most Catholics did not even enter into the
controversy. They were supported in their position by the hierarchy and by the leading Catholic theologian, Archbishop Francis
P. Kenrick. In his volumes on moral theology, he opposed slavery
as a deprivation of freedom, but he did not see it as violating the

[10] D. Spalding, "Martin John Spalding's 'Dissertation on the American
Civil War,'" *Catholic Historical Review*, 52 (1956), 66–86.

[11] Cf. M. H. Rice, *American Catholic Opinion in the Slavery Controversy* (New York: Columbia University Press, 1944).

natural law. He felt that owners had a legal right to retain their slaves but that they should treat them humanely. On the question of political agitation for abolition, Kenrick was negative: "Nevertheless, since such is the state of things, nothing should be attempted against the laws nor anything be done or said that would make them bear their yoke unwillingly."[12]

Another reason why so few Catholics joined the abolitionist movement was the attitude of the Irish Catholics who immigrated in large numbers to the United States in the eighteenth century. The Irish, who were mostly unskilled laborers, felt that the liberation of slaves would be a grave economic threat. In the North, for example, the Irish had to compete on the labor market with freed slaves who worked for lower wages. Tensions between the two races accelerated, and riots broke out in Cincinnati in 1829, in Philadelphia in 1834, and in New York in 1863. Moreover, the Irish remained apathetic to the abolitionist movement because its leadership came principally from the Protestant Anglo-Saxon majority. Nativism and the anti-Catholic sentiments of many of the abolitionists did little to endear their cause to the Irish. Orestes A. Brownson criticized the hostility of the Catholic population to the abolitionists as "unwise, unpolitic, uncalled for." Catholics saw the abolitionists as enemies of religion and the state. Yet Brownson observed: "We do them [Catholics] an injustice if we suppose them to be really in favor of Negro slavery or opposed on principle to emancipation."[13]

III. *Conversion Process*

Once the Emancipation took place, Church leaders supported the new law of the land. In 1866, the bishops met at the Second Plenary Council of Baltimore. They issued several decrees dealing with the Negro apostolate and ordered that churches and schools be built for Negroes. It was left, however, to the local

---

[12] *Theologia Moralis* (Mechlin: H. Dessain, 1860), tr. v, cap. vi, no. 38. Cf. J. D. Brokhage, *Francis Patrick Kenrick's Opinion on Slavery* (Washington: Catholic University of America, 1955).

[13] *The Works of Orestes A. Brownson*, ed. H. Brownson (Detroit: Thorndike, Nours, 1884), 17:317.

bishops to decide whether or not they would be integrated.[14] The continued apathy and hostility among the clergy and laity prevented a speedy implementation of the decrees. The Third Plenary Council of Baltimore in 1884 established the Commission for Catholic Missions Among the Colored People and the Indians, and authorized that an annual collection be taken up in all churches for this purpose.[15] The most forthright and detailed statement on the moral and political rights of the Negro was the 1958 pastoral letter of the American bishops on "Discrimination and the Christian Conscience." The letter stated that "the heart of the race question is moral and religious" and that "segregation in our country has led to oppressive conditions and the denial of basic human rights for the Negro."[16]

While the hierarchy was making genuine efforts to ensure political, economic, educational, and social equality for the Negro, other enlightened segments of the Catholic population were also at work. Even before the Emancipation there were two Negro sisterhoods: the Oblate Sisters of Providence, founded in Baltimore in 1829, and the Holy Family Sisters, founded in New Orleans in 1842. In 1871, the English Mill Hill Fathers came to the United States to work with the Negroes, and they became the Josephites in 1893. Mother Kathrine Drexel founded the Sisters of the Blessed Sacrament for Indians and Colored People in 1893. Other orders that work with the Negro are the Sister-Servants of the Most Pure Heart of Mary, the Holy Ghost Fathers, and the Divine Word Fathers.

Many Catholic laymen have also dedicated themselves to the Negro apostolate. The first Catholic Interracial Council began in New York City in 1934 through the work of Jesuit John LaFarge. In the next thirty years, some sixty councils were formed. In 1959, these councils were organized on a nationwide basis as the National Conference for Interracial Justice, with headquarters in Chicago. There are now about one hundred local councils. Other Catholic organizations working for racial equality are the

---

[14] *Decreta concilii plenarii Baltimorensi II* (Baltimore: J. Murphy, 1886), pp. 243–247.

[15] *Acta et decreta plenarii Baltimorensis tertii* (Baltimore: J. Murphy, 1886), pp. 135–136.

[16] H. J. Nolan, ed., *Pastoral Letters of the American Hierarchy, 1792–1970* (Huntington, Ind.: Our Sunday Visitor, 1971), pp. 507–508.

Catholic Worker movement, founded by Dorothy Day in 1933, and the Friendship House movement, begun by Baroness de Hueck in 1939.

Progress toward racial equality has been slow. Catholic indifference and at times open hostility toward Negroes is still present more than a hundred years after their emancipation. William A. Osborne, in his book *The Segregated Covenant*, summarizes the contemporary situation: "Clearly, the thinking and actions of the Catholic people lag behind the Church's moral teaching on interracial justice, behind the official statements of the bishops, behind the progressive positions taken by laymen in the Catholic interracial movement."[17] This moral lag, however, should not be surprising in view of the fact that the teaching of the American Hierarchy had lagged far behind that of other churches until the United States Government had itself abolished slavery, and that the Catholic layman had contributed little to the changing of the American Catholic Church's position on interracial justice.

IV. *Evaluation*

The changing posture of the American bishops on the slavery question illustrates the role of environmental input on the conversion process. Here are the basic conclusions:

1. A change in policy took place. The hierarchy moved from its neutral acceptance of the political fact of slavery to its vigorous assertion of the moral and political rights of the Negro.

2. Environmental inputs, rather than inputs from within the system, contributed to this change in hierarchical output.

3. The bulk of the input came from other Christian churches and from Protestant lay groups. But the decisive input was the legislative change, the abolition of slavery.

4. The authoritative output of the American Hierarchy was first an acceptance of the political change, then a moral rationalization of it, and finally, a gradual imposition on its own members of the implication of this moral and political principle of human equality and freedom.

[17] New York: Herder and Herder, 1967, p. 42.

4

The Birth Control
Debate

No CYBERNETIC ANALYSIS of the contemporary Church would be complete without a study of the continuing birth control controversy. Never before in the history of the Church has a moral doctrine evoked such widespread and heated reaction. The amount of feedback, both positive and negative, is vast and unabated. Even though it is not a classic example of negative input forcing the Church to change, it is a fascinating and valuable study of interacting forces within the Church. Our aim in this chapter is not a theological evaluation of the arguments for or against contraception. Rather we wish to concentrate on the communication processes operative in the *Humanae vitae* debate and to analyze their cybernetic meaning. We will begin first with the output from the decision-making body.

I. *Output*

Over the last forty years, the official Church has spoken frequently on the morality of contraception. The teaching of Pope Pius XI's encyclical *Casti connubii* (December 31, 1930) was a landmark pronouncement. The Pope reaffirmed the traditional Catholic position on the subject and insisted that regulation of birth through artificial means is a violation of the primary end of marriage, which is the procreation of children. Contraception, he asserted, is an unnatural act that is contrary to reason, intrinsically evil, and not permissible under any circumstances. The Pope's teaching of "the uninterrupted Christian tradition" was unambiguous:

> No reason, however grave, may be put forward by which anything against nature may become conformable to nature and morally good. Since, therefore, the conjugal act is designed of its very nature for the generating of children, those who, in exercising it, deliberately deprive it of its natural power and capacity act against nature and commit a deed which is shameful and intrinsically immoral.[1]

The next pope, Pius XII, repeated this ban on contraception several times during his pontificate. For example, in an address to the Italian Catholic Union of Midwives in 1951 he quoted from *Casti connubii* and said: "This prescription holds good today just as much as it did yesterday. It will hold tomorrow and always, for it is not a mere precept of human right, but the expression of a natural and divine law."[2] He permitted the use of nonfertile periods for married couples if there are "medical, eugenic, economic, and social 'indications' "[3] for not having children. In 1958, the Pope referred to the progesterone pills at the Seventh International Congress of Hematology. He distinguished between their use for therapeutic reasons and their use solely for the control of contraception. The former is permitted, the latter forbidden as a direct and therefore illicit sterilization.[4]

John XXIII in *Mater et magistra* (1961), without mentioning specific methods of birth control, rejected every solution to the population problem which would "offend against the divinely established moral order or which would attack human life at its very source." Man, he said, "is not permitted to use certain ways

---

[1] *Acta Apostolicae Sedis*, 22 (1930), 559.
[2] *Ibid.*, 43 (1951), 843.
[3] *Ibid.*, 845–846.
[4] *Ibid.*, 50 (1958), 732–740.

and means which are allowable in the propagation of plant and animal life."[5] In March 1963, Pope John established, without public notice, a Pontifical Study Commission on Family, Population, and Birth Problems. Its original task was to study the policies of the United Nations and to make recommendations to the Holy See on questions dealing with birth control and population questions.

In June 1964, Pope Paul VI expanded the commission to about sixty members, including several theologians, sociologists, doctors, and demographers. Their added duty was to study in depth the teaching of the Church on the morality of birth control with special reference to the progesterone pill. In the same month, the Pope addressed a group of cardinals and expressed the hope that he would soon be able to announce the results of the study commission. "In the meantime," he added, "we must say openly that up to now we have not sufficient reason to consider the rules laid down by Pope Pius XII in this matter to be out-of-date and therefore not binding."[6] The Pope's statement drew mixed reactions. Advocates of a continuance of the Church's ban on contraception read the pronouncement as a reaffirmation of the traditional norms. Proponents of change were disappointed, but they felt that the Pope at least was keeping an open mind about the mutability of the Church's position. However, it would be another four years before the Pope spoke definitively on the question.

At the Second Vatican Council the Fathers debated the contraception issue, and in the *Constitution on the Church in the Modern World* reference was made to it. The final text reads: "Sons of the Church may not undertake methods of regulating procreation which are found blameworthy by the teaching authority of the Church in its unfolding of the divine law."[7] A footnote (No. 14 of the Latin text) cited statements of Pius XI, Pius XII, and Paul VI (his address to the cardinals on June 23, 1964). It also mentioned the papal study commission and a future judgment by the Pope when the commission had com-

---

[5] *Ibid.*, 53 (1961), 446–447.
[6] *Ibid.*, 56 (1964), 588.
[7] *Constitution on the Church in the Modern World*, Art. 51.

pleted its task. The note ended by stating: "With the doctrine of the magisterium in this state, this holy Synod does not intend to propose immediately a concrete solution."

The Birth Control Commission met for the last time in the spring of 1966. In June, the final report of twelve volumes was handed to the Pope. The contents of this report was never officially released, but some of the most important documents were obtained by the *National Catholic Reporter*. On April 19, 1967, it published three documents: the working papers of the conservative minority ("The State of the Question: the Doctrine of the Church and Its Authority"), the liberal majority's reply ("Summary Document on the Morality of Birth Control"), and the report from the theological section ("An Outline for a Document on Responsible Parenthood"). The most dramatic element about these documents was the fact that the majority of the Commission members (some reporters put the figure at 80 percent) favored a change in the Church's position on contraception.

The Pope once again returned to the problem of contraception in an address to the Italian Society of Obstetricians and Gynecologists on October 29, 1966. He reminded his audience that "the norm taught until now by the Church and integrated by the wise instructions of the Council, demands a faithful and generous observance. It cannot be considered not binding, as if the magisterium of the Church were in a state of doubt at the present time, when in fact the magisterium is in a period of study and reflection on what has been presented to it as worthy of the most attentive consideration."[8]

Two years later the Pope finally spoke definitively. On July 29, 1968 Pope Paul issued his 7,500-word encyclical *Humanae vitae*, which unequivocally denied the use of artificial birth control methods for Catholics. While the Pope wrote with compassion and stressed the concepts of conjugal love, responsible parenthood, and the personalistic elements in marriage, he left no doubt of his conviction that contraception does not fit into the Church's vision of married life. He expressed gratitude for the work of the Commission but added that their conclusions "could not be considered by us as definitive, nor dispense us from a per-

[8] *Acta Apostolicae Sedis*, 58 (1966), 1169-1170.

sonal examination of this serious question. . . ."[9] The Pope went
on to say that the unitive and procreative aspects of the conjugal
act are inseparably joined and therefore, "each and every marriage act must remain open to the transmission of life."[10] The
crux of the encyclical is in paragraph No. 14, where the Pope
discussed illicit ways of regulating birth. Besides abortion and
direct sterilization, he also excluded "every action which, either
in anticipation of the conjugal act, or in its accomplishment, or
in the development of its natural consequences, proposes,
whether as an end or as a means, to render procreation impossible."

The teaching of the Church on the regulation of birth is,
according to *Humanae vitae*, a promulgation of the divine law.[11]
The practice of contraception, therefore, is a contradiction of
God's plan and of nature[12] and is intrinsically dishonest.[13] The
Pope also addressed himself with warmth and gentleness to hus-
bands and wives and exhorted them to follow the teaching of
the Church. Mindful of the grave difficulties this could cause
them, he urged them to pray often and to receive the Eucharist.
He added: "And if sin should still keep its hold over them,"[14]
they should avail themselves of the grace of the sacrament of
Penance.

II. *Input*

The sheer bulk of feedback, positive and negative, to the
question of contraception makes any full analysis difficult. We
will restrict ourselves, therefore, to the recent history of the
debate and attempt to focus on the major sources of input.[15]

[9] No. 6. The Latin text of *Humanae vitae* can be found in *Acta Apostolicae Sedis*, 60 (1968), 481–503. An English translation was published by the
United States Catholic Conference (1968).

[10] No. 11.

[11] No. 20.

[12] No. 13.

[13] No. 14.

[14] No. 25.

[15] For a thorough historical analysis of the contraception issue see J. T.
Noonan, *Contraception: A History of its Treatment by the Catholic*

Our survey is not exhaustive, nor does it attempt to give a detailed evaluation of the theological positions involved, but rather an objective statement of the arguments of both sides. In the first part of this survey we will discuss the input before the encyclical appeared, and in the second part the input in the years following its issuance.

A. INPUT BEFORE *Humanae vitae*

Bishops. Throughout the twentieth century, national hierarchies all over the world condemned contraception as a violation of God's law which admitted of no exceptions. Bishops in the following countries issued collective pastorals: Germany (1913), Belgium (1920), United States (1920 and 1959), India (1960), England (1964), and Honduras (1966). In 1963, however, the Dutch bishops issued a short statement on the morality of the birth control pill which departed somewhat from the position taken by previous episcopal pronouncements. The bishops showed concern over the problems facing married Catholics. They noted that the individual conscience, after listening to the Church's interpretation of divine law, must make the final decision. Because of new ideas on man and human sexuality and because of the recent discoveries by science of means to regulate fertility, the Church, they asserted, "has no immediately appropriate answers ready that meet all situations."[16] But they denied that oral contraceptives would be the solution, and they added that Catholic theologians "are discussing the question whether these means could be acceptable in certain circumstances."[17]

Theologians and Canonists (Cambridge: Harvard University Press, 1965). The more recent history of the problem is discussed by the following authors: A. Valsecchi, *Controversy: The Birth Control Debate, 1958-1968* (Washington: Corpus, 1968); W. H. Shannon, *The Lively Debate: Response to Humanae Vitae* (New York: Sheed and Ward, 1970); and N. St. John-Stevas, *The Agonising Choice: Birth Control, Religion and the Law* (Bloomington, Ind.: Indiana University Press, 1970). These studies have proved most helpful in writing this section.

[16] Quoted in L. Pyle, *The Pill and Birth Regulation* (Baltimore: Helicon, 1964), p. 34.

[17] *Ibid.*

The Dutch bishops, while not approving of the pill, seemed to leave the question open for further study.

Theologians. Until 1963 it was the unanimous opinion of Catholic theologians that birth control was intrinsically immoral and against the explicit teaching of the Church. In 1965 two Jesuit theologians, John C. Ford and Gerald Kelly, surveyed theological opinion on this question. They concluded that: "The Church is so completely committed to the doctrine that contraception is intrinsically and gravely immoral that no substantial change in this teaching is possible. It is *irrevocable*."[18]

This theological consensus changed rapidly, with opposition coming initially from Northern European theologians. In 1963, three articles appeared that jolted the Catholic world. Louis Janssens of Louvain,[19] Willem van der Marck of Nijmegen,[20] and Bishop J. J. Reuss of Mainz,[21] all wrote on the morality of the birth control pill. Although they used different arguments, they agreed substantially that the use of the pill could be morally justified. Janssens, for example, tried to show that *morally* there is no difference between the use of anovulant pills and the practice of rhythm. Both methods, he argued, are used with the positive intention of excluding conception, and yet both preserve the intrinsic nature of the conjugal act.

Also during 1963 in the United States, Dr. John Rock, one of the developers of the anovulant pill, and Professor Emeritus of Harvard University, published a book entitled *The Time Has Come.*[22] In it, this Catholic physician contended that the pill was not an artificial but a physiological means of regulating birth. As such it should not fall under the Church's condemnation and should be judged in the same way as the rhythm method.

---

[18] *Contemporary Moral Theology* (Westminster, Md.: Newman, 1963), II, 277.

[19] "Morale conjugale et progestogènes," *Ephemerides theologicae Lovanienses*, 39 (1963), 787–826.

[20] "Vruchtbaarheidsregeling: poging tot antwoord op een nog open vraag," *Tijdschrift voor theologie*, 3 (1963), 378–413.

[21] "Eheliche Hingabe und Zeigung," *Tübinger theologische Quartalschrift*, 143 (1963), 454–475.

[22] New York: Knopf, 1963.

American Catholic theologians lost little time in reacting to the proposals of Rock, Janssens, and others. The main line of defense was manned by Jesuit moralists. Joseph S. Duhamel[23] and John J. Lynch[24] rejected Rock's position and Fathers Ford and Kelly categorically stated: "Dr. Rock's opinions in this matter have no standing whatever with Catholic theologians and directly contravene the authoritative teaching of the Catholic Church which is binding on all Catholics."[25] Janssens' position did not fare any better. Fathers Lynch,[26] Ford,[27] and Kelly[28] were unmoved by Janssens' arguments, rejecting them as specious and in direct contradiction of clear papal statements. Two other American theologians, Charles E. Curran[29] and Felix F. Cardegna,[30] considered the theses of Janssens, van der Marck, and Reuss more positively and were generally in agreement with the main lines of their arguments.

The debate gained momentum in 1964 when several books appeared on contraception. The majority called for a complete rethinking of the Church's ban on contraceptive methods. In *Contraception and Holiness*, edited by Archbishop Thomas D. Roberts,[31] various authors argued that the Church should modify its stand on birth control and that by so doing it would make a genuine contribution to the development of sexual morality. Many of the essays written by lay Catholics in *The Experience of Marriage*, edited by Michael Novak,[32] and in *What Modern Catholics Think about Birth Control*, edited by William Birmingham,[33] made similar suggestions. Two philosophical

---

[23] *America*, April 27, 1963, pp. 608–611.

[24] *Marriage*, 45 (1963), 16–17.

[25] Ford and Kelly, *op. cit.*, pp. 376–377, footnote 43.

[26] "Notes on Moral Theology," *Theological Studies*, 25 (1964), 232–253.

[27] *NC News Service (Domestic)*, February 15, 1964. Also in *Pyle, op. cit.*, pp. 21–22.

[28] "Confusion: Contraception and the Pill," *Theology Digest*, 12 (1964), 123–130.

[29] "Christian Marriage and Family Planning," *Jubilee*, 12 (1964), 8–13.

[30] "Contraception, the Pill and Responsible Parenthood," *Theological Studies*, 25 (1964), 611–636.

[31] New York: Herder and Herder, 1964.

[32] New York: Macmillan, 1964.

[33] New York: New American Library, 1964.

studies also appeared, both written by professors at Georgetown University. Germain C. Grisez wrote *Contraception and the Natural Law*, in which he elaborated his own ethical theory and concluded that "he who practices contraception acts directly against one of the principles which make human action meaningful."[34] Louis Dupré, however, in his book *Contraception and Catholics*, disagreed with Grisez and was critical of the Augustinian or biologistic view of human nature. The marriage act, he argued, must be seen in the total context of man's nature and in relationship to the many values of marriage. While Dupré admitted that permanent exclusion of procreation from the marital act would be wrong, "to exclude occasionally the fertility of their love when circumstances prevent them from taking proper care of new offspring, does not necessarily contradict the objective meaning of the marital act."[35]

Fuel was added to the debate among theologians by the Pope's address on October 29, 1966, referred to earlier, in which he stated that the norm which has been taught by the Church "cannot be considered as not binding, as if the magisterium of the Church were in a state of doubt at the present time." Some theologians argued that this papal statement on contraception had doctrinal force. Thus, Fathers Ford and Lynch discussed the problem whether the morality of contraception is in a state of practical doubt and whether one may resolve this doubt by practicing contraception in certain circumstances. They answered clearly: "As of today (March 1968) this theological state of affairs does *not* obtain, and the doctrine of the Church on contraception is *not* 'in a state of practical doubt' in this sense."[36] Other theologians denied that the October address was an authentic teaching statement. For that reason, Richard A. McCormick concluded: "I would agree with the many theologians who contend that the matter of contraception is as of now, at least for situations of genuine conflict, just what it was before the papal address—in a state of practical doubt."[37]

---

[34] Milwaukee: Bruce, 1964, p. 92.

[35] Baltimore: Helicon, 1964.

[36] "Contraception: A Matter of Practical Doubt?" *Homiletic and Pastoral Review*, 68 (1968), 563–574. Cf. also N. Halligan, "Doubt or No Doubt— The Papal Question," *American Ecclesiastical Review*, 156 (1967), 257–267.

[37] "Notes on Moral Theology," *Theological Studies*, 28 (1967), 800.

Protestants. In the first three decades of this century all Christian churches took a united stand against contraception. This ended abruptly in 1930, when the Anglican bishops met at the Lambeth Conference on August 15, 1930. They became the first Christian church to approve contraception officially. In their 1908 and 1928 meetings the bishops had condemned contraception, but in 1930 they took a much more liberal view. In Declaration 15 of the Conference, the Anglican hierarchy proposed abstinence as the primary method of family limitation, but went on to say: "Nevertheless, in those cases where there is such a clearly felt moral obligation to limit or avoid parenthood, and where there is a morally sound reason for avoiding complete abstinence, the Conference agrees that other methods may be used, provided this is done in the light of the same Christian principles." The bishops warned, however, that it is wrong to use any contraceptive method "from motives of selfishness, luxury, or mere convenience."[38]

The Catholic reaction to the Lambeth declaration was predictably vehement. The Archbishop of Westminster, Cardinal Bourne, referred to "this destructive resolution" through which the Anglican prelates "have abdicated any claim which they may have been thought to possess to be authorized exponents of Christian morality."[39] Bourne took his case to Rome and found willing support. A short time later Pius XI published *Casti connubii* which, in a clear reference to the Lambeth Conference, mentioned those who "openly departing from the uninterrupted Christian tradition have recently judged it possible solemnly to declare another doctrine regarding this question."[40]

During the next thirty years other Protestant denominations followed the lead of the Anglicans and approved the use of contraceptives for married couples. Among the principal churches

---

[38] *The Lambeth Conferences, 1867–1948* (London: SPCK, 1958), p. 166. The Anglo-Protestant position is discussed by G. Kelly, "Contraception and the Natural Law," in *Proceedings of the Catholic Theological Society of America, 1963 Convention* (Yonkers, N.Y.: CTSA Editorial Offices, 1964), pp. 33–36. Kelly cited a 1961 dissertation from the Gregorian University, Rome: R. E. Murray, *An Historical and Critical Study of the Lambeth Conferences' Teaching on Contraception.*

[39] R. J. Dingle, *Cardinal Bourne at Westminster* (London: Burns and Oates, 1934), p. 165.

[40] *Acta Apostolicae Sedis*, 22 (1930), 560.

were: United Church of Canada (1936), Methodist Church of Great Britain (1939), Church of Sweden (1951), Methodist Church of the United States (1956), Disciples of Christ (1968), and the World Council of Churches (1959).[41]

Other Factors. In the two decades that preceded *Humanae vitae* there were many other developments that brought the question of family limitation through contraception to a controversial peak for Catholics. First, a more personalistic view of marriage emerged emphasizing mutual fulfillment and enduring love between the partners. Catholic scholars, such as Herbert Doms and Dietrich von Hildebrand, rejected the former preoccupation with the biological element in marriage and viewed sexual intercourse rather as deriving its meaning from the total personal commitment of the couple.[42] Neither Doms nor von Hildebrand, however, advocated contraception; in fact, they were completely opposed to it. Yet their theories of marriage, which gained wide acceptance by Catholic theologians, did later—indirectly, at least—encourage others to rethink the whole problem of the morality of contraceptive intercourse. Second, certain social changes focused the attention of many Catholics on family limitation. Fears of overpopulation, the financial burden of raising and educating large families, and the respectability of contraception among non-Catholics created an atmosphere which put Catholic couples on the defensive. Finally, the development of the progesterone pills, which were first sold commercially in the United States in 1960, provided a simple and effective method of contraception. This discovery further unsettled Catholic couples who had found that the rhythm method was often unreliable and caused problems in their married lives.

On the eve of *Humanae vitae*, the Catholic world was sharply divided on the morality of contraception. Some, encouraged by the majority report of the Birth Control Commission, favored a modification of the Church's position. Others, supported by the previous tradition of the Church which was repeated frequently

---

[41] Cf. R. M. Fagley, *The Population Explosion and Christian Responsibility* (New York: Oxford University Press, 1960).

[42] Cf. D. von Hildebrand, *In Defense of Purity* (New York: Sheed and Ward, 1935) and H. Doms, *The Meaning of Marriage* (New York: Sheed and Ward, 1939).

by Paul VI, adamantly opposed any change. This latter group felt vindicated when *Humanae vitae* appeared. The encyclical did not, however, end the debate. It merely lifted it to a new level of intensity.

B. INPUT AFTER *Humanae vitae*

Humanae vitae was made public at a press conference on July 29, 1968. The spokesman for the Vatican was Msgr. Ferdinando Lambruschini, professor of moral theology at the Lateran University in Rome. He had been a member of the pontifical Birth Control Commission and had supported the majority report. The choice of Monsignor Lambruschini by the Vatican was undoubtedly deliberate, and his statement at the press conference certainly reflected the thinking of the Holy See. He said that the encyclical "is not infallible, but it does not leave the question concerning birth regulation in a condition of vague problematics."[43] *Humanae vitae*, he explained, is an authentic and authoritative teaching of the Church and so demands a full assent both interior and exterior.

Scarcely had the encyclical been published when reaction to it came from all parts of the world. One thing became immediately apparent: full assent, both interior and exterior, was lacking among many. Outspoken critics and advocates of the encyclical launched a vigorous battle unprecedented in the Catholic Church. It began with the bishops.

Bishops. Nearly every national hierarchy met in the months following the publication of the encyclical to discuss its pastoral implications and to issue guidelines for its interpretation. It soon became clear that there was no universal acceptance of the Pope's decree that "each and every marriage act must remain open to the transmission of life." Unanimity was simply not present among the bishops. The bishops did more than repeat the Pope's words, they interpreted them. And their interpretations differed. All the bishops agreed that the encyclical was an authoritative and authentic teaching of the Church, even though it was noninfallible. They also held that it should be interpreted

---

[43] *NC News Service* (*Documentary*), August 8, 1968, p. 7.

in the light of Vatican II (Art. 25 of *Lumen gentium*). The main problem centered on the precise nature of the assent required. A wide variety of subtle interpretations appeared.

The bishops' statements have been classified by William Shannon as left, right, and center.[44] The *leftist* or liberal hierarchies, such as those of Austria, Belgium, Canada, France, Holland, and Scandinavia, while stressing the authority of the encyclical in the formation of conscience, emphasized the primacy of the individual conscience. The Canadian bishops, for example, taught the objective right of dissent from the encyclical. The French bishops, in a more guarded statement, argued that contraception can never be a good; it is always a disorder, but not always culpable. Married couples must carefully reflect on the encyclical and on their own circumstances, and then decide which duty is the greater. The *rightist* or conservative hierarchies demanded full and complete obedience to the encyclical and saw the failure to comply a serious wrong. Although they admitted the primacy of conscience, the bishops insisted that a properly informed conscience is one that follows the teaching of the Church. The following national episcopal conferences held this view: Ceylon, India, Ireland, Mexico, the Phillipines, Scotland, and Spain. Other hierarchies took a *centrist* or moderate position: England, Germany, Italy, Japan, Switzerland, and the United States. Some of the bishops in these countries discussed the possibility of dissent, but were circumspect about giving clear support to it. Others argued that circumstances may be such that Catholics who do not obey the papal decree may not be guilty of serious sin.

The statement of the bishops of the United States on *Humanae vitae* provides us with a good illustration of the perils of interpretation. On November 15, 1968, the American bishops issued an 11,000-word document on birth control and war. They supported *Humanae vitae* as a positive, authoritative, and obligatory pronouncement on the nature of married life and responsible parenthood. The bishops recognized the possible conflicts in conscience that Catholic couples may face, but reminded them "that however circumstances may reduce moral guilt, no one following the teaching of the Church can deny the objective evil of

---

[44] *The Lively Debate*, pp. 145–146.

artificial contraception itself."[45] They also urged those individuals who have used contraceptive methods "never to lose heart, but to continue to take full advantage of the strength which comes from the Sacrament of Penance and the grace, healing, and peace in the Eucharist."[46]

What did the bishops mean by these two statements? Was birth control permissible in some circumstances? The newspaper reports of the meeting reflected the confusion. The *Washington Star*'s headline was "Bishops Back Birth Edict,"[47] while the *Washington Post*'s headline was "Catholic Bishops Ease Restriction on Birth Control."[48] Individual members of the hierarchy reacted vigorously: Archbishop John J. Carberry of St. Louis was "utterly amazed" at some of the media reports;[49] Cardinal Krol of Philadelphia was "completely shocked by the very grave distortions";[50] Cardinal McIntyre stated that "what the bishops have said is not compromise";[51] and Bishop Robert F. Joyce of Burlington, Vermont, also argued that there was no compromise in the bishops' statement on *Humanae vitae*. It does not, he insisted, leave it to the individual consciences whether or not to practice birth control. Contraception is objectively evil, but those who practice it should get help from the sacraments. Bishop Joyce drew a parallel between a person who practices contraception and a person who steals: "We don't condone stealing, but we do urge that the person who steals go to the sacraments."[52] Bishop John J. Wright also stressed the objective malice of contraception, and when asked if confession was obligatory for those who practiced contraception he replied: "Whether they are in a state of sin . . . is a matter between them and their God."[53] He was also quoted as saying that he could "not conceive of circumstances under which a person could use

[45] *Human Life in Our Day* (Washington: United States Catholic Conference, 1968), p. 16.
[46] *Ibid.*
[47] November 16, 1968, p. 1.
[48] November 16, 1968, p. 1.
[49] *NC News Service (Domestic)*, November 21, 1968, p. 17.
[50] *Washington Star*, November 16, 1968, p. 11.
[51] *NC News Service (Domestic)*, November 23, 1968, p. 1.
[52] *Ibid.*, p. 18.
[53] *Washington Star*, November 16, 1968, p. 11.

artificial contraception and not think of himself as committing a grave sin."[54]

Most news reports in the secular press, however, considered the bishops' statement a compromise effort. They focused on the words "circumstances may reduce moral guilt" and "never lose heart" as a victory for liberal bishops who preferred a more permissive attitude toward those couples who felt obliged to practice contraception. The *New York Times*, for example, quoted one unnamed bishop as saying that "if you talk about reduction, you have to allow for the possibility that it could be reduced to nothing." The sinfulness of contraception, he said, "still depends on circumstances."[55]

Theologians. The first public dissent to the encyclical came from Washington the day after its publication. On July 30 Father Charles E. Curran read a statement supported by 87 theologians (later the number exceeded 600) that was highly critical of *Humanae vitae.* The theologians took issue with the ecclesiology and methodology of the encyclical. Furthermore, they found it deficient for several reasons: its narrow notion of papal authority; its inadequate concept of the natural law; its overemphasis on the biological aspect of marriage; and finally, its failure to acknowledge the witness of other Christian churches, of many Catholic couples, and of the ethical contributions of modern science. For these and other reasons, the theologians concluded: "Spouses may responsibly decide according to their conscience that artificial contraception in some circumstances is permissible and indeed necessary to preserve and foster the values and sacredness of marriage."[56]

Several theological faculties also expressed dissent from the encyclical. Among them were: Fordham University, St. Peter's College, Marquette University, and Alma College. At The Ca-

---

[54] *New York Times*, November 16, 1968, p. 1.

[55] *Ibid.*, p. 21.

[56] Found in C. E. Curran, R. E. Hunt, et al., *Dissent In and For the Church: Theologians and Humanae Vitae* (New York: Sheed and Ward, 1969), p. 26. This work gives a history of the Catholic University Inquiry. The companion volume should also be consulted: J. F. Hunt, T. R. Connelly, et al., *The Responsibility of Dissent: The Church and Academic Freedom* (New York: Sheed and Ward, 1969).

tholic University of America twenty professors who had signed the Washington statement became the subjects of a year-long inquiry procedure. The aim of the inquiry, instituted in September 1968 by the Board of Trustees, was to discover whether the professors had violated their responsibilities to the university and had acted within accepted norms of academic freedom. The Faculty Board of Inquiry reported in April 1969 that the statement of the professors regarding *Humanae vitae* "represents a responsible theological dissent from the teaching of the Encyclical . . . and this dissent is reasonably supported as a tenable scholarly position."[57]

Other theologians joined the chorus of dissent. Hans Küng saw the encyclical as "a second Galileo case."[58] John L. McKenzie said that "with this pronouncement on birth control, the papacy is going to lose its leadership, which will take 200 years to recover—if ever."[59] Bernard Häring, one of the signers of the Washington statement, said that *Humanae vitae* was a "diminution of the teaching of Vatican II," and called for the Pope to retract his statement. "It would be much more honorable," he wrote, "for him to retract his statement than to leave it to his successor."[60] Gregory Baum asserted that while Catholics are not rebels, "when their tested convictions demand it, they are free to dissent from an authoritative, non-infallible position of the Church."[61] This is close to Karl Rahner's position that if a Catholic after serious reflection on the Church's teaching arrives at a contrary opinion, "then such a Catholic needs to fear no subjective guilt nor to consider himself as formally disobedient to the Church authority."[62] The comment by St. John-Stevas from England summed up what many theologians felt about the papal decree: "I feel that it is extreme, that it is partial, that it is inadequate."[63]

Among the many theologians who found serious difficulties

---

[57] In Curran, Hunt, et al., *Dissent In and For the Church*, p. 221.
[58] *National Catholic Reporter*, August 7, 1968, p. 7.
[59] *Time*, August 9, 1968, p. 48.
[60] *Pilot* (Boston), August 24, 1968, p. 1.
[61] "The Right to Dissent," *Commonweal*, August 23, 1968, p. 554.
[62] "Zur Enzyklika Humanae vitae," *Stimmen der Zeit*, 182 (1968), 208–209.
[63] *National Catholic Reporter*, August 7, 1968, p. 7.

with *Humanae vitae,* one of the most balanced presentations was that of Jesuit moralist Richard A. McCormick of the Bellarmine School of Theology in North Aurora, Illinois. He discussed the traditional view that authentic, noninfallible statements are presumed to be correct. He noted, however, that the presumption of correctness exists only until "it becomes clear that a large number of loyal, docile, and expert Catholics"[64] find it difficult to justify the doctrinal conclusion. In such a case the doctrine could be said to be doubtful and the presumption weakened. He felt that the doctrine of *Humanae vitae,* which viewed contraception as intrinsically evil, fell into this category. McCormick clearly but carefully gave his own opinion:

> The intrinsic immorality of every contraceptive act remains a teaching subject to solid and positive doubt. This is not to say that this teaching of *Humanae vitae* is certainly erroneous. It is only to say that there are very strong objections that can be urged against it and very little evidence that will sustain it. One draws this conclusion reluctantly and with no small measure of personal anguish.[65]

Other theologians spoke out in support of the encyclical. Austin Vaughan of St. Joseph's Seminary in Yonkers, New York, argued that *Humanae vitae,* though not infallible, demands an internal religious assent and that this obligation is incumbent on all Catholics—the faithful, confessors, and moral theologians. The encyclical, he felt, manifests "what the Holy Spirit . . . wants and expects of us as Catholics, at this moment in the plan of salvation."[66] One must follow his conscience, "but a Catholic accepts the guidance of the Church as an obligatory way of forming his conscience. . . ."[67] Charles R. Meyer of St. Mary of the Lake Seminary in Mundelein, Illinois, disagreed strongly with the arguments and the conclusions of the Washington statement as a misinterpretation of the papal decree. He denied that dissent is the privilege of every Catholic. Only those who are experts may withhold assent, and even they have to

---

[64] "Notes on Moral Theology," *Theological Studies,* 29 (1968), 732.
[65] *Ibid.,* 737.
[66] *National Catholic Reporter,* August 7, 1968, p. 9.
[67] *Ibid.*

propose "to the proper authorities reasons which have not yet been considered by the magisterium in reaching its decision."[68]

Anthony T. Padovano of Immaculate Conception Seminary in Darlington, New Jersey, also defended the encyclical and disagreed with the Washington theologians. He accepted *Humanae vitae* without qualification, affirmed its enduring validity, and was confident that "the vast majority of clergy and laity will stand with Pope Paul and with the majority of his brother bishops."[69] As to the criticism that the Pope did not accept the majority report of the Birth Control Commission, Padovano replied: "No theological principle and no historical precedent requires the Bishop of Rome to repeat, endorse, or accept the majority opinion of his consultors."[70] He also insisted that the doctrine was collegially arrived at and that it was erroneous to claim otherwise: "A majority of the episcopate was heard before and after this decision and have collegially supported it."[71] Padovano finally appealed to the lesson of history as a reason for accepting the encyclical: "History is against those who resist the papacy and the episcopate in a matter of such urgency and solemnity."[72]

The English theologian Lawrence L. McReavy concentrated on the "essential doctrine" of the encyclical as an authoritative interpretation of natural law. The doctrine, he contended, is not based on natural reason alone, but on natural reason in the light of divine revelation. Man's supernatural vocation is "a factor of cardinal importance in judging how he is to exercise his sexual faculty in his present temporal situation."[73] In stronger terms, Swiss theologian Cardinal Journet, in a front-page article in *L'Osservatore Romano*, called it absurd for a son of the Church to oppose the authority of the Church on the basis of his own fallible conscience. He characterized the opponents of *Humanae*

[68] Found in *The Birth Control Debate*, ed. R. G. Hoyt (Kansas City, Missouri: National Catholic Reporter, 1970), p. 197.

[69] "In Defense of the Encyclical," *Catholic World*, 208 (1968), p. 113.

[70] *Ibid.*

[71] *Ibid.*

[72] *Ibid.*, p. 116.

[73] "The Essential Doctrine of *Humanae vitae*," *Clergy Review*, 53 (1968), 863.

vitae: "Those who are against the encyclical are those who love sin. They love sin so much that they pretend it should be legalized and declared to be a virtue."[74] Finally, Germain G. Grisez found the basic grounds for assent in the fact that the encyclical is presented by the magisterium with the assistance of the Holy Spirit: "If one is a Catholic, one is a papist. . . . One has to say, 'Rome has spoken, the cause is finished.' "[75]

Priests and Laity. Not far behind the theologians came the reaction from the clergy and faithful. Like the theologians, some gave their assent and others dissented. Five days after *Humanae vitae,* some fifty Washington priests endorsed the statement of the Washington theologians and asserted that couples must decide on the basis of their own conscience whether or not to practice contraception. Cardinal O'Boyle had earlier urged his priests "to follow without equivocation, ambiguity, or simulation the teaching of the Church on this matter."[76] His admonition was unheeded; for on September 15, forty-four members of the Association of Washington Priests reaffirmed their stand. Cardinal O'Boyle, after lengthy interviews with each of the dissenting priests, imposed sanctions ranging from suspension to restriction of one or more priestly functions, such as preaching or hearing confessions. Later, nineteen of the disciplined priests took their case to Rome for arbitration. Support for the dissenters came from many quarters: the National Liturgical Conference, the National Association of Laymen, the National Federation of Priests' Councils, and the Committee for Freedom in the Church. A poll of the Washington area's Catholic laymen revealed that nearly half of those interviewed supported the dissenting priests.[77]

Other diocesan priests were also heard from. The Vancouver Association of Priests, for example, accepted *Humanae vitae* and pledged to teach "without ambiguity" the principles it contains.[78] One group of Newark, New Jersey, priests signed a statement supporting the Pope's authority, but another group

---

[74] *NC News Service (Foreign),* October 10, 1968, p. 2.
[75] *National Catholic Reporter,* August 7, 1968, p. 8.
[76] *Time,* September 13, 1968, p. 58.
[77] *Washington Post,* November 10, 1968, p. 1.
[78] *NC News Service (Domestic),* September 17, 1968, p. 3.

dissented from the papal directives.[79] Twenty-four priests from Evansville, Indiana, maintained that Catholic spouses should decide according to their consciences.[80] In England and Wales, fifty-five priests asserted that they could not "give loyal internal and external obedience to the view that all such means of contraception are in all circumstances wrong."[81] At the same time the Cephas Association of Priests in England supported the encyclical and protested against what they felt was the liberal position taken by the English hierarchy.[82]

The faithful's response to *Humanae vitae* reflected the general polarization in the Church. Voices came from both sides. Letters to editors alone would fill volumes. In support of the encyclical, L. Brent Bozell, editor of *Triumph*, had an immediate solution: "Any person who refuses submission to an authoritative teaching by the Supreme Pontiff on faith and morals is a schismatic."[83] A similar sentiment was expressed by Dietrich von Hildebrand: "If anyone assumes that the Pope is wrong and he knows better, he is clearly disavowing his belief in the teaching authority of the Church in morals and thereby ceases to be an authentic Catholic."[84] William Marra, professor of philosophy at Fordham University, praised the Pope for his courage in making such an unequivocal statement. He also called for a new document: "The formal anathema hurled at the infidel priests and theologians who continue their scandalous assault on the one true faith."[85] Several lay associations supported the Pope. Thus, the Catholic Daughters of America, the Human Life Committee, the Catholics United for the Faith, and the National Conference of Catholic Women of India, to name a few, all came out in defense of the Pope's position.

Disappointment with the encyclical was expressed by many laymen. John T. Noonan, a consultor to the Birth Control Com-

[79] *Ibid.*, September 5, 1968, p. 18.

[80] *Ibid.*, September 7, 1968, p. 13.

[81] *NC News Service (Foreign)*, October 2, 1968, p. 1.

[82] *Ibid.*, p. 2.

[83] *National Catholic Reporter*, August 7, 1968, p. 9.

[84] *The Encyclical Humanae Vitae—A Sign of Contradiction* (Chicago: Franciscan Herald Press, 1969), p. 80.

[85] *National Catholic Reporter*, August 7, 1968, p. 8.

mission, stated that the encyclical "suffers from both internal inconsistency and from inadequate preparation."[86] He found a contradiction in two teachings of the Pope: one, that every conjugal act must remain open to the transmission of life; and the other, that rhythm may be used in certain circumstances. Dr. John Marshall, a member of the Commission, criticized *Humanae vitae* for its failure to give sufficient evidence for its position, especially since both the majority and the minority reports of the Commission agreed that the intrinsic evil of contraception could not be demonstrated on a natural law basis.[87] Another member, Dr. André E. Hellegers, considered the rejection of the Commission's findings as meaning that "the scientific method of inquiry is irrelevant to Roman Catholic theology."[88] Michael Novak, Mary Perkins Ryan, John Rock, Daniel Callahan, Robert Hoyt, and Robert Nowell were among others who expressed dissatisfaction with the encyclical.

The National Association of Laymen called *Humanae vitae* "tragic, most particularly because it has widened the credibility gap within the Church."[89] Severe criticism of the encyclical also came from 2,600 scientists who felt that the Pope was insensitive to the problems of overpopulation, famine, and poverty. "The world," they stated, "must quickly come to realize that Pope Paul . . . has sanctioned the death of countless numbers of human beings with his misguided and immoral encyclical."[90] In England, seventy-six educators, scientists, lawyers, and liter-

---

[86] *Ibid.*, p. 9. The following observation of Noonan, although made in reference to usury, may well apply to the contraception issue: "The theologians were to have the last word, because acts of papal authority are inert unless taught by theologians, because those who cared consulted them, because they taught the next generation, and because the very categories in which the papal teaching was put were shaped by Christian experience and theological analysis" ("The Amendment of Papal Teaching by Theologians," in *Contraception: Authority and Dissent*, ed. C. E. Curran [New York: Herder and Herder, 1969], p. 75).

[87] "The Council and the Commission," *The Tablet* (London), September 21, 1968, pp. 933–934.

[88] "A Scientist's Analysis," in *Contraception: Authority and Dissent*, p. 217.

[89] *National Catholic Reporter*, August 7, 1968, p. 11.

[90] *NC News Service (Domestic)*, December 30, 1968, p. 10.

ary figures challenged the papal ruling and found the distinction between rhythm and other contraceptive methods "untenable and the arguments used to support it unconvincing."[91] The choice of a method of birth control should be made, according to them, by husband and wife "in the conscientious exercise of their responsibility before God to uphold and foster a creative love."[92] At the eighty-second Katholikentag, a conference of German Catholics in Essen, about three thousand laymen asked for a revision of the papal decree and said that parents "cannot follow the demand of obedience"[93] to Pope Paul's decision. During the same conference a thousand members of the Legion of Mary sent a telegram to the Pope thanking him for the encyclical and pledging their loyalty.

Feedback from the laity appeared in several opinion polls that were taken immediately after *Humanae vitae* was released. A Gallup poll of lay Catholics in the United States found that 54 percent opposed the Pope's ruling and only 28 percent supported it.[94] In Holland a similar sampling discovered that 80 percent of Dutch Catholics accepted the use of contraception, including the pill and *coitus interruptus*.[95] In England two surveys were conducted. The *London Sunday Times* poll by the Opinion Research Center reported that a small minority of Catholics in Britain (one in five) supported the Pope's encyclical.[96] A Gallup Poll of Catholics in England, Scotland, and Wales revealed that a small majority believed that Catholics *should* obey the Pope, but they were evenly divided as to whether *in fact* Catholics would accept his directives.[97]

Two significant surveys of the attitude of priests on *Humanae vitae* were also published in the United States. In October 1968, the Center for the Study of Man at the University of Notre Dame reported the findings of a survey of American diocesan priests sponsored by the *National Catholic Reporter* and other

[91] *NC News Service (Foreign)*, November 4, 1968, p. 11.
[92] *Ibid.*
[93] *Ibid.*, September 7, 1968, p. 1.
[94] *Pilot* (Boston), September 7, 1968, p. 15.
[95] *Ibid.*
[96] *London Sunday Times*, August 4, 1968, p. 1.
[97] *London Sunday Telegraph*, August 11, 1968, p. 1.

organizations. It found that priests were almost exactly divided in their support of the Pope. Fifty-one percent of the priests said that before the encyclical they held that artificial contraception was permissible in some circumstances. Forty-nine percent reported that after the encyclical they held the same view. One percent said they were undecided.[98]

Another survey was part of the *Bishops' Report on Priestly Life and Ministry*. It found that only 40 percent of American priests accepted the teaching of *Humanae vitae* and only 13 percent would not give absolution to penitents who refused to promise to avoid the use of contraceptives. Twenty-seven percent of the priests surveyed said they had become more liberal since the encyclical and only 3 percent had become more conservative.[99]

Protestants. A brief survey of Protestant reaction to the encyclical shows that it was predominantly negative. Archbishop Ramsey, primate of forty million Anglicans, referred to the 1958 Lambeth Conference which did not exclude artificial means of contraception and held that "the means adopted to limit the number of children in a family are a matter for the consciences of each husband and wife."[100] He felt that the teaching of the Anglican Church had been reinforced by "the changes in human society and world population, as well as the development in the means available for contraception."[101]

More spirited criticism came from other Protestants. Albert C. Outler, a Methodist observer at Vatican II, said that the Pope "has finally fallen . . . into the eager arms of the Roman *immobilisti*."[102] Eugene Carson Blake, Secretary of the World Council of Churches, noted wryly that the re-examination of five years "seems to have ended up approximately where it

[98] *National Catholic Reporter*, October 9, 1968, p. 1.

[99] Cf. The National Opinion Research Center, *The Catholic Priest in the United States: Sociological Investigations* (Washington: United States Catholic Conference, 1972), pp. 81–131, and A. Greeley, *Priests in the United States: Reflections on a Survey* (New York: Doubleday, 1972), pp. 65–76.

[100] *London Times*, July 31, 1968, p. 1.

[101] *Ibid.*

[102] *National Catholic Reporter*, August 7, 1968, p. 9.

began."[103] Bishop J. R. Moorman, an Anglican observer at Vatican II, called the encyclical "ecumenically, a disaster for Christianity."[104] Robert McAfee Brown, a Vatican II observer for the World Alliance of Reformed and Presbyterian Churches, viewed *Humanae vitae* as "a tragedy for the Catholic Church and for the contemporary world."[105] Yet he called the encyclical an "ecumenical boon" because "its reception shows conclusively that traditional views of papal authority simply cannot be taken seriously any more, and that Catholics feel no greater sense of being bound to unquestionable doctrine than do Protestants."[106]

In the preceding pages, we have attempted to describe the input over the last decade to the Church's past and present prohibition of contraception. The feedback to *Humanae vitae* has come from within and without the Church in a flood of signed statements, articles, demonstrations, sanctions, and boycotts. Emotions ran high and charges and counter-charges were hurled from podia all over the world. Intemperance unfortunately marked some of the debate. Some dismissed the Pope as old, celibate, and ignorant of marriage, while others pleaded for the excommunication of those who disagreed with him. Yet apart from occasional polemical outbursts like these, thousands of serious and reasonable Catholics found themselves faced with an agonizing personal decision: to agree with the Pope or not. The result was widespread polarization within the Church. This was further compounded by the interpretations of the national hierarchies.

Supporters of the Pope based their decision on the fact that the Pope as head of the Church had issued, after extensive consultation, an unambiguous, authoritative, and authentic teaching, even if it was noninfallible. Thus, Catholics had an obligation to obey it, convinced that the Holy Spirit had guided the Pope in forming his judgment. Furthermore, the Pope's defense of the sacredness of human life was consistent with the previous

---

[103] *Time*, August 9, 1968, p. 46.

[104] *Ibid.*

[105] *"Humanae Vitae:* A Protestant Reaction," in *Contraception: Authority and Dissent*, p. 198.

[106] "An Ecumenical Boon?" *Commonweal*, September 6, 1968, p. 505.

tradition of the Church on the evil of contraception. Loyalty to this tradition and to the sacred authority of the Supreme Pontiff demanded that Catholics accept the Pope's encyclical, however difficult that might be.

Dissenters to the Pope's directives argued that no conclusive theological argument for the natural law can be adduced to show the intrinsic immorality of *every* act of contraception. The Pope in making his decision had not consulted sufficiently with the college of bishops, had been too hasty in rejecting the majority view of the Birth Control Commission, had neglected the witness of modern science and married couples, and had been inconsistent in allowing rhythm and banning contraception. For these reasons, a substantial number of bishops, theologians, and priests and laymen argued that a Catholic should be free, after seriously weighing the Pope's position, to dissent from this noninfallible statement and to follow the dictates of his own conscience.

It is impossible to give precise statistics of the acceptance or nonacceptance of *Humanae vitae* among Catholics. Such a tally sheet is not available, and it is not likely to be. Even professional pollsters would hesitate to undertake the formidable task of making a global survey of five hundred million Catholics. Undoubtedly there are many Catholics who continue to practice contraception, but it is also true that there are many who do not. What is beyond dispute is the division among Catholics on the question which cuts across every level of Church membership. Reputable and representative spokesmen for both sides have articulated their stand with fervor and candor.

III. *Conversion Process*

How did Pope Paul VI react to the vast input of negative criticism that greeted *Humanae vitae?* The answer must be that his response was confident, hopeful, and optimistic. In the months following the publication of the encyclical, he revealed his own feelings on the matter in several addresses. In general, he felt that the faithful had generously accepted his directives. He had occasional harsh words for unnamed theologians, but by and large his tone was positive. There was no threat of disciplinary action, but rather a paternal exhortation that all members of the Church obey the words of the Vicar of Christ.

On July 31, 1968, the Pope spoke publicly for the first time since the encyclical to a general audience at Castelgandolfo. The encyclical, he noted, was not only a statement of a negative moral law, but "above all the positive presentation of conjugal morality."[107] The long period of preparation, which caused "spiritual suffering," was devoted, he said, to extensive study, consultation, and the weighing of evidence that came from all sources: "We have studied, read, and discussed all we could. We have also prayed much."[108] At times, he said, "we had the impression of being almost overwhelmed by this mass of documentation."[109] The feeling of grave responsibility to the Church and of deep sensitivity to the difficulties faced by Catholic couples weighed heavily upon him. Yet "we had no doubt regarding our duty to pronounce our decision in the terms expressed in the present encyclical."[110] The Pope concluded his address with the hope that the encyclical would be well received despite the difficulties it presents to those "who want to follow it faithfully."[111]

On August 4, 1968, at another papal audience, he referred to the worldwide response to the encyclical. "As far as we remember," he said, "never before as on this occasion did the Pope receive, from all over the world and from every class of people, so many spontaneous messages of thanks and approval for the publication of a document issued by him."[112] Many, he acknowledged, opposed his teaching since it was austere. But he reminded his hearers that the norm given "is not our own, but pertains to the structures of life, of love, and of human dignity."[113]

At the end of August, when the controversy over the encyclical was reaching crisis proportions, the Pope again returned to

[107] *NC News Service (Documentary)*, August 6, 1968, p. 1.
[108] *Ibid.*, p. 2.
[109] *Ibid.*
[110] *Ibid.*
[111] *Ibid.*, p. 3.
[112] *NC News Service (Documentary)*, October 22, 1968, p. 1.
[113] *Ibid.*

the subject. Addressing the General Assembly of Latin American Bishops during his trip to Colombia, the Pope called his encyclical "ultimately a defense of life," and was confident that "the great majority of the Church has received it with favor and trusting obedience."[114] Earlier in the talk the Pope, without explicitly mentioning *Humanae vitae*, had severe words for those theologians who "have recourse to ambiguous doctrinal expressions . . . and even consent that each one in the Church may think and believe what he wants."[115] He lamented the fact that today "we are tempted by historicism, relativism, suggestivism, neopositivism which introduce into the field of faith a spirit of subversive criticism."[116]

In a letter to the participants of the Katholikentag in Essen, the Pope once more defended his encyclical. The letter was dated August 30 and was read at the end of the conference which earlier, as we have seen, rejected the papal directive concerning contraception. In the letter, the Pope stated as a fact that "the overwhelming majority within the Church welcomed our word with assent and obedience."[117] He also referred critically to those who propose their own personal views on the subject "with an authority which evidently they deny to him who alone has received this charism from God."[118] These individuals would prefer "everyone in the Church to think or believe what one pleases."[119]

In his final summer audience at Castelgandolfo, the Pope spoke of a "corrosive spirit of criticism."[120] He asked rhetorically what should be his response to the protests against his own encyclical. His answer was also in the form of a question: "Where is the coherence and dignity proper to true Christians? Where is the sense of responsibility towards one's own Catholic profession and that of others? Where is the love for the Church?"[121]

---

[114] *Catholic Review* (Baltimore), August 30, 1968, 10 A.
[115] *Ibid.*
[116] *Ibid.*
[117] *NC News Service (Documentary)*, September 13, 1968, p. 2.
[118] *Ibid.*
[119] *Ibid.*
[120] *NC News Service (Documentary)*, September 20, 1968, p. 1.
[121] *Ibid.*, p. 2.

Other addresses of the Pope in defense of *Humanae vitae* continued to appear during the rest of 1968. One further papal statement deserves mention. In an end-of-the-year review of the Holy See's activities, the Pope in an address to the papal family briefly discussed *Humanae vitae*. The message expressed the same tone of hope: "We are confident as of now that our teaching will be accepted with a genuine spirit of faith . . . that it will be accepted as a provident defense of the honesty and dignity of love."[122] Five months after the encyclical, the Pope's attitude had not weakened.

Nor did papal policy change in subsequent years. On November 16, 1970, the Pope visited the Roman headquarters of the United Nations' Food and Agriculture Organization (FAO) on the occasion of its twenty-fifth anniversary. In his address he praised the efforts of the FAO to alleviate hunger and misery and to increase the world food supply. But he also mentioned the birth control programs sponsored by international organizations as a radical solution to the problems faced by developing nations. The Church, he said, was "firmly opposed to a birth control which, according to the just expression of our venerable predecessor Pope John XXIII, would be in accordance with 'methods and means which are unworthy of man.' "[123] He called for a "rational control of births by couples who are capable of freely assuming their destiny.[124] In a confidential 10,000-word document sent to papal nuncios in November 1970, the Vatican continued its campaign against artificial birth control as a solution to population problems. It criticized the United States, "the leader of the ranks of promoters of an international birth control policy,"[125] and disagreed with policies of the United Nations. The nuncios were told to discourage governments and the United Nations from promoting artificial birth control programs and to "express clearly and more unanimously" the Church's position on the question.[126]

The Vatican's 1971 decision concerning the nineteen dissent-

---

[122] *NC News Service (Documentary)*, February 7, 1969, p. 5.
[123] *National Catholic Reporter*, November 27, 1970, p. 3.
[124] *Ibid.*
[125] *New York Times*, January 27, 1971, p. 7.
[126] *Ibid.*

ing priests from Washington, D.C., presents an interesting example of how Rome handled a delicate situation. It will be recalled that shortly after *Humanae vitae* appeared some fifty
Washington priests publicly stated that they would respect the
consciences of Catholic couples who decided to practice contraception. Many of them received severe sanctions. Nineteen of
them, supported by a team of canon and civil lawyers, took
their case to the Vatican, claiming that they had failed to find
adequate due process through the appropriate Church courts in
the United States. In May 1971, the Congregation for the Clergy
finally settled the dispute. It required that the priests accept the
"findings" of the Congregation's report and personally request
from Cardinal O'Boyle the restoration of their full priestly
faculties. It demanded no oral or written explanations of their
understanding of the "findings," nor did it ask for a retraction
of their former public statement.

The Vatican document stated among its "findings" that
Humanae vitae was an authentic expression of the Church's
teaching on contraception and that the Pope and the bishops
have the duty to teach those matters pertaining to faith and
morals. It further affirmed that *Humanae vitae* should be understood according to the dogmatic tradition of the Church concerning the assent due to the teaching of the ordinary magisterium. The decision also mentioned the right of conscience. It
is not a law unto itself, but "in the final analysis, conscience is
inviolable and no one is to be forced to act in a manner contrary
to his conscience, as the moral tradition of the Church at-
tests."[127] In counseling married persons, inside and outside the
confessional, the priest is obliged to follow these principles. Yet
the counselor should not "too quickly presume either complete
innocence on one hand, or, on the other, a deliberate rejection
of God's loving commands in the case of a person who is
honestly trying to lead a good Christian life."[128]

The decision from the Vatican was a carefully worded reply
that attempted to solve a thorny practical problem. It evaded
the real problem of dissent and couched its statements in such a

[127] *National Catholic Reporter*, May 7, 1971, p. 4.
[128] *Ibid.*

way that several interpretations were possible. Both sides saw it as a victory and an amicable solution. The news media correctly analyzed it. The *New York Times* called the decision "a draw"[129] and the *National Catholic Reporter* termed it a "no-win conclusion."[130] Father Donald E. Heintschel, one of the canon lawyers in the case, felt that "it was a breakthrough in the very fact that the context and content of the procedures were totally revealed."[131]

IV. *Evaluation*

The birth control debate, as we mentioned earlier, is not a classic example of negative input finally effecting a change in the Church's teaching. The ban on contraception has remained in spite of opposition. In view of our analysis of slavery, this result may well appear surprising. There were and still are many of the critical ingredients required for a revision: concerted demands from the faithful; dissent by the hierarchy; an impressive contrary opinion among theologians; the opposing Protestant tradition; and pressure from world governments and modern science. The one ingredient lacking was on the side of the Pope, who was unconvinced by the arguments advocating change, and as a result, resolutely reaffirmed the traditional teaching. In evaluating the controversy up to this date, a few conclusions are appropriate.

1. Loyalty to the uninterrupted tradition of the Church on contraception seems to have been the most persuasive argument for Pope Paul. He referred to it in *Humanae vitae* and in several post-encyclical addresses. It was clear that in conscience he felt he could not override the teaching of his predecessors. This was, to be sure, a formidable obstacle, and in the final analysis it proved insurmountable for the Pope. The deluge of opposing theological, scientific, and public opinion was no match for it.

2. The Pope was certainly aware of the intense and wide-

[129] *New York Times*, May 4, 1971, p. 10.
[130] *National Catholic Reporter*, May 7, 1971, p. 3.
[131] *Ibid.*, p. 4.

spread negative input to the Church's position both before and
after the encyclical. There are some who question this and claim
that he was a "prisoner of the Vatican" and isolated by his overly
conservative consultors. The charge of isolation is one that is
commonly used against those in authority. In this instance, there
seems to be no evidence to back it up. It is a strain on one's
credulity to think that the Pope had failed to study thoroughly
the report of the Birth Control Commission and to evaluate the
evidence in it which was in favor of a change. One must accept
the veracity of the Pope, when he says that he spent the years
before the encyclical studying, reading, and listening to suggestions from all sides. Progressives, of course, ask how he could do
this and still write a document like *Humanae vitae*. But this
does not alter the basic presumption that the Pope was well
informed but obviously not convinced by arguments demanding
relaxation of the prohibition on contraception.

3. The intensity of opposition to *Humanae vitae* was due in
no small part to the poor timing of Pope Paul. If the Church had
settled the question at Vatican II or if the Pope had spoken out
in 1966 after the Birth Control Commission had completed its
report, rather than waiting another two years, the reaction
would have been less violent. The long delay only served to
increase tensions, to foster confusion, and to raise false expecta-
tions. By the time the Pope finally issued *Humanae vitae* in 1968
the battle lines were already firmly drawn and the subsequent
response was predictable.

4. The reaction of the Holy See to the open dissent and defiance of the encyclical was remarkably restrained. A few individual bishops in Europe and the United States suspended some
priests, but the Vatican issued no excommunications or censures.
The Pope spoke harshly on occasion about those theologians
who refused to accept the guidance of the magisterium, but no
names were mentioned and no investigations were initiated by
Rome. Liberals saw in the attitude of the Holy See some legiti-
mization of dissent, while conservatives were chagrined that
more stringent action was not taken.

5. *Humanae vitae* has stimulated a total rethinking of several
critical theological issues: responsible dissent, the Church and
academic freedom, the role of *consensus fidelium*, and the obedi-

ence due to papal and episcopal authority. There is already a sizable literature on these problems, and it is still growing. This is one of the most fruitful effects of the encyclical and represents a possibility for genuine development of doctrine.

6. There is little likelihood that the Church will, in the immediate future, revise its teaching on birth control. This is especially true of Pope Paul. Yet the possibility of revision exists, in theory at least, since Rome has admitted that the doctrine is noninfallible and hence reformable. Perhaps the final word from Rome has not yet been heard. Perhaps when the heat of the debate has cooled and the value of the input has endured the test of time, further output will emerge.

5

The Ecumenical Movement

Dividation CHRISTIANITY is not something new. In nearly every century of the Christian era, there have been individuals and groups who, for doctrinal or disciplinary reasons, have separated themselves from the Church. The two great divisions among Christians, the eleventh-century one in the East and the sixteenth-century one in the West, have still not been healed. Yet ecumenism, the fostering of unity among Christians, while it is an accepted part of Catholicism today, is a fairly recent phenomenon. Not until the middle of the twentieth century did the Catholic Church positively approve genuine dialogue among Christians. A radical change took place between the time of Pius XI, who prohibited Catholics from participating in pan-Christian activities, and the time of John XXIII, who encouraged the unity of all Christians and began the Second Vatican Council with this goal in mind. What are the factors that caused the Church to change its position? To answer this question we will begin with a survey of papal output.

I. *Output*

Pope Leo XIII (1878–1903) has been called "the first Pope to take up ecumenism."[1] During his pontificate of twenty-five years, he wrote over thirty documents dealing with ecumenism. In his writings he referred not to "schismatics" and "heretics," as had his predecessors, but to "dissidents" and "separated ones." Leo XIII was especially sympathetic to Orthodox Christians. For example, in his apostolic letter *Praeclara gratulationis*, of 1894, he wrote: "It is not for any human motive, but impelled by divine charity and a desire for the salvation of all, that we advise the reconciliation and union with the Church of Rome."[2] He showed a deep respect for the rites and traditions of the Eastern Church and assured the Orthodox that they would not have to surrender their liturgical practices if they returned to the fold.

However, Leo XIII was extremely critical of late nineteenth-century liberal Protestantism and felt that it was eroding the faith by its rationalistic approach to doctrine. Nevertheless, in many of his letters to the Protestants of England, Scotland, and Germany, he spoke in a kindly manner. To the Anglicans, for example, he wrote: "God is witness to the lively hope we entertain of seeing our efforts help promote and bring about this great work of obtaining Christian unity in England."[3] He was convinced, moreover, that eventual reunion depended on the common dedication of all Christians to the love of Christ and a deep devotion to Scripture.

Pope Pius XI (1922–1939) was also warm in dealing with the dissident Christians of the East. He showed a high esteem for Orthodox theology and liturgical life and issued over twenty documents concerning the Eastern Church. Furthermore, he reorganized the Pontifical Oriental Institute under the direction of the Jesuits and established the Ethiopian, Ruthenian, and Russian Colleges in Rome. In several addresses he admitted that both the East and the West share the blame of divided Christi-

---

[1] G. H. Tavard, *Two Centuries of Ecumenism* (Notre Dame, Ind.: Fides, 1960), p. 91.

[2] *Acta Sanctae Sedis*, 26 (1893–1894), 709–710.

[3] *Ibid.*, 27 (1894–1895), 583.

anity and that holiness and divine help exist outside the visible confines of the Roman Church. In what has come to be a classic passage, the Pope stated his views on reunion with the Oriental Churches:

> For a reunion it is above all necessary to know and to love one another. To know one another, because if the efforts of reunion have failed so many times, this is in large measure due to mutual ignorance. If there are prejudices on both sides, these prejudices must fall. Incredible are the errors and equivocations which persist and are handed down among the separated brethren against the Catholic Church; on the other hand, Catholics have sometimes failed in justly evaluating the truth or, on account of insufficient knowledge, in showing a fraternal spirit. Do we know all that is valuable, good, and Christian in the fragments of ancient Catholic truth? Detached fragments of a gold-bearing rock also contain the precious ore. The ancient Churches of the East have retained so true a holiness that they deserve not only our respect but also our sympathy.[4]

A more rigorous view was expressed by the Pope concerning Protestant ecumenical efforts. In the 1928 encyclical *Mortalium animos*, he severely criticized the ecumenical movement for its apparent disregard of truth. Calling it a "pan-Christian" movement that fostered doctrinal indifference, he forbade Catholic participation. He also firmly stated that reunion must be rooted in the complete acceptance of Christian revelation, and that consequently any movement which considers doctrine unimportant works contrary to the unity of faith. Referring to the disagreement that exists between Anglicans and Protestant Christians on such critical questions as the episcopate, the priesthood, and the role of Mary, the Pope said: "We cannot understand how this wide variation of opinions can open up the way to unity of the Church, when this unity can be born of but one single authority, one sole rule of faith, and one identical Christian belief."[5]

The position taken by *Mortalium animos* may have disturbed many Christians, both Catholic and Protestant, who were working for unity, but it was consistent with Rome's long-standing policy regarding inter-Church dialogue. In 1864 and 1865, for example, the Holy Office had condemned the English Associa-

---

[4] From an address of Pope Pius XI, January 11, 1927. Cited in G. Baum, *That They May Be One* (Westminster, Md.: Newman, 1958), p. 110.

[5] *Acta Apostolicae Sedis*, 20 (1928), 13.

tion for the Promotion of the Unity of Christendom. The principal reason for this condemnation was that the A.P.U.C. espoused the "branch theory," which held that Photianism, Anglicanism, and Roman Catholicism were three forms of the one true Catholic religion. In the mind of Rome this implied "baneful indifference in matters of religion . . . and hence no proof is needed that Catholics who join this Society are giving both to Catholics and non-Catholics an occasion of spiritual ruin."[6]

Furthermore, the 1917 Code of Canon Law decreed that Catholics are to avoid any discussions or conferences on matters of faith with non-Catholics, especially public disputations. The permission of the Holy See was required, or in cases of emergency, the local Ordinary.[7] This policy was tested by the Protestants themselves when on May 16, 1919, a deputation from the Episcopal Church in the United States went to Benedict XV and requested that he send Catholic representatives to the forthcoming Faith and Order Conference. His response was unambiguous: "The teaching and practice of the Roman Catholic Church regarding the unity of the visible Church of Christ is well known to everybody, and therefore it would not be possible to take part in a Congress such as the one proposed. His Holiness, however, by no means wishes to disapprove of the Congress in question for those who are not in union with the Chair of Peter."[8]

Our examination of the outputs from the Holy See concerning ecumenical dialogue reveals that greater hope characterized the relations with Orthodox Christianity. The Vatican was cautious and at times critical in dealing with the Protestant West. Apparently the fiery days of the Reformation and the centuries of polemics and counter-polemics were not easily forgotten. Robert McAfee Brown, the Protestant ecumenist, points out that the Catholic Church had no "ecumenical problem" with Protestants, since they had willingly left the Church. He writes: "They were always welcome to return . . . but since they could not be forced to return, the next move was up to them."[9]

[6] *Acta Sanctae Sedis*, 2 (1867), 660.

[7] Canon 1325. Cf. S. J. Kelleher, *Discussions with Non-Catholics* (Washington: Catholic University of America Press, 1943).

[8] Cited in R. Rouse and S. Neill, eds., *A History of the Ecumenical Movement 1517–1948* (Philadelphia: Westminster, 1954), p. 416.

[9] *The Ecumenical Revolution* (New York: Doubleday, 1967), p. 48.

Another factor that impeded ecumenical relations with Protestants was their own obvious disunity. The some two hundred varieties of Protestantism made dialogue with the Catholic Church difficult if not impossible. In spite of this obstacle, Protestants considered Rome's stand on reunion as monolithic and intransigent. They were resentful of the Roman aloofness from the Protestant world and were doubtful that it would ever change. The observation of H. E. Root, Anglican observer at Vatican II, accurately reflects this attitude: "Even if we keep to the modern period and go no further back than 1928 and the encyclical *Mortalium animos*, Rome's attitude to the ecumenical movement had ever been (to put it as gently as possible) distinctly chilly."[10]

II. *Input*

The ecumenical movement is a child of the twentieth century and is a direct outgrowth of Protestant concern over divided Christendom. Ecumenism as we know it today is due principally to the patient and dedicated efforts of Protestants over the last sixty years. Cardinal Bea acknowledged this debt: "I should like to say that it is our separated brethren, Orthodox, Anglican, and Protestant, who gave the first impulse to the modern ecumenical movement and that we have learned much from them, and can learn still more."[11] Inputs from Protestantism created an atmosphere which made wider ecumenism possible. Let us briefly discuss first the Protestant input, then Catholic contributions, and finally other supportive factors that encouraged the development of the ecumenical movement.

A. PROTESTANT EFFORTS

In this century, four important Protestant organizations were begun that contributed greatly to the development of the ecu-

[10] "Ecumenism," in *The Second Vatican Council—Studies by Eight Anglican Observers*, ed. B. C. Pawley (London: Oxford University Press, 1967), p. 112.

[11] *Unity in Freedom* (New York: Harper and Row, 1958), p. 205.

menical movement. The first of these was formed in 1910, when Anglicans and Protestants met at the World Missionary Conference in Edinburgh. They were aware of the lack of unity which hampered Protestant missionary activities in Asia and Africa and sought to work out a common strategy. Hostility and competition among the various Protestant churches working in the missions was seen as a scandal and unworthy of Christians. As a result of this meeting, the International Missionary Council was established, whose task was to offer mutual assistance to the different churches and to eliminate competitive efforts. Doctrine was not discussed, and they concentrated on working out effective methods that would benefit all the churches in the mission areas.

A second ecumenical venture, the Life and Work Movement, was organized in 1925 and held its first world conference in Stockholm under the leadership of the Swedish archbishop Nathan Söderblom. Its emphasis was social and not theological, as its motto indicates: "Service unites, but doctrine divides."

The third major ecumenical organization was the Faith and Order Movement, which recognized that doctrinal questions had to be settled before unity was possible. It met for the first time in 1927 at Lausanne, Switzerland, with representatives from 108 churches, including the Eastern Orthodox.

A fourth ecumenical organization, the World Council of Churches, was organized in 1948, after ten years of planning. It eventually incorporated the International Missionary Council, the Life and Work Movement, and the Faith and Order Movement. The World Council of Churches has become the largest and most influential non-Catholic organization working for Christian unity. Its members represent all the major Christian communions with the exception of Roman Catholics, Southern Baptists, and some Lutheran and Pentecostal groups. The World Council does not claim to be a church unto itself, but, as its first General Secretary, W. A. Visser 't Hooft, explained, "it is essentially an instrument at the service of the churches to assist them in their common task to manifest the true nature of the Church."[12]

[12] W. A. Visser 't Hooft, ed., *The Evanston Report* (London: SCM Press, 1955), p. 25.

B. CATHOLIC EFFORTS

During most of this century, Catholic contributions to the growth of the ecumenical movement were less significant than those of their Protestant brethren. There were, however, important developments in this country and in Europe that should be noted. In the United States, Father Paul Wattson, an Episcopalian convert, established in 1910 the Chair of Unity Octave—eight days of prayer dedicated to reunion. It was approved by Pope Pius X and supported by all of his successors. In France, Father Paul Couturier adapted the Octave to permit Protestant participation. In Germany, Father Max Metzger founded the Una Sancta Movement in 1920, which was devoted to a Lutheran-Catholic dialogue. Finally, in Belgium, Cardinal Mercier began the famous Malines Conversations between Anglican and Catholic theologians.

Other contributions in the years before Vatican II were made by religious orders, ecumenical journals, and theologians. The Benedictines of Amay-Chevtogne in Belgium and Niederaltaich in Germany; the Assumptionists in France; and the Paulists and Friars of the Atonement in the United States, all worked actively to promote ecumenism. Furthermore, journals like *Irénikon*, *Catholica*, *Revue d'Orient*, *Eastern Churches Quarterly*, and *Unitas* provided scholarly forums for ecumenical research. Finally, there were many theologians who wrote perceptively and sensitively on the question of unity: Gregory Baum, Cardinal Bea, Charles Boyer, Louis Bouyer, Yves Congar, Bernard Leeming, Hans Küng, Gustave Weigel, and Cardinal Willebrands.

C. OTHER FACTORS

Besides the work concerned directly with Christian unity, other inputs influenced the ecumenical movement. First, there were the two World Wars in which Christians, Protestant and Catholic, were victims of the same suffering, losses, and destruction. Out of the common crucible of pain emerged a new spirit of camaraderie that transcended petty denominational differences. Fascism, Communism, and materialism were viewed as evil forces that all believers in the Sonship of God and the dignity of man must fight against: their negative assault, since it threatened Christian values, fostered a genuine ecumenical spirit of survival. Second, the profound social changes in the last few decades have acted as a catalyst which brought Christians of all faiths closer together. The acceptance of religious plurality on the part of an increased and more mobile population and the now accepted interfaith marriage have broken down many of the traditional barriers of religious separatism. Third, cross-confessional scholarship in biblical studies, liturgy, and history (especially of the Reformation and the Eastern Schism) has moved ecumenical activity beyond mutual polemics to a serious and objective common effort for reunion.

III. *Conversion Process*

Beginning with Pope Pius XII, the Catholic Church accelerated its ecumenical efforts. In his first encyclical, *Summi pontificatus,* the Pope in 1939 set the tone for future dialogue with non-Catholics. He stated: "We cannot pass over in silence the profound impression of heartfelt gratitude made on us by the good wishes of those who, though not belonging to the visible body of the Catholic Church, have given noble and sincere expression to their appreciation of all that unites them to us, in love for the person of Christ or in belief in God."[13] In dozens of other addresses Pius XII stressed the good will of the "separated brethren" and prayed that "they enter into Catholic unity and, joined with Us in the one, organic Body of Jesus Christ, may they with us run on to the one Head in the society of glorious love."[14]

In 1949, a year after the World Council of Churches was formed, the Holy Office issued an *Instruction on the Ecumenical Movement.* It was, as Gregory Baum has pointed out, "the first Roman document acknowledging the holiness of the worldwide ecumenical movement, and encouraging Catholics to take part

[13] *Acta Apostolicae Sedis,* 21 (1939), 542.
[14] Denzinger-Schönmetzer, 3821.

in it."[15] Catholics were urged to pray for its success, and bishops were instructed to appoint suitable priests in their dioceses to study ecumenical problems. The *Instruction* permitted Catholics, when authorized by competent authority, to discuss doctrinal questions with non-Catholics and to begin and end these meetings with common prayer. The permission of the Holy See was required for interdiocesan, national, and international ecumenical gatherings. While this document did repeat many of the early warnings about the possible dangers of "false irenicism," it urged that "this excellent work of reunion of all Christians in the one true Faith and Church . . . be made an object of concern that the whole Catholic people take to heart and recommend to God in fervent supplications."[16] One of the concrete results of Rome's new attitude was the presence of official Catholic observers at the Faith and Order Conference at Lund in 1952.

Pope John XXIII (1958–1963) began a new age for Catholic ecumenism. His warm personality and deep concern for Christian unity became clear in his speeches, and especially in his two major encyclicals, *Mater et magistra* and *Pacem in terris*. In one of his addresses early in his pontificate he cleared the air of any misunderstanding when he stated: "We do not wish to put anyone in history on trial: we shall not seek to establish who was right and who was wrong. Responsibility is divided. We only want to say: let us come together, let us make an end of our divisions."[17] To implement his plans he did two things: he established the Secretariat for the Promotion of Christian Unity in 1960, and he opened the Second Vatican Council in 1962. The Council was one of "reform and reunion." The guiding theme was that the Church should first renew itself and adapt its apostolate to the needs of modern man. Inner reform is the best possible preparation for eventual reunion. At the Council there were representatives from the Orthodox Churches, various Protestant communions, the Anglican Church, and the World Council of Churches.

---

[15] *Progress and Perspectives* (New York: Sheed and Ward, 1962), p. 38.
[16] *Acta Apostolicae Sedis*, 42 (1950), 146–147.
[17] Cf. *Herder-Korrespondenz*, 13 (1959), 274–275.

On November 21, 1964, Vatican II promulgated the *Decree on Ecumenism*, which elaborated the principles and practices of ecumenism for Catholics. Its very first sentence revealed the serious intention of the Church: "The restoration of unity among all Christians is one of the chief concerns of the Second Vatican Council." The *Decree* made the following critical assertions: (1) the division among Christians contradicts the will of Christ; (2) all Christians share the blame for this division; (3) the Catholic Church accepts those who have been baptized as brothers; (4) other churches and communities, although not in full communion with the Roman Catholic Church, possess an "ecclesial reality"; (5) the unifying elements among Christians should be discovered; (6) common dialogue, action, and worship (in some circumstances) can be of great value; (7) in Catholic teaching there exists a "hierarchy of truth" which vary in their relationship to the Christian faith; and (8) Catholic doctrine must be clearly and honestly expressed, for to do otherwise would be harmful to the ecumenical spirit.

Pope Paul VI has continued the ecumenical policy of his predecessor; and bishops, priests, and laity have taken significant steps to make it a living reality. The most encouraging and far-reaching development of the post-Conciliar era has been the many official bilateral consultations between Roman Catholics and other Christians. These theological dialogues have sought clarification and consensus. The most successful of them has been the Anglican–Roman Catholic dialogue which reached a substantial agreement on the essential doctrine of the Eucharist. It has been called "the most important statement since the Reformation for Anglicans and Roman Catholics."[18]

IV. *Evaluation*

The worldwide ecumenical movement illustrates, from a cybernetic viewpoint, the role of input in changing ecclesial attitudes.

[18] From an official explanatory section which accompanied the joint declaration quoted in the *New York Times*, December 31, 1971, p. 1. For the text of the declaration see *Origins* (*NC Documentary Service*), January 6, 1972, vol. 1: no. 29, 486–488.

It is possible to summarize the development in the following statements:

1. In somewhat over twenty years, the Catholic Church has made a radical change in its ecumenical position. The conversion process resulted in a sharp break with centuries of tradition.

2. The major input was primarily the work of Protestant ecumenical organizations. Other churches, like the Orthodox, were involved but not intensely.

3. Catholic input was in the beginning mainly derivative, gaining its inspiration from Protestant efforts. Eventually Catholic theologians became involved, and Catholic ecumenical organizations were formed. The demands of the Catholic laity were generally limited to disciplinary matters of marriage and worship.

4. The evolving output of the hierarchy was fourfold: the statement of ecumenical goals in the spirit of fellowship; the permission for participation in ecumenical organizations; the relaxation of disciplinary rules concerning mixed marriage and mixed worship; and, finally, the fostering of efforts to find areas of doctrinal unity.

5. These authoritative outputs of the hierarchy have received the support of the Catholic clergy and laity, who no longer express the polemical attitude toward non-Catholics that formerly characterized their interdenominational contacts.

6

The Priestly Celibacy Controversy

Ⅾ URING THE LAST DECADE there has been an intense debate on the question of priestly celibacy. Should it be retained as a requirement of the Roman Catholic priesthood or should it be made optional? Advocates of both positions appeal to Scripture, history, psychology, and sociology. Negative input here, however, has not effected a change in the law, as it did in two of the examples we have analyzed. Celibacy is still obligatory for priests of the Latin rite. Nevertheless, a cybernetic analysis of this critical issue is valuable, because it reveals the forces in conflict within the Church.

I. *Output*

In the New Testament, there is no evidence that celibacy was required of the Lord's followers, even though Jesus, John the Baptist, Paul, and Barnabas were celibate. We know, however, that Peter and some of the disciples were married (I *Cor.* 9:5) and a bishop must be "faithful to his one wife" (I *Tim.* 3:2; *Tit.* 1:8). Celibacy, however, was proposed as an ideal for the sake of the Kingdom of Heaven. It was a special gift from God, not given to everyone. St. Paul, for example, says that "better be married than burn with vain desire" (I *Cor.* 7:9) and Matthew advises: "Let those accept it who can" (*Matt.* 19:12). Consequently, it seems that in the New Testament celibacy is presented as a counsel rather than as an obligation.

In the Western Church, our concern here, the earliest law imposing clerical continence is found in the Spanish Council of Elvira, around 300. Thus, Canon 33 states: "All bishops, priests, deacons, and all clerics engaged in the ministry are forbidden entirely to live with their wives and to beget children; whoever shall do so will be deposed from their clerical dignity."[1] In the fourth and fifth centuries, several popes and provincial councils in Italy, France, and Africa decreed that priests, deacons, and subdeacons should not be allowed to marry. If they were married before their ordination, they were to live in continence with their spouses.

In spite of this tradition, clerical morality began to decline in the ninth century, and by the eleventh century the situation was chaotic. Pope Benedict VIII in 1023, for example, denounced the clergy who had wives or concubines;[2] Pope Leo IX in 1040 ordered the wives and concubines of priests, "*damnabiles feminae*" he called them, to be servants in the Lateran Palace in Rome;[3] and Pope Nicholas II in 1059 forbade the faithful to attend Masses offered by married priests and ordered the people not to accept the sacraments from them.[4] It was during the pontificate of Gregory VII (1073–1085) that a strong policy was formed to restore sacerdotal celibacy. He vigorously reaffirmed the traditional view and took firm steps to reform the clergy.

In the twelfth century, the question of clerical marriages came to a head. Lateran I (1123), the first general council held in the West, forbade priests, deacons, and subdeacons to live with concubines or with any woman except their mother, sister, aunt,

---

[1] Denzinger-Schönmetzer, 119.

[2] *Monumenta Germaniae Historica*, V, I, 70.

[3] In A. de Roskovany, *Coelibatus et breviarium* (Pest: I. Beimel and B. Kozma, 1861), I, 260.

[4] *Sacrorum conciliorum nova et amplissima collectio*, ed. J. D. Mansi, V, 19: 897–898. Hereafter cited as Mansi.

or any such person above suspicion.[5] The Fathers also decreed that clerics in major orders and monks were forbidden to have concubines or to contract marriage. Any cleric already married must have his marriage dissolved and do penance.[6]

The precise canonical status of clerical marriages was clarified in the Second Lateran Council (1139), which declared that such marriages are invalid. In decreeing that sacred orders are a diriment impediment to marriage, the Council concluded: "For a union of this kind which has been contracted in violation of the ecclesiastical law, we do not regard as matrimony."[7] With the Second Lateran Council, the obligation of clerical celibacy became the universal law of the Western Church. This obligation was reaffirmed at the Council of Trent in 1563[8] and in the Code of Canon Law in 1917 (Canon 132.1 and 1072). Furthermore, the Congregation of Sacraments in 1930[9] and 1955[10] and the Congregation of Religious in 1931[11] and 1961[12] have both issued decrees requiring the candidate for the subdiaconate to be carefully instructed about the obligation of celibacy and demanding a signed statement that he is aware of the implications of the law of celibacy.

At Vatican II, before the celibacy question could be publicly discussed, Pope Paul intervened. In a letter to Cardinal Tisserant, Dean of the Council Presidency, the Pope said that it was inopportune to discuss the matter at the Council and suggested that the bishops submit their views in writing. Moreover, the Pope made clear his own position. He said that he intended "not only to maintain this ancient, sacred and providential law . . . but to strengthen its observance by reminding priests of the Latin Church of the reasons and causes—particularly pertinent today

---

[5] Canon 7; *Conciliorum oecumenicorum decreta*, ed. J. Alberigo et al. (Freiburg: Herder, 1962), p. 167.

[6] Canon 21, *ibid.*, p. 170.

[7] Canon 7, *ibid.*, p. 174.

[8] Sess. 24, canon 9, *ibid.*, p. 731.

[9] *Acta Apostolicae Sedis*, 23 (1931), 120–129.

[10] Not published in the *Acta* but an English translation of it can be found in T. L. Bouscaren and J. O'Connor, *Canon Law Digest* (Milwaukee: Bruce, 1958), IV (1953–1957), 305–315.

[11] *Acta Apostolicae Sedis*, 24 (1932), 74–81.

[12] Found in Bouscaren-O'Connor, *op. cit.*, V (1958–1962), 452–488.

—for the supreme stability of this law."[13] In view of this background, it was not surprising that the Council reaffirmed the tradition of the Latin Church.[14] Celibacy is called a spiritual gift which enables clerics to have an undivided love of Christ, to witness to the future resurrected state, and to become all things to all men.[15] The Council, however, admitted that celibacy "is not demanded by the very nature of the priesthood, as is evident from the practice of the primitive Church and from the tradition of the Eastern Churches."[16]

Every pope in this century has written in support of priestly celibacy. For example, Benedict XV in a letter to the Archbishop of Prague in 1920, rebuked a Bohemian group that advocated abolition of the celibacy requirement. The Pope firmly stated that the Church would not change or mitigate this obligation.[17] John XXIII, in an address to the Roman Synod in 1960, reiterated the long-standing tradition of the official Church on clerical celibacy: "It deeply hurts us that . . . anyone can dream that the Church will deliberately or even suitably renounce what from time immemorial has been, and still remains, one of the purest and noblest glories of her priesthood."[18] His words set the tone for the subsequent treatment of the issue at the Second Vatican Council.

Paul VI returned to the topic numerous times after the Council. He devoted an entire encyclical, *Sacerdotalis caelibatus* (June 24, 1967), to a lengthy discussion of priestly celibacy, which he termed "a brilliant jewel," and a "golden law." He affirmed that "the present law of celibacy should today continue to be linked to the ecclesiastical ministry."[19] The Congregation for the Clergy issued a letter, dated November 4, 1969, which recommended that each year, preferably on Holy Thursday,

[13] Quoted by F. Wulf in *Commentary on the Documents of Vatican II*, ed. H. Vorgrimler (New York: Herder and Herder, 1969), IV, 283.

[14] *Decree on the Ministry and Life of Priests*, Art. 16.

[15] *Ibid.* and *Decree on Priestly Formation*, Art. 10.

[16] *Decree on the Ministry and Life of Priests*, Art. 16.

[17] In an allocution Benedict XV said: "We solemnly testify that the Holy See will never in any way mitigate, much less abolish, this most sacred and salutary law" (*Acta Apostolicae Sedis*, 12 [1920], 585).

[18] *Ibid.*, 52 (1960), 235–236.

[19] *Ibid.*, 59 (1967), 662.

priests renew their ordination promises, especially those of obedience and celibacy. The Pope also made a very strong statement defending the celibacy of priests at a public audience on February 1, 1970. He called it a "capital law in our Latin Church." "It cannot," he insisted, "be abandoned or subject to argument. That would be to retrogress."[20]

The official position of the Catholic Church regarding the celibate priesthood in the Western rites is clear: the law will not be changed. This output, however, did not end the controversy. In fact, it only caused further feedback.

II. *Input*

Sharp ideological division on the problem of married priests troubles the Church today. Demand for change and support for tradition are in public conflict. We will consider briefly both forms of this informational input.

A. DEMANDS

Many priests were greatly disappointed with the Second Vatican Council's stand on celibacy, as well as by the repeated attempts of Paul VI to discourage further discussion of the issue. Moreover, the alarming rate of defections from the priesthood has made the topic a popular and often sensational one for the secular and religious press. Since the Council, therefore, there has emerged a widespread assault on the traditional laws of the Latin Church concerning obligatory celibacy. This negative feedback will be examined under three headings: conferences, opinion polls, and theological writings.

Conferences. The National Association for Pastoral Renewal was formed in 1966 and became the first national organization of priests and laymen in the United States devoted to changing the celibacy legislation. It has conducted several surveys on what

---

[20] *NC News Service (Documentary)*, February 3, 1970. The Pope's address came less than two weeks after the Dutch Pastoral Council had voted for optional celibacy.

American priests think about a married priesthood, and in 1967 it sponsored a Symposium on Clerical Celibacy at the University of Notre Dame. Present were 211 priests and laymen who discussed the possibility of optional celibacy for priests in the Latin rite. The Symposium recommended that "diocesan priests of the Latin rite have the individual option of the celibate or married state while retaining their active ministry" and that married priests "if they so choose . . . be returned to the active ministry, after due consideration of their individual cases."[21]

The most dramatic statement on optional celibacy came from the Dutch National Pastoral Council on January 7, 1970. The Dutch bishops and representatives from the clergy, religious, seminarians, and laity discussed the celibacy problem. The assembly, with the bishops abstaining, passed four motions by an overwhelming majority: that the obligation of celibacy as a condition of the priesthood be abrogated; that priests should be allowed to marry while keeping their priestly functions and that married priests should be readmitted to the active ministry; that married men should be admitted to the priesthood; and that celibacy should no longer be a condition for entering the priesthood.[22] It was later reported that two weeks before the Dutch Council, Paul VI had written to the Dutch bishops urging them to defend priestly celibacy in view of Church tradition and the teachings of Vatican II.[23] This apparently had little effect on the episcopal leadership but perhaps explains their abstentions. On January 19, the Dutch bishops issued a statement in which they affirmed their allegiance to the universal Church and agreed that they would consult with the Holy Father and the rest of the Church before any change would be made. Yet they also said that it would be better for the Church community if, besides celibate priests, married priests were also allowed in the Latin rite.[24]

Less than a month after the Dutch statement, two European

---

[21] The full statement of the conference can be found in *Celibacy: The Necessary Option*, ed. G. H. Frein (New York: Herder and Herder, 1968), pp. 15–16.

[22] *New York Times*, January 8, 1970, p. 1.

[23] *NC News Service (Foreign)*, January 13, 1970, pp. 1–2.

[24] *NC News Service (Documentary)*, January 30, 1970.

groups reacted. In February, 84 Swiss, German, and Austrian theologians issued a letter to their individual bishops expressing solidarity with the Dutch and urging their bishops to discuss the problem with the Holy See.[25] Also a group of 140 Swiss priests, from German-speaking areas, rejected an earlier statement of the Swiss hierarchy which defended celibacy for priests as not being truly representative. The Swiss priests urged that men entering the seminary should be free to choose either celibacy or marriage.[26]

In the United States, the celibacy topic was discussed by the delegates of the National Federation of Priests' Councils who met in Baltimore in March 1971. The NFPC, which claims to represent 60 percent of the country's 57,000 priests, resolved that obligatory celibacy for priests be eliminated immediately and that former priests be reinstated. "We are convinced," they said, "that the present law of mandatory celibacy in the Western Church must be changed."[27]

Opinion Polls. The first wide-scale survey of the attitude of American priests on a married clergy was done by Jesuit sociologist Joseph H. Fichter. His preliminary findings were first released in December 1966.[28] He discovered that 62 percent of the 3,000 priests who replied favored optional celibacy, but only 5 percent would marry if given that option. A *Newsweek* survey, undertaken by the Louis Harris Associates, revealed that 48 percent of the Catholic laity interviewed felt that the Pope should give priests the right to marry.[29] The National Association for Pastoral Renewal in 1967 conducted a survey among priests in New York, New Jersey, and Connecticut which showed that 47 percent of the priests interviewed believed that diocesan priests should have the freedom of choice to marry or to remain celibate.[30] In 1970, the National Federation of Priests' Councils

[25] *New York Times*, February 12, 1970, p. 12.

[26] *Ibid.*

[27] The full text of the NFPC statement can be found in *National Catholic Reporter*, April 2, 1971, p. 8.

[28] *Ibid.*, December 12, 1966. For the complete survey see J. M. Fichter, *America's Forgotten Priests—What They Are Saying* (New York: Harper and Row, 1968).

[29] *Newsweek*, March 20, 1967, pp. 68–75.

[30] Cited in Frein, *op. cit.*, p. 14.

Study announced the results of a two-year investigation which found 56 percent of the priests replying in favor of a married clergy, but only 36 percent would consider marriage if permitted.[31]

The most ambitious study of American priests was commissioned by the National Conference of Catholic Bishops at a cost of $500,000. This four-year study began in 1967, and preliminary reports were made in 1971. The sociological part of the *Bishops' Report on Priestly Life and Ministry* was prepared by the National Opinion Research Center, which is affiliated with the University of Chicago. It concluded that a majority of priests (54 percent) felt that celibacy should be a matter of personal choice for diocesan priests. Yet most priests (four-fifths of those interviewed) would not get married even if the law were changed.[32] The psychological study reached similar conclusions.[33]

The above studies clearly show that a little over half of the Catholic priests in the United States want the law of obligatory celibacy changed. One should not overlook, however, the fact that relatively few priests would take advantage of this change and get married. The psychological report of the bishops' study explains this paradox by noting that it was the question of freedom of choice rather than the celibacy issue itself that was considered most important. The report also mentioned that there are other factors that influence departures from the priesthood: loneliness, conflicts with bishops, job dissatisfaction, restrictive structures, and maldeveloped emotional maturity.

Theological Writings. Beginning about 1965, a flood of books and articles on the celibacy question appeared all over the world.[34] The majority of them favored optional celibacy, or at

[31] *National Catholic Reporter*, March 26, 1971, p. 16.

[32] Cf. The National Opinion Research Center, *The Catholic Priest in the United States: Sociological Investigations* (Washington: United States Catholic Conference, 1972), pp. 233–266 and A. M. Greeley, *Priests in the United States: Reflections on a Survey* (New York: Doubleday, 1972), pp. 77–89.

[33] Cf. E. C. Kennedy and V. J. Heckler, *The Catholic Priest in the United States: Psychological Investigations* (Washington: United States Catholic Conference, 1972), pp. 12–14.

[34] Extensive bibliographies on priestly celibacy can be found in the continuing publications from 1966 of the Centre de Documentation et de

least argued that the whole problem should be thoroughly researched and discussed.

A theological study was also part of the *Bishops' Report on Priestly Life and Ministry*. It was prepared by a committee under the chairmanship of Father Carl J. Armbruster. In reference to the question of married priests, it said: "The simple theological fact is that celibacy is a charism bestowed by the Holy Spirit and it does not necessarily coincide with the charism of priestly service." While admitting that optional celibacy will not be a panacea for all the problems of the priesthood, the report concludes that it is "an authentic element of priestly renewal."[35]

B. SUPPORTS

The principal input supporting the Church's position on obligatory celibacy came from the bishops themselves. For example, they promptly and publicly defended the Pope's negative view of the resolutions of the Dutch pastoral council. In February 1970, several national hierarchies declared their solidarity with the Pope by reaffirming the traditional ban against married priests. The United States bishops cabled the Pope on February 10 and said: "The bishops of this country wholeheartedly join

Recherche in Montreal. Other bibliographies are given in the following studies: H. C. Lea, *An Historical Sketch of Sacerdotal Celibacy in the Christian Church*, 4th. ed. rev. (Hyde Park, N.Y.: University Books, 1966); J. Blenkinsopp, *Celibacy, Ministry, Church* (New York: Herder and Herder, 1968); M. Boelens, *Die Klerikerehe in der Gesetzgebung der Kirche unter besonderer Berücksichtigung der Strafe* (Paderborn: Schöningh, 1968); R. Gryson, *Les origines du célibat ecclésiastique du premier au septième siècle* (Gembloux: J. Duculot, 1970); J. E. Lynch, "Marriage and Celibacy of the Clergy: The Discipline of the Western Church: An Historico-Canonical Synopsis," *The Jurist*, 32 (1972), 14–38, 189–212.

[35] *National Catholic Reporter*, April 30, 1971, p. 12. The Administrative Committee of the National Conference of Catholic Bishops voted not to publish this theological study. They gave the following reason: "The bishops on this committee simply do not agree with some of the conclusions of the study and therefore feel it would be misleading for them to authorize its publication" (*National Catholic Reporter*, September 29, 1972, p. 20). Excerpts from the study were published by the *National Catholic Reporter*, October 8, 1971, p. 14, and May 12, 1972, p. 9.

Your Holiness again in supporting the ideal and discipline of consecrated celibacy which have served the priesthood and the Church so well."[36] Earlier, at their semi-annual meetings in November 1967 and November 1969, the bishops had also endorsed the celibacy rule.

Also in Europe, bishops reaffirmed priestly celibacy. The French episcopal conference in February 1970, for example, declared: "We are calling to the priesthood only men who have decided to lead a consecrated celibate life. Priests released from their obligations cannot exercise their priestly ministry."[37] The Scottish bishops in a joint declaration stated that they were "in complete accord with the Holy Father in his courageous defense of this sacred and treasured tradition. . . ."[38] Similar pronouncements of loyalty came from bishops from Ecuador, Austria, North-Rhine-Westphalia, and the Pacific. Cardinal Suenens of Belgium said that in Belgium former priests will not be reinstated to the priestly ministry, nor will seminarians be accepted who wish to get married at a later date.[39] The Cardinal, however, regretted that the Pope had suppressed discussion of the celibacy problem and urged that it should be a subject of dialogue between the Pope and the bishops.[40]

Strong words against those who advocate a married clergy came from Cardinal Daniélou in an article in *L'Osservatore Romano*, January 31, 1970. His main argument was that the attacks on celibacy were nothing else but an attack on papal authority. "Smoothly," he wrote, "appeals have been addressed to the world episcopate to close ranks with the Dutch, in an endeavor to shake loose the authority of the Pope, to blackmail it, and finally suppress it."[41] He denied the validity of surveys favoring optional celibacy, since they did not correspond to the real mind of the Christian community but only to specific groups. Claiming that "hatred of Rome's authority" motivates many who campaign against celibacy, the French Cardinal pleaded for support of the Pope.

---

[36] *NC News Service (Domestic)*, February 12, 1970, pp. 1–2.
[37] *NC News Service (Foreign)*, February 7, 1970, p. 10.
[38] *Ibid.*, February 28, 1970, p. 1.
[39] *NC News Service (Domestic)*, March 14, 1970, p. 5.
[40] *NC News Service (Foreign)*, May 5, 1970, pp. 9–10.
[41] *NC News Service (Documentary)*, February 9, 1970, p. 3.

An argument frequently used by supporters of obligatory celibacy is based on the experience of the Eastern and Protestant married clergy. However, these groups are also suffering from a dearth of candidates for the ministry. In fact, Protestant clergymen are leaving the ministry at a rate which parallels the departures from the Catholic priesthood. The manpower drain among Protestant clerics has not received great publicity, but studies have confirmed it. According to a report directed by Rev. Dr. Gerald J. Jud of the United Church, at least three thousand ministers leave every year.[42] The two-year project, entitled "Ex-Pastors: Why Men Leave the Ministry," gave some of the reasons for the departures: lack of a private life, outmoded theology, church bureaucracy, and low salaries. Marital problems were also cited as a contributing factor.

Many among the Catholic clergy and laity have felt that priests should continue to be celibate. This supportive input has not received the same publicity as the statements of those advocating change. Those who agree with existing legislation do not feel it necessary to form an organization to defend it. Vocal opponents of any long-standing tradition will always be more audible than those who simply accept it. Consequently it is difficult to learn the comparative strength of the two input positions.

III. *Conversion Process*

The Catholic hierarchy had to make some reply to the mounting demands for optional celibacy. This was done by both the United States bishops and the world synod of bishops. At these meetings the demands were acknowledged, but they were not converted into favorable outputs.

In April 1971, the bishops of the United States met in Detroit to discuss, in closed session, the comprehensive study on the priestly ministry they had sponsored. Unconvinced by the fact that over half the priests under their jurisdictions favored optional celibacy, the bishops reacted negatively. Most of them agreed with Cardinal Krol's assessment of the study: "Psycho-

[42] *Washington Post*, February 14, 1970, p. B 6.

logical and sociological data cannot be used as a criterion of truth or as a norm of action."[43] The consensus was that the present discipline on clerical celibacy should be maintained, but that the question should be openly discussed at the synod in Rome in September 1971. A further indication of the mind of the American bishops was their selection of conservative delegates to represent them at the Rome meeting.

Catholic reaction to the bishops' stand was mixed. Liberals criticized them for their inflexible attitude, while conservatives praised them for their courageous defense of tradition. The strongest criticism came from two priests' organizations and from one bishop. The National Federation of Priests' Councils attacked the bishops for failing to discuss the celibacy issue fully and predicted that their position would only encourage secret marriages among the clergy. If the matter was not treated at the Roman synod, the statement warned, then support for clandestine marriages would "come from the laity and the rest of the priests."[44] Another negative reaction came from the Association of Chicago Priests, who represented 900 of the 2,400 priests in the archdiocese. It censured Cardinal Cody and the five auxiliary bishops "for failing to speak out on behalf of the needs of priests" at the April meeting.[45] The most dramatic response, however, was that of Bishop Bernard M. Kelly, Auxiliary Bishop of Providence. Two months after the April meeting he resigned from the active ministry. In his June 14 letter of resignation, he expressed displeasure with the bishops' conference during which they " 'studied' the priesthood for three days and then reaffirmed the status quo, ignoring the serious recommendations of the National Federation of Priests' Councils, of their own regional input, and of their own scientific report calling for serious changes in priestly ministry and life style."[46]

The synod of bishops met in Rome in September 1971 with over two hundred delegates in attendance. Priestly ministry, with special reference to celibacy, was one of the items on the agenda. Before the meeting, the bishops had received a Vatican

---

[43] *New York Times*, April 23, 1971, p. 30.
[44] *National Catholic Reporter*, May 21, 1971, p. 4.
[45] *Washington Post*, June 6, 1971, p. A6.
[46] *New York Times*, June 15, p. 28.

survey that was ordered prepared by the Congregation for the Doctrine of the Faith. The survey revealed that between 1963 and 1969 about eleven thousand priests had abandoned the ministry. Among those who requested laicization, the desire to marry was given as the principal reason. The study also gave projections for the future based on the data collected. It was estimated that between 1970 and 1975 some twenty thousand priests would leave. During the same period there should be about fifteen thousand ordinations. Thus, the net loss of priests during this period would be about a thousand a year.[47]

Some observers felt that the Vatican estimate was inaccurate and that the actual number of departed priests was much higher. Father François Houtart, a Belgian sociologist, studied the eight-year period between 1963 and 1970. He concluded that the total number of priests who have left the priesthood was closer to twenty-five thousand. This would be five percent of all the priests in the world.[48] Another survey was prepared by the American Jesuit sociologist Eugene Schallert, whose findings showed that in the United States a remarkable change had taken place between 1965 and 1971. In 1965, four men were ordained for every three who were lost through death, retirement, or defection. In 1971, however, twice as many priests left as were ordained.[49]

During the synod, the bishops debated the celibacy issue. Two principal questions emerged: (1) should priests be allowed to marry? and (2) should married men be ordained? In regard to the first question there was virtual unanimity among the bishops, who concluded that in the Latin Church the law of priestly celibacy should be kept in its entirety. The final vote was 168 in favor of the motion, 21 in favor but with some reservations, and 10 against it. In regard to the second question, a division developed. Finally, after much debate, two formulas were proposed. The first formula stated that, granting the right of the pope, married men should not be ordained even in particular cases. A majority of the bishops, 107, voted for this. Cardinals Conway of Ireland and Wyszynski of Poland were the chief

[47] *Ibid.*, August 9, 1971, p. 1.
[48] *National Catholic Reporter*, April 30, 1971, p. 13.
[49] *Ibid.*, September 10, 1971, p. 7.

spokesmen for this group. The second formula proposed that the pope should in particular cases, and for the good of the Church, allow the ordination of mature and qualified married men. A minority of 87 voted for this. Its main support came from Eastern rite bishops and from some of the delegates representing Canada, Asia, and Africa. The ordination of married men thus became the only issue at the synod which failed to get the agreement of at least two-thirds of the bishops. Nevertheless the closeness of the vote left hope that the pope might permit such ordinations eventually. Bishop Alexander Carter, for example, considered the vote as the beginning of further discussion. He said: "It effectively throws the question back to the national bishops' conferences to make their minds felt to the Pope."[50]

IV. *Evaluation*

The celibacy controversy illustrates the cybernetic interaction over matters of discipline. This example differs from the others in that it centers on a law that the decision-makers have the power to change. Some of Christ's apostles were married. Some married men, usually convert ministers, have been ordained as Catholic priests. The Uniate Churches, in communion with Rome, have a married clergy. The change desired, therefore, has many precedents. Here are the major points of the analysis:

1. Celibacy has a long tradition in the Roman Catholic Church. It is rooted in Scripture and the example of Christ. It has both witness value and intrinsic spiritual value. The proponents of optional celibacy do not deny its value in the Church. They wish to preserve it, but to make it voluntary.

2. The demand looks to a relatively small group of persons, the clergy, who assert the right to self-determination in disciplinary matters. A slight majority of the clergy want a change. Moreover, many laymen have supported these demands although they are certainly not directly involved.

3. The news media have kept up a steady flow of information on the issue, some of it sensational. Their impact on Church

---

[50] *New York Times*, November 7, 1971, p. 22.

authorities is lessened, however, by the fact that they do not speak from a shared faith or religious commitment.

4. The output has consistently fostered priestly celibacy and denied optional celibacy. The reason given for this firm stand is concern for the good of the whole Church. However, two things have occurred: the Church now permits married men to be ordained to the diaconate; and the Church has finally discussed a married priesthood on a high collegial level, the bishops' synod in Rome.

5. The informational input is continuing and is stronger and better organized than ever. The drop in priestly vocations is intensifying the critical aspects of the problem.

CONCLUSION

The four instances analyzed above illustrate the function of that key concept in cybernetics, the feedback loop, which involves the communication flow influencing the conversion process.

The subject matter of these instances is diverse: human equality (slavery), sexual ethics (birth control), religious diversity (ecumenism), and disciplinary law (priestly celibacy). In each case there was intense input. Surprisingly, the Church changed its view in the two instances (slavery and ecumenism) where the input was predominantly from those outside the Church; whereas, in the two instances (birth control and celibacy) where the input was predominantly from Church members, the ecclesial decision-makers refused to change their position.

What conclusions can be drawn from this sampling? First, all input is important, even that coming from outside the ecclesial system. Secondly, Catholics are involving themselves more and more in ecclesial decisions, even though their contribution is only on the level of input. Thirdly, even minor success in influencing decision-making increases the quantity of input. Fourthly, since Vatican II and its emphasis on liberty and collegiality, the move for participation in decision-making has intensified.

In brief, these cases reflect the growing demand for ecclesial democratization. In the next part, we examine the historical and theological justifications for such a radical change.

PART THREE

Traditional Ecclesial Democracy

T HE FOUR CYBERNETIC ANALYSES in the preceding part revealed certain communication deficiencies in the ecclesial system. Too many informational messages from within the system and from its parameters were either rejected, delayed, or inadequately converted into creative outputs. This failure caused, as we have seen, polarity and stagnation. In the past, the reluctance of the Church to react decisively to demands has often restricted its evolutionary potential. The situation today is not substantially different. Many observers see the present crisis in the Church as attributable primarily to a communications breakdown.[1] The increasing loss of confidence in the Church and in

---

[1] In spite of the overstatement, the following remark is typical: "At a time when virtually every other organized society, even the most primitive, makes some kind of obeisance to the principle of government by consultation of the governed, the Church, almost alone, stands firm for autocracy—an autocracy based on the theory of divine election and inspiration of the autocrat, the Pope" (R. C. Doty, *New York Times*, January 19, 1969, p. 6E). A very negative view of ecclesial democratization is taken by J. Eppstein, *Has the Catholic Church Gone Mad?* (New Rochelle, N. Y.: Arlington House, 1971).

its leadership appears to be proportioned to the level of influential informational flow. Can this be improved by a greater participation of the faithful in the decision-making process? In other words, can there be any kind of ecclesial democracy?

This part will attempt to answer this question by discussing three areas: first, the meaning of political democracy; second, the historical evidence for ecclesial democracy with special reference to the election of Church leaders; and third, the theological foundation of ecclesial democracy.

7

The Meaning of Democracy

THE WORD *democracy* first appeared in the writings of
Herodotus some twenty-five hundred years ago.[1] Etymologically,
it derives from two Greek words: *demos*, the people; and *kratos*,
rule. Democracy, then, is a form of government in a civil community in which the people control the power. Cybernetically,
democracy may be defined as an open political system in which
societal decisions (outputs) are made according to the will (input) of the majority, either directly or through representatives
who are subject to periodic control through elections. Power
in a democracy is rooted in the consent of the governed. The
philosophical justification for this is that in a civil society the
people are the first bearers of authority. Consequently the people
have the right to control the system through a variety of inputs
—the principal one being a regular free election. Democracy,
therefore, emphasizes a close interaction and communication
among the members of the system and establishes input channels.

Two basic types of political democracy exist: direct and indirect. Both involve active citizen participation and both acknowledge the right of the people to control their own destiny.

[1] *History*, Book III.

Direct democracy is that form of government in which the citizens, acting as a whole, personally and immediately exercise their right to make decisions. Indirect democracy is that form of government in which the citizens elect representatives who are accountable to them. The fundamental difference between direct and indirect democracy is succinctly explained by Giovanni Sartori: "In direct democracy there is continuous participation of the people in the direct *exercise* of power, whereas indirect democracy amounts to a system of *limitation* and *control* of power."[2]

I. *Direct Democracy*

Direct or self-governing democracy, its origins lost in pre-history, first appeared in the western world in the Greek city-states.[3] According to the Greek ideal, all citizens could attend legislative sessions, vote, and be elected to office. The privilege of citizenship, however, was limited to free males over twenty. Women, children, slaves, and resident aliens were excluded from political activity.

The main legislative body in Greek democracy was the General Assembly, which met ten times a year to make laws for the city and to discuss questions of finance, foreign trade, war, and diplomacy. All matters were decided by vote. There were some public officials who were elected by the assembly and paid for their work. Two other governmental bodies functioned in the city-state: the Council and the Council of the Five Hundred. The Council, a kind of executive committee formed from representatives from the General Assembly, met regularly to discuss policies and to draft resolutions that were submitted to the General Assembly. The Council of the Five Hundred, fifty elected members chosen from the ten Athenian tribes, met between regular sessions of the General Assembly. Among its duties was seeing that the decrees of the Assembly were faith-

[2] *Democratic Theory* (New York: Praeger, 1965), p. 252.

[3] For further details on this subject see A. E. Zimmern, *The Greek Commonwealth* (Oxford: Oxford University Press, 1931); W. Jaeger, *Paideia: The Ideals of Greek Culture* (New York: Oxford University Press, 1939); and W. W. Fowler, *The City-State of the Greeks and Romans* (London: Macmillan, 1952).

fully carried out. The judicial acts of the government were conducted either during the General Assembly or in special courts
where the judges and jurors were chosen by lot from a group of
six thousand that had been previously elected.

Athenian democracy had its supporters and its critics. Pericles,
for example, saw it as the ideal form of government in which
the citizen's participation in the political life of the city made him
fully a person.[4] Furthermore, it was argued, a collective decision
is more apt to be correct than the decision of one man. An issue
that is publicly debated can utilize the experience and wisdom of
all the participants. Democracy was also seen as giving greater
protection against tyrannical rule, suppression of minorities, and
misgovernment by dishonest officials. Yet, on the other hand,
Aristotle considered democracy as among the corrupt forms of
government[5] and Plato ranked it second only to tyranny as an
undesirable political system.[6] These philosophers reasoned that
since the majority of the citizens were poor and uneducated,
democracy, the rule of the many, was bound to be a failure.
Plato favored a rationalistic ideal, a "noocracy" or aristocracy of
the wise. He lamented the incompetence of the ordinary citizen
and feared that the emotional character of mass meetings encouraged demagogy.

Direct democracy, with its rapid conversion of feedback, is no
longer feasible on a large scale. The Greek *polis* was small and
cannot be compared with the mass society of the modern state.
The size of modern countries and cities makes face-to-face

[4] Thucydides, *The History of the Peloponnesian War*, trans. R. Crawley
(London: J. M. Dent, 1923), p. 123.

[5] *Politica*, trans. B. Jowett in *The Works of Aristotle*, Vol. X (Oxford:
Clarendon Press, 1921), Book III, 7, 1279 a. Aristotle, *ibid.*, called democracy
a "government of the needy." G. Sartori would agree with Aristotle's
observation and argues that the failure of Greek democracy was due primarily to economic paralysis. He explains: "The more perfect their democracy became the poorer the citizens became. And the Greek *polis* could
not escape from the vicious circle of seeking a political solution to
economic distress by confiscating wealth in order to make up for insufficient production of wealth. The democracy of antiquity was fated to
be destroyed in the class struggle between rich and poor, because it had
produced only a political animal and not a *homo oeconomicus*" (Sartori,
op. cit., p. 254).

[6] *The Republic*, trans. A. Bloom (New York: Basic Books, 1968), Book
VIII, 544, p. 222.

democracy impossible. The increased population, the complexities of contemporary living, and governmental bureaucracy are resistant to direct control. The fragmentation and mobility of society today have created an environment hostile to a direct democratic system. Rousseau's words on this point are still apropos: "If there were a people of gods, they would govern themselves democratically. So perfect a government is not suited to men."[7]

For two thousand years after the fall of the Greek democratic system, there was almost a total absence of any theory or practice of democracy. The oligarchic Roman republic and the autocratic empire were succeeded by monarchies and various forms of absolutist rule. Democracy had only historical interest up to the time of the French and American revolutions. Since then, however, political theorists the world over have analyzed every facet of democracy. Although the literature on the subject is vast, this has not deterred modern scholars. Articles and books on democracy continue to appear with relentless regularity.[8] Most of them deal with the second type of political democracy, which is called indirect democracy.

II. *Indirect Democracy*

Indirect democracy, in name at least, is widely accepted throughout the world. This is clear from the results of a symposium sponsored by UNESCO in 1949 which attracted over a

---

[7] *Du contrat social* (Aubier: Editions Montaigne, 1943), Book III, ch. iv, p. 277.

[8] Some significant works on democratic theory are A. D. Lindsay, *The Modern Democratic State* (London: Oxford University Press, 1943); R. M. MacIver, *The Web of Government* (New York: Macmillan, 1947); J. A. Schumpeter, *Capitalism, Socialism, and Democracy* (New York: Harper, 1947); W. Lippmann, *The Public Philosophy* (Boston: Little, Brown and Company, 1954); C. J. Friedrich, *Constitutional Government and Democracy* (Boston: Ginn, 1950); Y. R. Simon, *Philosophy of Democratic Government* (Chicago: University of Chicago Press, 1951); H. B. Mayo, *An Introduction to Democratic Theory* (New York: Oxford University Press, 1960); R. A. Dahl, *Political Oppositions in Western Democracies* (New Haven: Yale University Press, 1966); and R. Niebuhr and P. E. Sigmund, *The Democratic Experience* (New York: Praeger, 1969).

hundred scholars from both the East and the West. One of the questions debated was the ideal form of government. The reported consensus was surprising: "There were no replies adverse to democracy. Probably for the first time in history, democracy is claimed as the proper ideal description of all systems of political and social organization advocated by influential proponents."[9] Since nearly 40 percent of the world's population lives under totalitarian regimes, this was an astonishing agreement. It indicates how broadly democracy can be defined even in our age of conflicting ideologies and how much of a status symbol democracy has become. Nearly every nation in the world wants to be known, at least nominally, as a democracy. Stalin called his tyrannical rule "democratic centralism." The most rigid of Eastern European satellites, East Germany, is officially called the German Democratic Republic. Other nations in the Communist bloc use the term "people's democracies." In Rhodesia, the fact that 250,000 whites have power over 4 million blacks does not prevent Premier Ian Smith from calling his government a "responsible democracy."

For a democratic system to be established and to prosper, the members of the system should agree on two fundamental principles: that all members share a common human dignity and that the government exists for the people and not vice versa. The role of the government, as the controlling subsystem in society, is to allow men to exercise their rights and to maximize their total potential as persons. Consequently, arbitrary use of force, deprivation of basic freedoms, and discrimination are contrary to the democratic ideal. Where there is no respect for order and a poor understanding of individual responsibility and of compromise without violence, democracy cannot succeed.

Democracy must emerge from a community's consciousness; it cannot be imposed from without. The United States has discovered through experience that democracy is not easy to export. Many fledgling governments are too unstable to adapt to the mechanisms of a democratic system. Their initial task is to achieve minimal public order. As James Madison noted in the *Federalist Papers*, the first requirement of a government is to control the governed. Severe disagreement among citizens on the

9 *Democracy in a World of Tensions* (Paris: UNESCO, 1951), p. 527.

nature of a particular political philosophy can lead to subversion and eventual revolution. Many developing Asian and African countries that had aspired to democracy have taken that route. For serious unemployment, a high illiteracy rate, and inadequate educational and housing facilities create an environment inimical to democracy, as do certain cultural and political traditions. The formation of an educated and enlightened middle class, the involvement of the working class, and general economic security are not easily achieved; yet without them, democracy is unstable, if not unobtainable.[10]

Political scientists enumerate, besides free elections, other requirements for a successful democratic system: the presence of organized opposition parties; a guarantee of the freedoms of speech, religion, press, and assembly; an independent judiciary system; freedom from coercion and arbitrary arrest; and, finally, a sound economic system that provides for the good of all the citizens. There are, however, three aspects of democracy which deserve special attention: the principle of majority rule, the need for leadership, and the value of decentralization.

The first aspect, the majority principle, is linked, though not necessarily, to the idea of universal suffrage which assures the involvement of the people in the political system. Since the people elect their leaders through a competitive struggle, they control indirectly the decision-making process. The ballot is a powerful form of input which allows the citizens to elect or dismiss their representatives. Moreover, voting establishes a regularized communication channel between the people and their representatives and requires from the political elites a continual accounting to their constituents. Another great advantage of the elective system is that it fosters processes of homeostasis and evolution. The stability of the system is maintained in spite of frequent change of office-holders. A peaceful and orderly transferral of power that is controlled avoids the disruptive consequences which often accompany the emergence of a new regime in monarchic or totalitarian countries. Therefore, progress and

---

[10] Religion is another factor that may foster or impede democracy. On the relationship between Catholicism and democracy see S. M. Lipset, "Some Social Requisites of Democratic Development and Political Legitimacy," *American Political Science Review*, 53 (1959), 69–105.

an arrest of entropy can result when new leaders with creative ideas are elected to face the ever-changing problems of political life.

The majority principle, of course, is not an absolute guarantee that the best candidate will always be elected. Taine once remarked: "Ten million ignorances do not make up one knowledge."[11] To this should be added Jefferson's statement: "Although the will of the majority is in all cases to prevail, that will to be rightful must be reasonable."[12] It is not true, as history has proven countless times, that "the people always know best." Even apart from fraudulent elections, the people can make collective errors. The average voter knows little about the candidates or the issues. His voting habits are often determined, though less so today, by his membership in a particular family, class, peer group, or church. He may also be a victim of saturation advertising through the media. Notwithstanding these drawbacks, it still seems reasonable to entrust the people with decisions about matters that affect them directly. In the long run, it is hoped, the people will be more often right than wrong. The chance of a disastrous choice of delegates appears to be relatively infrequent.

The majority rule, built on the existence of one or more opposition parties, helps assure a genuine choice of representatives. A common objection, however, is that those elected are not really representative. How many Congressmen and Senators, the argument goes, are women, blacks, or blue-collar workers? This question suggests that a statistical representation based on sex, race, occupation, or religion is the ideal. Most democracies, however, have found this plan unworkable. The greater the number of people and issues in a democratic system, as Bruno Leoni has observed, "the less the word 'representation' has a meaning referable to the actual will of actual people."[13] In a

---

[11] H. A. Taine, *Origines de la France contemporaine* (Paris, 1875), Preface.

[12] Thomas Jefferson in his first inaugural address in 1801. Found in S. K. Padover, *The Complete Jefferson* (New York: Duell, Sloan and Pearce, 1943), p. 384.

[13] *Freedom and the Law* (Princeton, N.J.: Van Nostrand, 1961), p. 18–19.

democracy elections take place in specific geographical regions, but representatives are seen primarily as representing persons and not interests. "The thing that matters most," according to Yves Simon, "is not so much sociological belonging to a group as intentional communion with it."[14]

The application of the majority principle gives a community an opportunity to correct its mistakes. Alexander Hamilton warned his contemporaries: "Give all the power to the many, they will suppress the few. Give all the power to the few, they will suppress the many."[15]

Democracy tries to avoid both of these extremes. Power is shared by both the many and the few through the mechanism of election. In the United States the separation of powers, constitutional checks and balances, as well as elections are designed to prevent despotic rule.

A second aspect of democracy is the type of leadership required. As J. Bryce puts it: "Perhaps no form of government needs great leaders so much as democracy does."[16] The leaders in a democracy must encourage shared decision-making; utilize the abilities and energies of the constituents; and direct the body politic to achieve its goals. On their part, the citizens must carefully scrutinize their leaders. There has to be, in Sidney Hook's words, "a skepticism, stubborn but not blind, of all demands for the enlargement of power."[17] A deification of office-holders or an abandonment of critical civic interest in their accomplishments can easily pave the way to excessive use of power. A healthy polarity should exist between the minority "out parties" and the controlling "in party," as well as between the general public and their representatives. A democracy that is satisfied with unworthy leaders has already abandoned its hope in the democratic ideal. A people, as the adage goes, gets the kind of government it deserves.

[14] Simon, *op. cit.*, p. 222.

[15] Alexander Hamilton in *Debates on the Adoption of the Federal Constitution*, ed. J. Elliot (Philadelphia: Lippincott, 1941), V, 203.

[16] *The American Commonwealth* (New York: Macmillan, 1888), III, 337. Sartori notes: "Democracy is the most daring experiment in man's faith that has ever been, or even can be tried" (*op. cit.*, p. 118).

[17] *Reason, Social Myths and Democracy* (New York: Harper Torchbooks, 1966), p. 290.

Every government, including a democracy, is ruled by a few. The governing subsystem is not a mere "coach driver" who makes no decisions but only takes orders. Elected representatives make judgments on the basis of their own intelligence, wisdom, and experience. Leaders must lead and not be led, even if it results in their not being reelected. Officials often have to face threats, bribes, failing popularity, and influences from pressure groups. A governing elite is not opposed to the democratic concept. "A society," as H. D. Lasswell writes, "may be democratic and express itself by a small leadership. The key question turns on accountability."[18] Leaders are accountable to the people who elect them, but they must decide on how best to serve the common interest.

A third aspect of the democratic system is the notion of decentralization. Where autocratic government tends to centralize power by concentrating it in the hands of a few, democracy seeks to decentralize it by distributing it to several groups. The federal system of the United States is based on this notion of subsidiarity: the larger society should not do what the smaller community or the individual person can do. Representational decentralization has several values: it engages the people in the decision-making process; it establishes communication channels through which demands and supports can flow; and it allows regional officials to cope with their own local problems.

Decentralization, however, also has the vices of its virtues. Critics of the democratic system point out that it is often unwieldy, inefficient, and financially debilitating. The cumbersome mechanisms of popular sovereignty, it is claimed, delay prompt action in critical situations. Responsibility is so diffused that often necessary things do not get done. Democracy, according to its critics, has failed to conquer inequality, poverty, and unemployment in spite of its highflown philosophical justification. Lobbyists seem to exert more influence on lawmakers than their constituents with all their voting power.

These arguments against democracy still have a certain validity. Democracy is not utopian government. It has the shortcomings of most human constructs. To be successful it needs con-

---

[18] H. D. Lasswell and others, *The Comparative Study of Elites* (Stanford: Stanford University Press, 1952), p. 7.

tinual review and reform. No one can deny that democracy has failed to achieve many of its goals. Nevertheless it has tried to safeguard the intrinsic dignity of the human person and to allow his potential to be maximized. "The critics of democracy," Henry B. Mayo asserts, "all too often fail to apply the same standard to democracy as to its rivals."[19] One cannot overlook the gross suppression of human rights and institutionalized corruption in totalitarian regimes. There elections are a sham. Dissent of any kind is ruthlessly eliminated. Only the outer trappings of democracy are present.

Can the Church incorporate some democratic elements into its governmental system? We know that the Church is not simply another political entity but a unique religious society. An application, therefore, of democracy to the Church has to take into account this uniqueness. Our task, then, is to inquire whether the democratic ideals of majoritarianism and decentralization are compatible with the hierarchic structure of the Church. The rest of this part will e devoted to a historical and theological analysis of this question.

[19] Mayo, *op. cit.*, p. 285.

8

The Historical Development of Ecclesial Democracy

ECCLESIAL DEMOCRACY is not a new thing. It has its roots deep in Christian tradition. Evidence of democratic elements in the open system which is the Church appears primarily in the selection of office-holders. The complete history of co-responsibility in the Church has not been written. Our efforts here are not intended to accomplish that formidable task. We wish, rather, to present a brief survey of democratization in the Church and to analyze its development and obsolescence. Contemporary advocates of shared responsibility frequently refer to the practice of the past as an ideal that should now be reintroduced. What role did the individual believer play in the governing of the Church and why was he gradually excluded from participation? The history of the Church provides many insights into this problem. We will begin by examining the data in the New Testament, then proceed to the patristic era, and, finally, examine later developments.

I. *The New Testament*

The New Testament Church, unlike the Church of today, was
not a thoroughly structured organization, but an evolving one
that gradually adapted itself to new challenges. Christ did not
reveal a complete code of managerial principles ready for application. Consequently the New Testament gives us few answers
to the specific juridical questions that developed in a later ecclesiastical tradition. There does, however, emerge from the New
Testament something of the internal dynamics of co-responsibility. This is most apparent in the Acts of the Apostles, but
there are also indications in other writings. The importance of
these texts is not so much the practical details as the theology
behind them.

The intense relationship of the early Christians to the community colored their attitude toward consensual decision-making.
They were bound together by a common profession of the
Lordship of Jesus, sealed by baptism, by love, and by the
eucharistic worship. The *koinonia*, or bond of union, is described by Luke: "The whole body of believers was united in
heart and soul."[1] The foundation of this unity was the Holy
Spirit, who instilled life in the Church, guided it, and enabled
it to grow. The first Christians felt that they were the Spirit-
filled, messianic People of God. They took for granted that they
should have an active role in making decisions that affected
them.

Two things must be kept in mind when discussing community
decisions in the early Church: first, the nature of the material
that was openly debated; and second, the unique position of the
Apostolic College. As to the first, there is no indication that the
entire community played any significant part in the formulation
of doctrinal matters. The fundamental Christian message was
revealed to the apostles, prophets, and teachers. It was not the
result of community discovery. For example, at Jerusalem, "at
a private interview with the men of repute" (*Gal.* 2:2), Paul

---

[1] *Acts* 4:32. In this passage Luke uses the expression *homothumadon*—of
one mind, purpose, or impulse. It is found several times in *Acts* to emphasize the unity of the believing community: 2:1 (variant reading); 2:46;
4:24; and 8:6.

willingly presented the teaching he received from God.[2] He did so for the sake of unity, to gain from them an acknowledgment that both he and they were teaching the same Gospel message. The Christian assembly, however, communicated but did not create doctrine. Its proper decision-making competence, therefore, concerned administration, discipline, and the application of doctrine to specific matters. Although the early Church considered the Gospel message as something received, it did judge the credentials of its teachers and the purity of their teaching. Everyone teaching the mystery of Christ was, in Paul's word, an "ambassador" (*Eph.* 6:20) of God, one held to an exact communication.

The second item to remember is the role of the apostles in the community. As Paul reminds the Ephesians: "You are built upon the foundation laid by the apostles and prophets, and Christ Jesus himself is the foundation-stone" (*Eph.* 2:20). In listing the special ministries, Paul always placed the apostles in the first place. The term *apostle* is used in a variety of ways in the New Testament.[3] In Luke, the apostles are identified with the twelve; but in Paul, Christian missionaries and community emissaries are also called apostles. The twelve apostles were directly commissioned by the risen Christ, but we cannot exclude the possibility that the emissaries were elected by the community. Granting the difficulty of forming a single concept of apostle in the New Testament, it does seem that the office implied definite authority and prestige.

Several instances in the New Testament refer to community participation. In the following pages we will discuss the five principal passages, which are found in the First Epistle to the Corinthians, the Gospel of Matthew, and the Acts of the Apostles.

A. THE EXPULSION OF THE INCESTUOUS MAN (1 *Cor.* 5:1–8)

St. Paul had learned that one of the members of the Corinthian community was having intercourse with his stepmother—a prac-

---

[2] Cf. I *Cor.* 11:23; 15:3; and *Gal.* 1:12.

[3] An excellent survey-article with an extensive bibliography on the problem of apostolicity has been written by R. Schnackenburg, "Apostolicity—The Present Position of Studies," *One in Christ*, 6 (1970), 243–273.

tice, he noted, that not even the pagans would condone. Paul was angry and—characteristic of his strong personality—he reacted vigorously. He wrote (v. 2 ff):

And you can still be proud of yourselves! You ought to have gone into mourning; a man who has done such a deed should have been rooted out of your company. For my part, though I am absent in body, I am present in spirit, and my judgement upon the man who did this thing is already given, as if I were indeed present: you all being assembled in the name of our Lord Jesus, and I with you in spirit, with the power of our Lord Jesus over us, this man is to be consigned to Satan for the destruction of the body, so that his spirit may be saved on the Day of the Lord.

Commentators disagree on the meaning of this text. J. C. Hurd,[4] H. Conzelmann,[5] and M. M. Bourke[6] suggest that the decision is Paul's alone and not the community's. C. K. Barrett[7] and G. W. MacRae,[8] however, feel that Paul does not impose his will on the community but rather urges them to judge the matter themselves and to be responsible for it. It would seem that from the text Paul has already judged the case, but in some way he wishes the community to be involved in the final judgment. Paul, therefore, is aware of shared responsibility and the necessity of community consultation.[9] Thus, Bourke notes that Paul "does want the members of the community to make his decision their own, so that the verdict will be that of the entire

---

[4] *The Origin of 1 Corinthians* (New York: Seabury Press, 1965), p. 178.

[5] *Der erste Brief an die Korinther* (Göttingen: Vandenhoeck und Ruprecht, 1969), p. 117.

[6] "Collegial Decision-Making in the New Testament," *The Jurist*, 31 (1971), 4–6.

[7] *The First Epistle to the Corinthians* (New York: Harper and Row, 1968), pp. 124ff.

[8] "Shared Responsibility—Some New Testament Perspectives," *Chicago Studies*, 9 (1970), 120.

[9] In reading other Pauline epistles one gets the impression that Paul often feels obliged to explain his actions, to listen to objections, and to reply to criticism. The same can be said of Peter. In *Acts* 11:1-18, for example, the Jewish Christians in Jerusalem demanded that Peter explain his table-fellowship with Gentiles. Peter gives a lengthy reply and "their doubts were silenced."

church."[10] The apostle is certainly encouraging a close relationship between apostolic authority and local decision-making.[11]

B. FRATERNAL CORRECTION (*Matt.* 18:15–18)

This text also deals with an internal community problem—an erring member. The process is carefully described:

> If your brother commits a sin, go and take the matter up with him, strictly between yourselves, and if he listens to you, you have won your brother over. If he will not listen, take one or two others with you, so that all facts may be duly established on the evidence of two or three witnesses. If he refuses to listen to them, report the matter to the congregation; and if he will not listen even to the congregation, you must treat him as you would a pagan or a tax-gatherer. I tell you this: whatever you forbid on earth shall be forbidden in heaven, and whatever you allow on earth shall be allowed in heaven.

Once again the experts disagree. The problem centers on the interpretation of v. 18. Bourke[12] and Schnackenburg[13] argue that this verse is addressed only to the disciples and not to the community. Consequently, it is probable that the leaders made the decision and sought agreement from the community. McKenzie[14] and MacRae,[15] on the contrary, contend that v. 18 applies to the whole community. According to this view, we have an explicit example of the entire community making the decision.

[10] Bourke, *op. cit.*, p. 6.
[11] A similar situation is described in II *Cor.* 2:1-11 dealing with the excommunication of a sinner and his later return to the community. Most commentators feel that the man mentioned is not the same one referred to in I *Cor.* 5.
[12] Bourke, *op. cit.*, pp. 7–8.
[13] *The Church in the New Testament* (New York: Herder and Herder, 1965), pp. 74–75.
[14] *The Jerome Biblical Commentary*, ed. R. E. Brown, J. A. Fitzmyer, and R. E. Murphy (Englewood Cliffs, N.J.: Prentice-Hall, Inc., 1968), II, 92, 95.
[15] MacRae, *op. cit.*, p. 122.

C. THE ELECTION OF MATTHIAS (*Acts* 1:12–26)

This pre-Pentecostal event took place, according to *Acts*, in Jerusalem. Present were 120 members of the brotherhood, including Mary, a group of women, the Twelve with the exception of Judas, and "the brothers of Jesus."[16] Peter presided over the assembly and announced that their first task must be to find a replacement for Judas. The one to be appointed would be selected from the group that was with Jesus from the ministry of John to the ascension; he would become with them a witness to the resurrection. This was to guarantee a continuity between the life and work of Christ and the nascent Church. Two names were put forward: Joseph and Matthias. The text seems to indicate that this nominating process was the action of the entire assembly and not just a select group of their leaders. They then prayed together and petitioned the Lord to declare who should be chosen to receive the apostolic ministry. There is an interesting parallel in *Luke* 6:12-16 which tells of Christ praying the whole night before he chose the Twelve. In *Acts* we find the assembly praying that the Lord guide them. They drew lots and Matthias was chosen. This choice was attributed directly to the Lord (v. 24).

The election of Matthias as an apostle is the first significant act taken by the community after the ascension of Jesus. It was a community action in which all participated. The selection of candidates may have been done through voting, open discussion, or by lots. The actual procedure is of secondary importance here. What is important is that the community agreed to this procedure and participated in it.

D. THE ELECTION OF THE SEVEN (*Acts* 6:1–6)

Here we see those in authority reacting positively to feedback from the assembly. A disagreement had arisen, demands were made, and the apostles calmly and decisively resolved the con-

---

[16] The number of 120 is mentioned apparently to signify the official character of the election. According to Jewish practice, there had to be at least 120 present for the Sanhedrin to have jurisdiction.

flict in a democratic way. The scene again was in Jerusalem. The Greek-speaking Christians resented the fact that their widows were not treated the same as the Jewish-speaking Christians in the daily distribution of alms. They made their complaints known to the apostles, who took steps to heal the dissension. The Twelve called "the whole body of the disciples together" (v. 2) and told them to select seven men of good reputation from the community, who were men of wisdom and filled with the Spirit. They would have the responsibility of waiting on tables, of distributing alms, and of administering. The apostles would then have time for prayer and for the ministry of the word.[17] The entire group accepted this proposal and elected the seven. They were presented to the apostles, who prayed and laid hands upon them.

The apostles showed confidence in the judgment of the fellowship. They did not hesitate to allow the members to elect the seven, nor did they interfere with their decision. The text, however, indicates that the apostles exercised strong leadership. It is they who convoked the assembly, decided on the solution, determined the number and qualifications of the candidates, and formally approved the choice. Nevertheless, the ideal presented here is one of community participation.

E. THE COUNCIL OF JERUSALEM
(*Acts* 15 and *Gal.* 2:1–18)

Here again we find the early Church facing a crisis and settling it through discussion. The issue was whether or not Gentile converts first had to become Jews: that is, to be circumcised according to the Law of Moses. It was a crucial question and had far-reaching ramifications: the legitimacy of the Gentile was again affirmed and the Church was liberated to become a "new creation" and not simply a sect of Judaism.

The historical accuracy of Luke's account of the Council of

---

[17] Throughout the rest of *Acts* Luke never mentions the seven taking care of the temporal goods of the community. Stephen and Philip both became preachers.

Jerusalem is questioned by many authors. They argue that what we have in *Acts* is not a single incident, but a combination of two separate meetings and decisions at Jerusalem that took place at different times.[18] At one meeting, presided over by Peter and the Twelve, a decision was made in agreement with Paul's view that Gentile converts did not have to be circumcised (cf. *Gal.* 2:1-10). At a second meeting, James decreed that some Jewish laws would not be obligatory for Gentile converts in Antioch, Syria, and Cilicia (cf. *Gal.* 2:11-18). Luke puts the two together. Even if we grant the dubious historical character of this passage, it still has significant theological value. It is part of the canon of Scripture and reveals Luke's vision of co-responsibility in the Church. According to Bourke, the description of Luke "can rightly be taken as a norm whereby the church's decision-making is to be guided."[19]

Luke begins and ends the story in Antioch. Certain Judaizers came to Antioch and taught that circumcision was necessary for salvation. Paul and Barnabas, who had just returned from missionary work among the Gentiles, disputed their teachings. The controversy reached such an impasse that "it was arranged" (v. 2) that Paul and Barnabas and others from Antioch would go to Jerusalem and see the apostles and elders. Whether this arrangement involved election is not clear from the text. When they reached Jerusalem they were welcomed by the Church. There some of the Pharisaic party spoke out in favor of circumcision.

The actual working of the Council presents two problems: Who were present at it? And who made the final decision? In regard to the membership of the Council, Luke is vague. Verse 6 gives the impression that only the apostles and presbyters held the meeting. Verses 12 and 22 indicate that the whole assembly was present. The common critical opinion favors the second explanation. Apparently there was a lively discussion among the participants. The text says that after a "long debate" (v. 7) Peter addressed the group, calling on his own experience. Paul

---

[18] Cf. Bourke, *op. cit.*, pp. 9–11, R. E. Brown, *Priest and Bishop: Biblical Reflections* (Paramus, N.J.: Paulist Press, 1970), p. 57.

[19] Bourke, *op. cit.*, pp. 12–13.

and Barnabas then spoke, and they were followed by James, who concluded by giving the four restrictions of the Mosaic Law that were applicable to the Gentiles: abstention from meat offered to idols, from blood, from fornication, and from anything that has been strangled (vv. 20-21).

Who made the final decision? In v. 28 the apostolic decree is attributed to the apostles and presbyters, and this is repeated in *Acts* 16:4. No reference is made to the community's role in formulating the decree. As regards its dissemination, however, the community is mentioned. The apostles and presbyters "with the agreement of the whole Church" (v. 22) resolved unanimously to send Judas and Silas as elected representatives to deliver the letter to the Church in Antioch. On their arrival there, they read the letter to the assembly "and all rejoiced at the encouragement it brought" (v. 30).

The Council of Jerusalem is an important description of decision-making in the early Church. It would seem that the community participated in the discussions, and perhaps even in the formulation of the decree. There are, therefore, democratic elements in some, if not all, phases of the meeting.

Our brief survey of the New Testament reveals that the democratic goal of shared responsibility was operative in the early Church. Two basic aspects of democracy are mentioned: the majoritarian principle and decentralization. The majoritarian principle is clearly present in the elections of Matthias and of the seven. It is not as clear in the other three passages, where exegetical interpretations differ. Decentralization, as the implementation of the principle of subsidiarity, is found in varying degrees in all the texts we have examined. Generally, the entire community was expected to participate in the decision-making process. Of course, the apostles were leaders of the community, but they recognized the value of input from the faithful in the exercise of their authority. What is important in these texts is the absence of authoritarianism and the atmosphere of openness that facilitated free discussion of issues crucial to the life of the community. From the New Testament evidence, therefore, we can conclude that every church assembly should have active lay representation when matters that affect them are under discussion.

II. *The Patristic Era*

As the Church expanded, it continued to function as an open system. The communitarian principles that were evident in the New Testament community remained. This is most apparent in the selection of Church leaders. Eusebius, for example, wrote that in the year 62, after the martyrdom of James, "the apostles, disciples, and those who were related to the Lord according to the flesh" unanimously selected Symeon to be the bishop of Jerusalem.[20] For centuries Christians were able to participate in the decision-making process by having an active voice in the naming of their pastors.

Before examining the patristic corpus, three observations are in order. First, the structures of the Church in the first five centuries were not uniform. Local assemblies enjoyed an autonomous status and were flexible in their organization. In the matter of episcopal appointments we find no clear-cut legislation applicable to the universal Church. The final court of appeal for all issues was apostolic tradition. Secondly, it is difficult to analyze this period from a strict canonical perspective. Most of the patristic texts we shall study fail to give us a detailed explanation of electoral procedures. The writers assumed that the process was familiar. They were writing pastoral exhortations, not a book of law. Thirdly, the Christian communities were often separated from one another by great distances, thus making communication slow and unreliable. The local Church, more the size of a modern parish than a diocese, became the very life of the people, who were involved in all its activities and who knew well their fellow believers and their bishop. This close relationship fostered participation in the government of the Church, even to the extent of having a voice in the appointment of bishops.[21] With these observations in mind, we will examine the patristic data from the first five centuries.

[20] *Historia Ecclesiastica*, 3, 11 (PG 20: 246).

[21] The following studies on the election of Church officials may be profitably consulted: E. Roland, "Élection des évêques," *Dictionnaire de théologie catholique*, IV, 2256:2281; A. Parsons, *Canonical Elections: An Historical Synopsis and Commentary* (Washington: Catholic University of America, 1939); J. Eidenschink, *The Election of Bishops in the Letters*

A. THE FIRST AND SECOND CENTURIES

The *Didache*, or Instructions of the Apostles, is the earliest noncanonical source dealing with the selection of bishops. This work appears to be of Syrian origin and, while its exact date is uncertain, reputable scholars place it at the end of the first century. There is one reference to election: "Accordingly, elect for yourselves bishops and deacons, men who are an honor to the Lord, of gentle disposition, not attached to money, honest and well-tried."[22] Nothing is said of how the election should be conducted. It may have been through antecedent voting or simply by subsequent community approval of a candidate chosen in another manner.

Clement of Rome, an Apostolic Father and pope in the last decade of the first century, mentioned the appointment of bishops in a letter to the Corinthian Church. Certain dissident members of the Church had, on their own authority, deposed some of the officials. Clement rebukes them for their actions. He made his point in strong terms:

Consequently, we deem it an injustice to eject from the sacred ministry the persons who were appointed by them [the apostles] or later, with the consent of the whole Church, by other men in high repute, and have ministered to the flock of Christ, faultlessly, humbly,

---

of Gregory the Great (Washington: Catholic University of America, 1945); Y. Congar, *Lay People in the Church* (Westminster, Md.: Newman, 1957), pp. 230–257 and "The Historical Development of Authority in the Church" in *Problems of Authority*, ed. J. M. Todd (Baltimore: Helicon, 1962), pp. 119–156; J. O'Donoghue, *Elections in the Church* (Baltimore: Helicon, 1967); H. Küng, "Participation of the Laity in Church Leadership and in Church Elections," *Journal of Ecumenical Studies*, 6 (1969), 511–533; J. A. Mohler, *The Origin and Evolution of the Priesthood* (Staten Island, N.Y.: Alba House, 1969); L. Swidler and A. Swidler, eds., *Bishops and People* (Philadelphia: Westminster, 1970); R. Eno, "Shared Responsibility in the Early Church," *Chicago Studies*, 9 (1970), 129–141; G. Thils, *Choisir les évêques? Elire le Pape?* (Paris: P. Lethielleux, 1970); J. E. Lynch, "Coresponsibility in the First Five Centuries: Presbyterial Colleges and the Election of Bishops," *The Jurist*, 31 (1971), 14–53; and T. F. O'Meara, "Emergence and Decline of Popular Voice in the Selection of Bishops," in *The Choosing of Bishops*, ed. W. W. Bassett (Hartford, Conn.: The Cannon Law Society of America, 1971), pp. 21–32.

[22] *Didache*, 15. *Die Apostolischen Väter*, ed. F. X. Funk and K. Bihlmeyer (Tübingen: J. C. B. Mohr, 1956), I, 8.

quietly, and unselfishly, and have moreover, over a long period of time, earned the esteem of all.[23]

"The consent of the whole Church" presumably refers to a subsequent approval of candidates that were selected by "men in high repute," rather than an actual election by the whole community. This consent may, however, have implied more than mere approval. The members of the community, since they knew the individuals who were appointed, probably had the opportunity to discuss their merits and to indicate a preference.

Ignatius of Antioch (d. *c.* 107), in his *Epistle to Polycarp of Smyrna*, gave several details of local Church organization in Asia Minor. Of special interest are his remarks on the relationship between the bishop and his people. In this, as in his other letters, Ignatius stated clearly that the bishop is the central authority in the Church. He reminded Polycarp that: "Nothing must be done without your approval."[24] Yet he insisted on community participation. "Let meetings be held as frequently as possible. Seek out all by name."[25] He encouraged Polycarp to send a representative to Syria and told him how to go about it: "It is fitting . . . to convene a council . . . and to appoint someone who is dear to you and untiring in his zeal, one qualified for the part of God's courier; then confer upon him the distinction of going to Syria and extolling for the glory of God, the untiring charity of your community."[26] Although the reference here seems to be to a representative or legate rather than a bishop, Ignatius considered it a community concern. A council, presumably with some lay voices, should discuss the matter and the opinions of all should be heard. Ignatius favored open discussion of serious issues even though he gave the right of making the final decision to the bishop.

B. THE THIRD CENTURY

Hippolytus of Rome (d. *c.* 235), in his *Apostolic Tradition*, gives us a comprehensive picture of Church order and liturgical

---

[23] *First Epistle of Clement*, #44 (Funk-Bihlmeyer, I, 59).
[24] Ignatius of Antioch, *Pol.* 4, 1 (Funk-Bihlmeyer, I, 111).
[25] *Ibid.*, 4, 2 (Funk-Bihlmeyer, I, 111–112).
[26] *Ibid.*, 7, 2 (Funk-Bihlmeyer, I, 112–113).

worship of the third-century Christian assembly in Rome. The work was held in high esteem in the East, especially in Syria and Egypt. Concerning the selection of the bishop and his ordination, he was quite explicit:

> Let the bishop be ordained after he has been chosen by all the people. When he has been named and shall please all, let him, with the presbytery and such bishops as may be present, assemble with the people on a Sunday. While all give their consent, the bishops shall lay their hands upon him, and the presbytery shall stand by, in silence.[27]

Cyprian of Carthage (d. 258), in several of his letters, revealed his deep commitment to community consultation in important matters. For example, in reply to the presbyters of Carthage, who had asked for his advice, he wrote that he has not answered them sooner because "from the beginning of my episcopate I decided to do nothing without the advice and consent of the people."[28]

His remarks on episcopal selection are most pertinent. In a letter written to the Church in Spain he urged them to retain "the divine traditions and apostolic observance" regarding electoral procedures which were practiced in Africa and "through almost all the provinces."[29] Cyprian explained that "it comes from divine authority that a bishop be chosen in the presence of the people before the eyes of all and that he be approved and worthy and fit by public judgment and testimony."[30] At the actual ordination "all the bishops of the same province should assemble and a bishop should be chosen in the presence of the people."[31] Cyprian exhorted the people to repudiate bad bishops: "A people who obey the precepts of the Lord and fear God ought to separate themselves from a sinful leader."[32] The same practice of selecting bishops was also observed in Rome. Cyprian told of the appointment of Pope Cornelius, who was made

[27] *The Apostolic Tradition of Hippolytus*, 2:1–4, trans. B. S. Easton (Cambridge: Cambridge University Press, 1934), p. 33.

[28] Cyprian, *Ep.* 14, 4. (*Corpus scriptorum ecclesiasticorum latinorum*, 3, 2:512). Hereafter cited *CSEL*.

[29] *Ibid.*, *Ep.* 67, 5 (*CSEL* 3, 2:739).

[30] *Ibid.*, *Ep.* 67, 4 (*CSEL* 3, 2:739).

[31] *Ibid.*, *Ep.* 67, 5 (*CSEL* 3, 2:739).

[32] *Ibid.*, *Ep.* 67, 3 (*CSEL* 3, 2:738).

bishop of Rome "by the testimony of almost all the clergy, by the vote of the people who were then present, by the college of venerable bishops and good men."[33]

From the letters of Cyprian it seems clear that the method of selecting bishops was similar in Rome, Africa,[34] and Spain. It involved the clergy, the people, and the neighboring bishops. The precise juridical role of each group is not delineated. Although Cyprian uses the term *suffragium*,[35] its meaning is debated by commentators. Some think that the clergy and people conducted a genuine election,[36] while others feel that they only gave testimony and subsequent approval of a candidate who was finally chosen by the bishop.[37] At any rate, there was active participation on all levels of the community, even though the exact role of each is uncertain.

C. THE FOURTH CENTURY

As persecutions waned and the Church grew, the bishops became more powerful. Even though the principle of lay participation in the selection of bishops was not rejected, the bishops assumed a greater role. The impetus came from councils, both provincial and general. The Council of Arles (314) decreed that no single bishop can ordain another bishop. The new bishop must be ordained by seven others; or if this is impossible, at least by three others (Canon 20). The Council of Nicaea (325)

---

[33] *Ibid., Ep.* 55, 8 (*CSEL* 3, 2:629–630).

[34] Origen (d. *c.* 253) also speaks of the electoral practice in the Egyptian Church. The bishop is to be ordained "in the presence of the whole laity in order that all may know for certain that the man elected to the episcopate is of the whole people the most eminent . . . and to avoid any subsequent change of mind or lingering doubt." *Homilia in Leviticum*, 6:3. (J.-P. Migne, *Patrologia Graeca*, 12:480). Hereafter cited as *PG* or *PL* (*Patrologia Latina*).

[35] Cf. *Ep.* 67, 5 (*CSEL* 3, 2:739); *Ep.* 59, 6 (*CSEL* 3, 2:673).

[36] Cf. F. X. Funk, *Kirchengeschichtliche Abhandlung und Untersuchungen* (Paderborn: F. Schöningh, 1897), I, 28, and H. Gerdes, *Die Bischofswahlen in Deutschland unter Otto dem Grossen* (Göttingen: Peppmüller, 1878), p. 2.

[37] G. Phillips and F. H. Vering, *Kirchenrecht* (Regensburg: G. J. Manz, 1889), VIII, 10. Lynch (*op. cit.*, p. 41), however, favors the idea of the community participating in elections beyond simple approval.

prescribed that the new bishop has to be appointed by all the bishops of the province and that the final ratification must come from the metropolitan (Canon 4).

The regulations of Nicaea were repeated by other councils. The Councils of Antioch (341), Sardica (343), Laodicea (*c.* 360), and Chalcedon (451) all stipulated that the synod of bishops must be present at episcopal elections. In the fifth century, Pope Innocent I[38] (402–417) and Pope Hilary[39] (461–468) referred to the binding force of Nicaea.

The councils of the fourth century did not exclude community participation in episcopal appointments but did tend to minimize it. Yet there is ample evidence in this century that the laity still had a significant voice. The Syrian *Apostolic Constitutions* (*c.* 380) prescribed that the consecrating prelate get popular approval of the candidate (8,4). Canon 20 of the Council of Hippo (392) and Canon 1 of the Fourth Council of Carthage (398) both referred to the testimony of the people.

In the East and in the West popular elections were held. John Chrysostom was made bishop of Constantinople in 398 "by the general consent of both clergy and laity."[40] In Egypt the Arians accused Athanasius of being elected secretly by a few bishops in 328. He replied to their charges by citing a letter of the Egyptian council of bishops who stated that "he was elected by a majority of our body in the sight and with the acclamations of all the people."[41] Martin of Tours, according to Sulpicius Severus, was opposed by several of the neighboring bishops. They had strong views on his qualifications, feeling that "Martin's person was contemptible, that he was unworthy of the episcopate, that he was a man despicable in countenance, that his clothing was mean and his hair disgusting."[42] The people, however, preferred Martin, and in 371 he was made bishop. Ambrose was chosen as the bishop of Milan in 373 by popular acclama-

---

[38] Pope Innocent I, Epistle to Victricius of Rouen (*PL* 20: 469–481).

[39] Pope Hilary in *Acta conciliorum et epistolae decretales ac constitutiones summorum pontificum*, ed. J. Hardouin (Paris: Ex Typographia Regia, 1714), II, 788.

[40] Socrates, *Historia Ecclesiastica* 6, 2 (*PG* 67:683).

[41] Athanasius, *Apologia contra Arianos*, 1, 6 (*PG* 25:258–259).

[42] Sulpicius Severus, *Vita S. Martini*, 9, 2 (*CSEL* 1:119).

tion, with the people crying out that "Ambrose was worthy of the bishopric."[43] St. Jerome[44] and St. Gregory Nazianzus[45] also mention the will of the people in choosing bishops.

In the fourth-century Church of North Africa the laity had responsibilities that extended beyond the role they played in elections. There existed a special group of laymen, representatives of the Christian community, who had important administrative and judicial duties.[46] They were called by various titles: *seniores locorum*,[47] *fideles seniores*,[48] *seniores plebis*,[49] and *seniores christiani populi*.[50] This structure was found in both the Catholic and Donatist churches. The senate of lay elders, apparently elected by the people, assisted the bishop in administering his diocese with special concern for church property. They ranked, according to Augustine, after the clergy but before the *"universa plebs."*[51] In some places they exercised disciplinary functions. In Nova Germanica in Numidia, for example, the *seniores* made an official complaint against their bishop. A council, presided over by the Bishop of Carthage, discussed the issue and decided that arbitrators should be appointed to settle

---

[43] Socrates, *Hist. Eccl.* 4, 30 (PG 67:544) and Paulinus of Milan, *Vita S. Ambrosii*, 6 (PL 14:29). Socrates reports that "all present came to a unanimous agreement crying out 'that Ambrose was worthy of the bishopric,' and demanding his ordination. . . . And inasmuch as such unanimity among the people appeared to the bishops then present to proceed from some divine appointment, they immediately laid hands on Ambrose." Gryson writes of community participation: "In practice, it was sometimes the bishops who ratified the choice of the people, as in the election of Ambrose himself, sometimes it was the people who approved the choice made by the bishops, as in the election of Eusebius of Vercelli. In any case, the combination of the two opinions is indispensable." (R. Gryson, *Le prêtre selon saint Ambroise* [Louvain: Imprimerie Orientaliste, 1968], pp. 227–228).

[44] Jerome, *Ep.* 125, 17 (PL 22:1082).

[45] Gregory Nazianzus, *Oratio*, 21, 8 (PG 35:1090).

[46] Cf. P. G. Caron, "Les seniores laici de l'église africaine," *Revue internationale des droits de l'antiquité*, VI (1951), 7–22, and W. Frend, "The Seniores Laici and the Origins of the Church in North Africa," *Journal of Theological Studies*, 12 (1961), 280–284.

[47] *Codex canonum ecclesiae Africanae*, Canon 91 (Hardouin, I, 914).

[48] Optatus, *De Schismate* 1, 17 (PL 11:918).

[49] *Gesta apud Zenophilum* (CSEL 26:189).

[50] *Acta Purgationis Felicis* (CSEL 26:198).

[51] Augustine, *Ep.* 76 (CSEL 34, 2:331).

the matter. The *seniores* had a voice in the selection.[52] Tertullian said that the *seniores* could excommunicate certain undesirable members of the community.[53]

Laymen also performed other duties in the assembly. Some acted as lawyers (*defensores ecclesiae*) and others were treasurers of local churches. The Council of Chalcedon, however, decreed in 451 that the treasurer must be a priest (Canon 26). Laymen also were teachers of Christian doctrine. The *Didache* referred to itinerant prophet-teachers. Justin of Rome, Clement of Alexandria, and Tertullian were all laymen. The fourth-century Syrian *Apostolic Constitutions* permitted a pious and qualified man to teach even if he were a layman (8,32).[54] In the next century, however, at least in Gaul, laymen were forbidden to teach in the presence of priests.[55] Gradually the teaching office was restricted to the bishop and his clergy.

D. THE FIFTH CENTURY

Popular participation in episcopal selection was still observed in Gaul during the fifth century. The testimony of two popes has special value. Pope Celestine I (422–432) admitted the necessity of final approbation by the metropolitan, but in a letter to the bishops of Gaul he wrote: "Let no bishop be given to a community against its will; the consent and desire of the clergy, people, and nobility is required."[56] A similar sentiment is expressed by Pope Leo I (440–461) in a letter to the bishops of Vienne in 445: "The approval of the clergy, the testimony of those in noble rank, and the agreement of the common people should be had. He who is in charge of all, should be chosen by all."[57] The same pope, however, made it clear that the clergy, the people, and the bishops work together closely: "No con-

---

[52] *Codex canonum ecclesiae Africanae*, Canon 100 (Hardouin, I, 882).

[53] Tertullian, *Apology*, 24, 4 (*Corpus christianorum—series latina*, I:134).

[54] *Apostolic Constitutions*, 8.32 (*Didascalia et Constitutiones Apostolorum*, ed. F. X. Funk [Paderborn: F. Schöningh, 1905], I, 539).

[55] *Statuta ecclesiae antiqua*, Canon 98 (*Corpus christianorum—series latina*, 148:183–184).

[56] Pope Celestine I, *Ep.* 4, 5 (*PL* 50:434).

[57] Pope Leo I, *Ep.* 10 (*PL* 54:634).

sideration allows making bishops of those who have not been chosen by the clerics, sought for by the people, and consecrated by the provincial bishops with the consent of the metropolitan."[58] This same view is contained in the *Statuta ecclesiae antiqua* (*c.* 480) of the Church in Gaul, a remarkable legislative summary of the Latin Church. Its influence endured for centuries. It codified the tradition of shared responsibility in selecting bishops: "Let the bishop be ordained with the consent of the clergy and lay people, and by the agreement of every province, especially by the authority or presence of the metropolitan."[59]

The patristic data show that for the first five centuries, both in the East and in the West, bishops were selected *"per clerum et populum."* The democratic ideals of majoritarianism and decentralization were incorporated into Church government. The majoritarian principle is evident, although procedural rules are not fully elaborated. It is clear that the whole community participated in selecting Church leaders. Even when the provincial bishops and the metropolitan assumed greater authority, the will of the people was not disregarded. The involvement of the laity and clergy reflected the ancient legal maxim: *"Quod omnes tangit, ab omnibus approbetur."*[60]

The decentralization of the early Church was also most striking. The individual churches selected their own leaders according to several different methods. A bishop was not unilaterally imposed on a community. The Roman See did not intervene and, in fact, several popes defended the autonomy of the local assembly. Besides Celestine I and Leo I, whom we earlier referred to, mention should also be made of Pope Julius (337–352). In denying the legitimacy of Gregory as bishop of Alexandria, he appealed to tradition. "What canon of the Church, or what apostolic tradition," he asked, permits Gregory to be sent to Alexandria, "a stranger to the city, not having been baptized there, not known to the general body, desired neither by the presbyters, bishops, nor laity?"[61]

[58] Pope Leo I, *Ep.* 167 (*PL* 54:1203).

[59] *Statuta ecclesiae antiqua* (*Corpus Christianorum—Series Latina*, 148:165–166).

[60] Cf. Y. Congar, "Quod omnes tangit . . . ," *Revue historique de droit français et étranger*, 35 (1958), 210–259.

[61] Anthanasius, *Apologia contra Arianos*, 30 (*PG* 25:297).

III. *Later Developments*

Lay involvement in episcopal elections remained, in theory at least, the law of the Church until the twelfth century. In the compilations of law used in the early Middle Ages the principles of Celestine I and Leo I were frequently quoted. Yet long before that time, contrary practices began to emerge. By the sixth century, the clergy and the bishops played the determinative role in the election of bishops. The change was gradual. The tendency to reduce lay participation was more pronounced in the East than in the West. Justinian, for example, decreed in 546 that only the *primores civitatis*, eminent members of the Church, and not the whole community, were to nominate three candidates for bishop and that the consecrating prelate would select the most suitable. Two ecumenical councils, a century apart, also contributed to the eventual suppression of lay and clerical input. Canon 3 of the Second Council of Nicaea (787) decreed that "he who is elevated to the episcopate must be chosen by the bishops."[62] Canon 22 of the Fourth Council of Constantinople (870) prescribed that the appointment of bishops belongs exclusively to the college of bishops and that no secular ruler nor any lay person shall intervene.[63] During the next few centuries the layman's participation dwindled and eventually disappeared. However, the intervention of the secular rulers increased.

In the West, at a later date, a similar development occurred. Like their Eastern brethren, the Latin laity were gradually excluded from an active role in episcopal selection. An underlying reason for this was the lack of an educated laity. This problem became acute at the time of the barbarian invasions in the fifth century, when the Roman Empire fell and along with it its educational system. This affected the Church in Europe severely. The clergy and laity were badly educated and little by little gave up their participatory role in the selection of bishops. Besides this general cultural atmosphere, two other reasons for the decline of lay involvement may be given: abuses in the traditional process and interference by secular authorities.

[62] *Conciliorum oecumenicorum decreta*, ed. J. Alberigo et al. (Freiburg: Herder, 1962), p. 116.
[63] *Ibid.*, p. 159.

First of all, intrigue, bribery, and violence often threatened the liberty and quality of episcopal elections.[64] Origen in the third century, for example, wrote against those bishops who attempted to appoint their relatives as successors or who used money or violence to influence people.[65] Henri Marrou's comments about the early fourth century are revealing: "The intervention of intriguing ladies, especially rich benefactors, in episcopal elections was often deplored."[66] Minority parties were at times unwilling to accept the duly elected bishop and continued to support their candidate, often with violence. In the contested elections of Pope Damasus in 366 and Pope Symmachus in 498, for example, rioting occurred in Rome and several people were killed or wounded. In the East, Chrysostom told of those who desired the episcopacy for worldly reasons,[67] and the Council of Laodicea warned that the unruly multitude should not be permitted to elect a bishop. Even Pope Leo I, the great defender of popular suffrage, was "astonished that the presumption of intriguers or the rioting of the populace has so much weight" with the African bishops. He lamented the fact that "those far from deserving the episcopal dignity were given the chief pastorate of the Church."[68] Abuses of this kind encouraged the synod of bishops to select the new bishops themselves. The eventual result was that the laity were effectively excluded. As J. Gaudemet observes: "An acclamation of popular joy finally will be all that will remain of election by the people."[69]

---

[64] The Second Council of Orleans (533) condemned simony and decreed that elections should be conducted by the provincial bishops, the clergy, and the people (Mansi, VIII, 836). The Council of Clermont in 535 warned against elections that involved bribery, violence, or deceit (Mansi, VIII, 860).

[65] Origen, *Homilia in Numeros*, 22 (PG 12:740–745).

[66] J. Daniélou and H. Marrou, *The First Six Hundred Years*, Vol. 1 of *The Christian Centuries* (New York: McGraw-Hill, 1964), p. 240.

[67] John Chrysostom, *On the Priesthood*, 3:9–10 in *A Select Library of the Nicene and Post-Nicene Fathers of the Christian Church*, ed. Philip Schaff (New York: Scribner, 1908), IX, 49–50.

[68] Pope Leo I, *Ep.* 12, 1–2 (PL 54:645).

[69] *L'Eglise dans l'empire romain aux IVe et Ve siècles* (Paris: Sirey, 1958), p. 332. Cf. also F. L. Ganshof, "Note sur l'élection des évêques dans l'empire romain au IVe et pendant la première moitié du Ve siècle," *Revue internationale des droits de l'antiquité*, 4 (1950), 467–498.

A second reason which caused profound changes in the electoral process was the interference of lay rulers in Church affairs. This became a serious threat in the sixth century. The Fifth Council of Orleans (549) prescribed the usual kind of election but added that royal consent was needed.[70] In the next century the Twelfth Council of Toledo (681) decreed that the bishop of Toledo can appoint as bishops "whomever the royal power selects."[71] There were occasional reactions to this development. The Council of Paris (557) insisted that the bishop be elected by clergy and people and that the prince should not appoint the bishop contrary to the will of the metropolitan and his fellow bishops.[72] The Synod of Aix-la-Chapelle (817) made a similar prescription and warned against the use of simony.[73] These efforts, however, had little effect in discouraging secular intervention. Royal dominance grew in Carolingian and feudal times. Bishops more and more became involved in secular politics and, like other government officials, were appointed by the king. By the tenth century this was a common practice. The role of the clergy and laity became largely ceremonial and their approval of the king's choice was only a formality.

In the eleventh century, a reform movement began which urged a return to traditional electoral procedures. Leo IX (1048–1054),[74] Nicholas II (1058–1061),[75] and Gregory VII (1073–1085)[76] attempted to reinstate episcopal elections by clergy and people, but with only limited success. By the middle of the twelfth century, the canons of the cathedral church assumed the responsibility of appointing bishops to vacant sees. This was apparently a well-established custom by 1139, when the Second Lateran Council (Canon 28) decreed that the canons must elect the bishops with the advice of "religious men," abbots, and

[70] Hardouin, II, 1443.
[71] *Ibid.*, III, 1715.
[72] *Ibid.*, III, 338.
[73] *Ibid.*, IV, 1213.
[74] Synod of Rheims (1049), Canon 1: "Without the election of the clergy and people, no one may be advanced to an ecclesiastical office" (Mansi, XI, 741).
[75] Synod of Tours (1060), (Mansi, XIX, 925–930).
[76] Synod of Rome (1080), (Mansi XX, 531–537).

other outstanding members of the clergy.[77] The Fourth Lateran Council (1215) clearly saw the cathedral chapter as the only body of electors (Canon 24).[78]

During the thirteenth century the move toward a centralized Roman Church became more pronounced. The papacy involved itself directly in the affairs of the local churches and in the appointment of bishops. The prerogatives of the cathedral chapter gradually disappeared. At first the Roman See only confirmed elections and settled disputed ones. Eventually it directly appointed bishops. By the middle of the fourteenth century this was the usual practice.

In the United States prior to 1833 several methods of selecting bishops were used.[79] Bishop Carroll, for example, was elected by his clergy. Other bishops were appointed either by the metropolitan, by suffragans without recourse to the metropolitan, or directly by the Holy See. In 1833, at the Second Provincial Council of Baltimore, a new procedure was adopted. The provincial bishops were to select candidates at their provincial meetings and submit the names to Rome. No provision was made for consultation with the clergy or laity. The Third Plenary Council of Baltimore in 1884 made for the first time an official policy that some diocesan priests participate in selecting bishops.

---

[77] *Conciliorum oecumenicorum decreta*, p. 179.

[78] *Ibid.*, p. 222. Also see E. Roland, *Les chanoines et les élections épiscopales du XIe au XIVe siècle* (Aurillac: Imprimerie Moderne, 1909), and R. L. Benson, "Election by Community and Chapter: Reflections on Co-responsibility in the Historical Church," *The Jurist*, 31 (1971), 54–80, and *The Bishop-Elect: A Study in Medieval Ecclesiastical Office* (Princeton, N.J.: Princeton University Press, 1968).

[79] There are several studies on the practice in the United States of selecting bishops. See C. F. McCarthy, "The Historical Development of Episcopal Nominations in the Catholic Church in the United States," *Records of the American Catholic Historical Society of Philadelphia*, 38 (1927), 337–359; J. T. Ellis, "On Selecting Catholic Bishops for the United States," *The Critic*, June–July 1969, pp. 43–55; R. F. Trisco, "An American Anomaly: Bishops without Canons," *Chicago Studies*, 9 (1970), 143–157, and "The Variety of Procedures in Modern History," in *The Choosing of Bishops*, pp. 33–60; F. J. Weber, "Episcopal Appointments in the U.S.A.," *American Ecclesiastical Review*, 155 (1966), pp. 178–191; and J. T. Finnegan, "The Present Canonical Practice in the Catholic Church," in *The Choosing of Bishops*, pp. 85–102.

It decreed that diocesan consultors and irremovable pastors meet when a diocese falls vacant and present three names of candidates to the metropolitan. Then the provincial bishops meet and discuss the list given by the clergy but retain the right to reject any candidate. The bishops vote and send their recommendations to Rome for final approval.

This practice continued until 1916 when the Consistorial Congregation issued new norms.[80] According to this legislation, the bishops every two years shall indicate to their metropolitan, after consultation with their diocesan consultors and irremovable rectors, the names of one or two priests whom they judge worthy of the office of bishop. The bishops may also consult with "prudent men, even of the regular clergy,"[81] concerning the proposal or qualification of any candidate. This inquiry must be conducted individually and not collectively, so that it does not have even the appearance of an election. Moreover, the reference to the "*prudentes viros*" is not clear. It may mean that the laity can be consulted, although there is no evidence that this was ever the regular practice.[82]

Vatican II only briefly mentioned the selection of bishops. It took a strong position in regard to any interference by secular powers in the process: "In the future no rights or privileges of election, nomination, presentation, or designation for the office of bishop be any longer granted to civil authorities."[83] The 1966 *motu proprio, Ecclesiae sanctae*, decreed that episcopal conferences should meet annually to discuss which priests are qualified for promotion to the episcopate. The list of candidates proposed is to be sent to the Holy See.[84] Nothing was said about lay consultation.

The most recent directives for the selection of bishops were issued by Rome in March 1972.[85] The new regulations state that

---

[80] *Acta Apostolicae Sedis*, 8 (1916), 399–404.

[81] *Ibid.*, 401.

[82] Cf. Finnegan, *op. cit.*, p. 92.

[83] *Decree on The Pastoral Office of Bishops*, Art. 20.

[84] *Ecclesiae sanctae*, I, 10, *Acta Apostolicae Sedis*, 58 (1966), 763.

[85] The norms are published in *Origins* (*NC Documentary Service*), May 25, 1972, vol. 2: no. 1, pp. 1, 3, 8, 9. An earlier draft of these norms can be found in Bassett, *The Choosing of Bishops*, pp. 103–107. The two

the residential bishop is to obtain information about candidates worthy of the episcopal office. To do this he may confer with the diocesan consultors; members of the priests' senate; other priests, diocesan or regular; and members of the laity. This consultation, however, must be done on an individual basis and not collectively. At the meeting of the provincial bishops, the candidates are discussed and a list of names, drawn up after a secret vote, is sent to the Holy See through the papal delegate. The names may also be sent to the national episcopal conference for further information and observations. Before a candidate is appointed bishop, the apostolic delegate must personally conduct an investigation. He is obliged to consult with the head of the ecclesiastical province (the metropolitan), the bishop of each diocese in the province (the suffragan), and the chairman of the national episcopal conference. He may also, but is not required to do so, consult individually with the diocesan consultors, members of the priests' senate, other priests and religious, and "prudent and generally reliable lay people." The delegate then selects three nominees and sends them to Rome. It should be noted that all phases of the process are conducted under the strictest secrecy. Furthermore, the pope, in virtue of his office, is always free to appoint someone as bishop whose name does not appear on the list.

The 1972 legislation was a disappointment, but hardly a surprise, to those Catholics who desired greater democratization in the Church. The *clerus et populus* are allowed only minimal participation, and always at the discretion of the bishop and papal delegate. Both have the option, but not the obligation, of consulting with the clergy and laity. Moreover, the insistence on individual, as opposed to collective, consultation avoids any

---

versions are substantially the same. We have reprinted the 1972 norms in Appendix B. Cf. R. Tucci, "La scelta del candidati all'episcopato nella Chiesa latina," *La Civiltà Cattolica*, 2 (1972), 422–439; articles by L. Orsy, J. Fahey, J. Hennesey, and L. J. Topel in *America*, September 2, 1972, pp. 111–120 and reactions by W. W. Bassett, A. Carter, J. T. Ellis, R. Goedert, and J. A. Coriden in *America*, October 14, 1972, pp. 287–291. The School of Canon Law at The Catholic University of America conducted a symposium on the new norms in May 1972 and urged that "the present document be rejected by the Church for the good of the churches and the progress of the ecumenical movement" (in *Origins, ibid.*, pp. 4 and 18).

semblance of the democratic process. Also the secret nature of the entire procedure fails to recognize any hierarchic accountability. The new norms, therefore, are substantially the same as the 1916 procedures. They are unresponsive to the ideals of collegiality and subsidiarity enshrined at Vatican II. Furthermore, they fail to implement the proposals made in *Ecclesiae sanctae* whereby episcopal candidates should be chosen collegially by the national conference. The present document gives far greater responsibility to the apostolic delegate than to the national conference. In short, the new norms are a feeble effort to restructure Church government. They make quite clear that a democratic selection of bishops involving the entire Christian community is not encouraged by the Vatican.[86]

IV. *The Issue of Conciliarism*

The theory of conciliarism is necessary in any discussion of participatory democracy in the Church. Briefly, conciliarism holds that the supreme organ of government in the Church is a representative general council. Cybernetically, the issue centers on the decision-makers within the system, those whose role is to issue the final authoritative outputs. For conciliarists, the role of the council was ultimately superior to that of the pope.[87]

Although the conciliarist crisis was not until the fifteenth

[86] Although consultation with the laity and clergy is optional according to the norms, an individual bishop may make it normative for his own diocese. Some have done so. It is encouraging to see that the U. S. Bishops' Ad Hoc Committee on Priestly Life and Ministry recommends this procedure. The report has not yet been published, but summaries of it indicate that all levels of Church membership should participate to some degree in the selection of bishops. Cf. *Origins* (*NC Documentary Service*), October 26, 1972, vol. 2: no. 18, pp. 285, 287, 299, 300.

[87] Brian Tierney has written extensively on the origin and development of medieval conciliarism. The following studies should be consulted: "Ockham, the Conciliar Theory and the Canonists," *Journal of the History of Ideas*, 15 (1954), 40–70; *Foundations of the Conciliar Theory* (Cambridge: Cambridge University Press, 1955); "Pope and Council: Some New Decretist Texts," *Mediaeval Studies*, 19 (1957), 197–218; and "Roots of Western Constitutionalism in the Church's Own Tradition," in J. A. Coriden, ed., *We, the People of God* (Huntington, Ind.: Our Sunday Visitor, 1968), pp. 113–128.

century, two hundred years earlier medieval canonists had
grappled with some aspects of the question, primarily the constitutional aspects of papal deposition. Thus in his *Decretum* (c.
1140) Gratian, while emphatically holding that the pope is beyond all human judgment, ecclesiastical or civil,[88] did grant that
for heresy, and heresy alone, the pope could be judged.[89]

Canonists after Gratian analyzed and developed this limitation
of papal power. In giving a larger role to the general council,
they established, in a variety of ways, the basic tenets of conciliarism. Huggacio (d. 1210), for example, extends the argument that a pope who publicly professes heresy can be deposed
by the Church. For him, the commission of notorious crimes
arc likewise grounds for deposition, for they are equivalent to
heresy in terms of the harm that is done to the Church. Another
canonist, Joannes Teutonicus (d. 1246), held a similar view.
Using Jerome's observation, *"Orbis maior est urbe,"* he concluded that since the universal Church is more important than
the Roman Church, a general council is superior to the pope in
matters of faith and for the good of the Church. A more extreme form of conciliarism—decidedly anti-papal—appeared in
the fourteenth century in the writings of William of Ockham
(d. 1349) and Marsilius of Padua (d. 1342). In the fifteenth century, the classical era of conciliarism, the number of canonists,
ecclesiastics, and even civil authorities supporting the supremacy
of the general council had increased. However, many of these
supporters, such as Franciscus Zabarella (d. 1417), Pierre d'Ailly
(d. 1420), Jean Gerson (d. 1425), and Nicholas of Cusa (d.
1468) advocated only a moderate conciliarism which limited the
legal intrusion of the general council to a very few extraordinary
situations.

The conciliarist and anti-conciliarist theories were put to the
test at the end of the fourteenth and the beginning of the fifteenth
centuries when the Church had fallen into schism. The immediate issue was not the determination of the respective roles of
pope and council within the ecclesial system, but rather the

---

[88] "Neque ab Augusto neque ab omni clero neque a regibus neque a
populo iudex iudicatur" (c.9 q.3 c.13).

[89] "[Papa] a nemine est iudicandus, nisi deprehendatur a fide devius"
(*Dist.* 40 c.6).

ascertainment of the specific person who was then and there legitimately filling the traditional role of pope. This Great Western Schism, which lasted for nearly forty years, began in 1378. The cardinals in Rome had elected Urban VI as pope. Later that year, claiming coercion, they rejected him and chose Clement VII, who then took up residence in Avignon. During the next three decades, several attempts at negotiation and compromise were made, all unsuccessful. Finally, in 1409, thirteen cardinals representing both parties convoked a council at Pisa. The two papal claimants were deposed, and a new pope, Alexander V, was elected. Nevertheless, the schism continued: the Church was tricephalic, with three claimants to the papal throne each maintaining his own residence and curia and exercising his supreme authority over his subjects.

Once again recourse was made to a general council as a means of healing this agonizing disunity at the heart of Christendom. No claimant was strong enough personally or politically to resolve this impasse, so John XXIII of the Pisan line convoked a council at Constance in 1414. It succeeded where Pisa had failed: structural unity was re-established in the Church. Drastic measures were applied. In 1415, the Council deposed John XXIII, declaring him guilty of perjury, simony, and scandalous living. In 1417, it deposed Benedict XIII of Avignon for perjury, heresy, and schism. Gregory XII of the Roman line abdicated in 1415 at the age of ninety, on condition that he be allowed to reconvoke the council. The Council, on November 11, 1417, elected Martin V as pope, and the schism came to an end.

The most important enactment of the Council of Constance for the history of the Church was the decree *Haec sancta* which was unanimously agreed upon at the fifth session on April 6, 1415. This decree, inspired by the principles of moderate conciliarism, was able to resolve the schism by affirming that a council, as representative of the Church, was superior to the pope in certain circumstances. The decree stated:

This holy synod of Constance . . . declares that, being lawfully assembled in the Holy Spirit and being a general council representing the Catholic and militant Church, it has its power immediately from Christ and that every person of whatsoever state or dignity, even the papal, is bound to obey in those matters which pertain to the general reform of this said Church in head and members. It also declares that any person of whatsoever condition, status, or dignity, even the papal, who, contumaciously refuses to obey the mandates, statutes, decrees, or instructions made or to be made by this holy synod or by any other lawfully assembled general council concerning the aforesaid matters or matters pertaining to them shall, unless he repents, be subjected to suitable penance and appropriately punished, recourse to other sanctions of the law being had if necessary. . . .[90]

To implement *Haec sancta*, the Council passed the decree *Frequens* on October 9, 1417 which scheduled future councils: the next council was to be held five years after the close of Constance; another was to be held seven years later, and future Councils were to be held regularly every ten years. Martin V faithfully carried out this decree. After Constance, the next council met at Siena-Pavia (1423–1424), followed by one at Basle (1431).

Modern theologians and historians are divided in their assessment of the validity and the significance of *Haec sancta*. Three interpretations have emerged. The first argues that *Haec sancta* is not a valid dogmatic degree because the decree was enacted before the council became legitimate through the convocation of Gregory XII and neither Martin V nor his successor Eugene IV ever confirmed it.[91] The second argues that *Haec sancta* is a valid dogmatic decree which binds the Church forever. Hans Küng, for example, dismisses the problem of papal approbation as unimportant because "at the time of the Council of Constance an express papal approbation was not deemed necessary."[92] Küng

---

[90] *Conciliorum oecumenicorum decreta, op. cit.*, p. 385. For a survey of the historical and theological literature on the Council of Constance see A. Franzen, "The Council of Constance: Present State of the Problem," Vol. 7 *Concilium* (Glen Rock, N. J.: Paulist Press, 1965), pp. 29–68, and R. E. McNally, "Conciliarism and the Papacy," *Proceedings of the Catholic Theological Society of America, 1970* (Bronx, N. Y.: Manhattan College, 1971), pp. 13–30.

[91] Cf. J. Gill, "The Fifth Session of the Council of Constance," *Heythrop Journal*, 5 (1964), 131–143.

[92] *Structures of the Church* (New York: Thomas Nelson, 1964), p. 271. A similar position is taken by P. de Vooght, *Les pouvoirs du Concile et l'autorité du Pape au Concile de Constance* (Paris: Editions du Cerf, 1965) and F. Oakley, *Council Over Pope?* (New York: Herder and Herder, 1969).

insists that the Fathers at Constance attempted to set some constitutional limits to papal authority and that their actions reflected the orthodox teaching of moderate conciliarism. The power of a general council is limited to those instances in which the pope abuses his authority. A general council would be superior to the pope "on the premise that a possible future pope might again lapse into heresy, schism, or the like."[93] The third argues that *Haec sancta* had a limited validity. Hubert Jedin contends that the decree must be seen in its full historical context. It was "an emergency measure to meet a definite exceptional situation."[94] The Council did not intend to promulgate a pronouncement that had a binding and permanent dogmatic force, but rather to resolve the scandal of a schism.

To unravel the historical and theological intricacies surrounding *Haec sancta* is difficult. Nevertheless, it seems probable that the decree does not possess the authority of a solemnly defined dogmatic statement from a legitimate general council. First of all, there is considerable ambiguity in the approbation of Martin V at the last session of the Council in which he said that "he would uphold and observe everything decided, concluded, and decreed in matters of faith (*in materiis fidei*) by the present Council acting in a conciliar manner (*conciliariter*) . . . and not otherwise." The pope made this statement during an emotional debate during which the Polish members interrupted the proceedings to demand that the pope condemn the German Dominican Falkenberg as heretical. One must ask: what meaning is to be given to terms *conciliariter* and *in materiis fidei? Does Haec sancta* fulfil these conditions? Moreover, the action of the Council of Constance is unparalleled in the history of general councils. It was a council that was alienated from the pope and acted independently of him. Finally, in the centuries after Constance, while there is no explicit rejection of *Haec sancta*, there are numerous instances of a clear denial of any appeal from the pope to a general council on the grounds that the pope has authority over all councils. It would indeed be a difficult task to reconcile

---

[93] Küng, *op. cit.*, p. 285.
[94] *Bischöfliches Konzil oder Kirchenparlament? Ein Beitrag zur Ekklesiologie der Konsilien von Konstanz und Basel* (Basel: Helbing and Lichtenzahn, 1963), p. 12.

Haec sancta, which affirmed the superiority of the episcopal college over the pope, with *Pastor aeternus* of Vatican I, which taught the supremacy of papal power.[95]

The conciliarist ideology continued long after Constance in spite of vigorous papal opposition. It was manifested principally in that complex of political and theological ideas which is known as Gallicanism.[96] In France, kings, ecclesiastics, and theologians, using the decrees of Constance and the writings of such canonists as Pierre d'Ailly and Jean Gerson, made a concerted effort to insure the independence of the French Church from Roman domination. By the seventeenth century, the main tenets of Gallicanism were systematically proposed and supported by King Louis XIV. The writings of Pierre Pithou (d. 1596) and Pierre Dupuy (d. 1651) elaborated this theory. It was not surprising, therefore, that the declaration of the French clergy was formally approved in 1682 by Louis XIV. The declaration made four major affirmations: (1) complete independence of the king and princes from ecclesiastical authority in temporal matters; (2) the superiority of the general council over the pope; (3) papal power must be exercised in accordance with the sacred canons and with the customs of the Gallican Church; and (4) papal judgments on matters of faith require for their validity the consent of the universal Church.

The 1682 declaration was condemned by Pope Alexander VIII in 1690[97] and by Pope Pius VI in 1794.[98] By the middle of the nineteenth century many French clergy and bishops had begun to desert the Gallican camp and to accept the ultramontanist (Roman or papal) position. The dogmatic decrees of Vatican I (1870) on papal primacy and infallibility made the principal claims of Gallicanism clearly incompatible with Church teaching.

Present canon law makes no provision for an appeal to authority superior even to an unworthy pope. Should there be

[95] Cf. H. Riedlinger, "Hermeneutische Uberlegungen zu den Konstanzer Dekreten," in A. Franzen and W. Muller, eds., *Das Konzil von Konstanz* (Freiburg: Herder, 1964).

[96] Cf. V. Martin, *Les origines du Gallicanisme* (Paris: Bloud and Gay, 1929).

[97] Denzinger-Schönmetzer, 2281–2284.

[98] *Ibid.*, 2700.

definite constitutional limitations on papal authority? A crippling illness, mental aberration, outright incompetence, immoral conduct, or heresy are still possibilities for the fallible head of an incarnational Church. What happens to the Church if such a pope cannot be induced to resign? Could a general council intervene for the good of the Church? Some insist that certain minimal limitations on papal primacy are necessary. Others feel that such limitations are impossible because of Vatican I. Others object that such limitations would only encourage constant turmoil in the Church, foment polarization, and reflect a near abandonment of trust in divine providence. Karl Rahner, in this context, admits to the possibility of a pope's acting in an autocratic manner independently of the College of Bishops, but he notes: "The simple answer is that he 'can' do so, but that he will not. The Catholic does not demand a juridical norm by which the pope could be impeached; he relies on the power of the grace of God and of the Holy Spirit in the Church."[99]

Conciliarism has been an enduring stimulus to ecclesial self-study despite its contextual limits and its authoritative demise. Somehow the idea of the superiority of council to pope has managed to survive radical social changes. For two centuries before Constance, canonists, reacting against an ultra-monarchic papacy, had worked out at best a kind of conciliaristic self-defense, and at worst a kind of aggressive anti-papalism. The Great Western Schism afforded a unique opportunity to test this theory by restoring unity to a Church with three claimants to the papal throne. Despite the success of the council, the conciliarist theory was never given full acceptance. But the idea persisted despite persistent Roman rejection. Conciliarism surfaced periodically as the ideology behind resistance to the papacy as, for example, in the Gallican controversy. It remained for a general council, Vatican I, to issue the definitive repudiation. Nevertheless, the assertation of the superiority of pope to council did not remove the problems occasioned by the concentration of ecclesial power in the hands of one man or by the possibilities, however remote, of papal incompetency, immorality, or heresy. More recently

[99] H. Vorgrimler, ed., *Commentary on the Documents of Vatican II* (New York: Herder and Herder, 1967), I, 203.

a radical step has been taken, however, which, although it does not solve all the problems, does provide for the major one. Vatican II has given us the vision of a collegial Church wherein authority is vested in the pope together with his bishops. Decision-making has become, to some extent, a shared responsibility. In the next chapter, we will examine the nature and implications of this great historical reform.

9

The Theological Foundation
of Ecclesial Democracy

The rich testimony of shared responsibility found in the New Testament and the Fathers was neglected for centuries. As the hierarchic control system grew stronger, lay participation decreased. Open channels of information were rare, and persistent demands were effectively eliminated or neutralized by the hierarchy. Papal and episcopal absolutism flourished, while an uneducated laity, unwilling and unable to assert any real power, accepted the status quo submissively. The official outputs of the hierarchy were frequently apologetic and anti-conciliarist. After Trent, ecclesiology consisted primarily of an analysis of the hierarchy.[1] The role of the laity as an active contributing force received scant attention.

In the nineteenth century, a new kind of ecclesiology developed. Johann Adam Möhler was a leading figure. After an intensive study of the Fathers, Möhler was convinced that a more scriptural vision of the Church was needed. He saw the Church as a spiritual reality, the Body of Christ vivified by the Holy

[1] This type of ecclesiology is called "hierarchology" by Yves Congar, *Lay People in the Church* (Westminster, Md.: Newman, 1957), p. 39.

171

Spirit. Other theologians, such as John Henry Newman, Victor Dechamps, and Matthias Scheeben, elaborated a biblical and patristic approach. Unfortunately, their works did not replace the solidly entrenched post-Tridentine ecclesiology. It was not until the twentieth century that their efforts bore fruit.

This movement continued in the twentieth century. Romano Guardini, Karl Adam, Columba Marmion, Abbot Vonier, Emile Mersch, and Sebastian Tromp made outstanding contributions to the theology of the Mystical Body. In the 1920s and '30s the renewed interest in biblical and liturgical scholarship supported this inquiry. The most important official contribution in this period was the encyclical *Mystici corporis* (1943) of Pope Pius XII. Yves Congar's *Jalons pour une théologie du laïcat* (1953) became a classic source for greater lay participation in the Church. Thus, on the eve of Vatican II, Catholic ecclesiology, while not fully liberated from its Counter-Reformation rigidity, had started to move in the direction of shared responsibility.

Vatican II began a new era for the theology of the Church. It presented a sound theological basis for ecclesial democratization by recognizing the role of the laity. Since the Council, a growing theological literature on the specific question of a democratized Church has developed.[2] In this chapter, using the documents of Vatican II, we will examine the theological foundation of ecclesial democratization. Three major aspects of the Church will be discussed: the egalitarian, the hierarchic, and the charismatic.

---

[2] The following studies may be consulted: J. M. Todd, ed., *Problems of Authority* (Baltimore: Helicon, 1962); A. Müller, *Obedience in the Church* (Westminster, Md.: Newman, 1966); J. L. McKenzie, *Authority in the Church* (New York: Sheed and Ward, 1966); J. E. Biechler, ed., *Law for Liberty* (Baltimore: Helicon, 1967); L.-J. Suens, *Co-responsibility in the Church* (New York: Herder and Herder, 1968); K. Rahner, "Demokratie in der kirche?" *Stimmen der Zeit*, 182 (1968), 1–15; J. A. Coriden, ed., *We, The People of God* (Huntington, Ind.: Our Sunday Visitor, 1968); D. E. Nicodemus, *The Democratic Church* (Milwaukee: Bruce, 1969); José de Broucker, *The Suenens Dossier* (Notre Dame, Ind.: Fides, 1970); *Studies in Co-responsibility*, *The Jurist*, 31 (1971); G. May, *Demokratisierung der Kirche—Möglichkeiten und Grenzen* (Wien: Herold, 1971); and A. Müller, ed., *Democratization of the Church*, vol. 63, *Concilium* (New York: Herder and Herder, 1971).

I. *The Egalitarian Aspect*

Contemporary ecclesiology stresses the egalitarian aspect of the ecclesial system.[3] Triumphalism, elitism, and separatism are rejected. The Church is no longer identified with the hierarchy. It is viewed as a community called by God, not one formed on the basis of prior service or holiness. Embracing all the faithful whether or not they have received Holy Orders, the ecclesial system, then, consists of a multiplicity of interacting members who share a common dignity and equality.

Scripture frequently refers to this equality. The People of God are "a chosen race, a royal priesthood, a dedicated nation, and a people claimed by God for his own" (I *Peter* 2:9–10). St. Paul also insists that "we are all brought into one body by baptism, in the one Spirit, whether we are Jews or Greeks, whether slaves or free men" (I *Cor.* 12:13). Or again: "Do you know that your body is a shrine of the indwelling Holy Spirit, and the Spirit is God's gift to you?" (I *Cor.* 6:19). These passages, which are referred to by Vatican II, are addressed to all the believers and not just to those in leadership roles. The Council uses them to emphasize the basic equality among all the members of the Church, thereby indicating the theological foundation of ecclesial democratization.

Doctrinally, the egalitarian aspect of the Church was never denied; but in practice, the laity were assigned a passive role by generations of popes and theologians. Gratian, the great medieval canonist of the twelfth century, makes a typical observation:

There are two kinds of Christians. On the one hand, those who are given up to the service of God and devoted to prayer and contemplation, and who ought to refrain from all worldly concerns; these are the clergy and those consecrated to God and the elect. . . . The second kind of Christians are the laity. . . . They are permitted to

[3] This is a favorite theme in Orthodox ecclesiology. For some perceptive observations on this problem see N. Nissiotis, "The Main Ecclesiological Problem of the Second Vatican Council," *Journal of Ecumenical Studies*, 2 (1965), 31–62.

marry, to cultivate the soil, to judge between men, to appear at law, to lay their offerings on the altar, and to pay tithes. In this way they too can achieve salvation, provided that they avoid vice by engaging in acts of charity.[4]

Gratian's separatist vision of roles in the Church was echoed for centuries in subsequent collections of canon law. It is reflected in the nineteenth century in the oft-quoted remark of Monsignor Talbot to Cardinal Manning: "What is the province of the laity? To hunt, to shoot, to entertain. These matters they understand, but to meddle with ecclesiastical matters they have no right at all."[5] Papal statements about this time are more sophisticated, but substantially the same. Leo XIII, for example, continued the image of two classes within the Church—the pastors and the flock. "The first of these classes has the function of teaching, of governing, of maintaining vital disciples, and of making laws: the second class has the duty of submitting, of obeying, of following the laws, and of showing honor."[6] Pius X also talked of two orders in the Christian community: "The hierarchy," he says, "alone has the right to move and to direct the members toward the society's goal; but the function of the multitude is to allow itself to be governed and to follow obediently the direction of its governors."[7]

Many variations of the ecclesiology outlined above developed. At different times in its history, the Church was modeled after a military organization, a father-son relationship, or a pyramid. In all of these there remained a sharp dichotomy between leaders and subjects. The ordinary believer was often treated as a minor, subservient to hierarchical control.[8] According to this clericalist structure, authority was unidirectional and paternalism became

[4] Gratian, C. 7, XII, I (*PL* 178:884, 885).

[5] Found in E. S. Purcell, *Life of Cardinal Manning* (London: Macmillan, 1895), I, 318.

[6] *Acta Sanctae Sedis*, 21 (1888), 322.

[7] *Ibid.*, 39 (1906), 8.

[8] The Code of Canon Law is indicative of this spirit. Canon 107 states: "By divine institution there are in the Church clerics distinct from laity. . . ." The passive role of the laity is expressed in Canon 682: "Lay persons have the right to receive from the clergy . . . spiritual benefits, especially the means necessary for salvation." See also *Lex Fundamentalis Ecclesiae*, Canons 26 and 29.

normative. The ideal layman, unquestioning and docile, was locked into a system in which there were no regular channels to communicate his demands.

This same rigid elitism is found in the classical treatment of the states of perfection. Thus, St. Thomas Aquinas wrote that one is in the state of perfection "because he binds himself permanently and with a certain solemnity to what leads to perfection."[9] This applies only to religious and bishops. Religious, by observing the evangelical counsels, are bound to tend to perfection to be acquired (*adquirenda*). The episcopate is an already acquired state of perfection (*adquisita*). In this context, Garrigou-Lagrange notes that it is most fitting that bishops be in the unitive way, in order that they may be able, through their pastoral duties, to lead others to perfection.[10] Clergy and laity are not in a separate state of perfection, although they are obliged to attain that perfection of the Christian life which consists in charity.

The secular political culture has also influenced the development of the Church as a closed, nonparticipatory system with limited informational flow and restricted adaptability. Political absolutism had no place for regularized dissent, allocation of power, and widespread involvement of the citizenry in the decision-making process. Even benevolent and enlightened rulers saw demands as a threat to the stability of the status quo. Throughout history the Church has incorporated many of the liabilities of secular culture into her own political system. The low priority that was traditionally given to the faithful is one sign of this. Today much of the tension in the Church stems from a conflict over political ideology with special reference to limited self-determination. The main agitation for political change comes from Northern Europe and North America, where the democratic experience has conditioned the faithful to demand a greater voice in the life of the Church.

The ecclesiology of the Second Vatican Council contains insights that logically lead to some form of ecclesial democratization. The most striking reason for this is the Council's insis-

---

[9] *Summa Theologica*, II–II, q.184, a.4.
[10] R. Garrigou-Lagrange, *The Three Stages of the Interior Life* (St. Louis: B. Herder, 1947), I, 219.

tence on the fundamental equality and dignity possessed by all members of the Church. The Church as the People of God is a partnership or fraternity.[11] Thus, pope, bishops, clergy, religious, and laity are all sacramentally united in the Church. The bonds of unity, shared by all, are enumerated by St. Paul: "There is one body and one Spirit, as there is also one hope held out in God's call to you; one Lord, one faith, one baptism; one God and Father of all, who is over all and through all and in all" (*Eph.* 4:4–6). All believers, the Council affirms, "share a common dignity from their rebirth in Christ" and "a true equality with regard to the dignity and to the activity common to all the faithful for the building up of the body of Christ." There is "no inequality on the basis of race or nationality, social condition or sex."[12] The Holy Spirit, dwelling within each Christian as in a temple, is the source of this equality. By his presence individuals are united to each other and to Christ. The Church as a Spirit-created fellowship of charity, life, and truth calls all its members to perfect holiness[13] and imposes on every disciple of Christ the obligation of spreading the faith.[14] These tasks are incumbent on every believer, not just on one segment of the Church.

The egalitarian character of the ecclesial community is elaborated by the Council in terms of the threefold mission of Christ as priest, prophet, and king. The laity as well as the hierarchy share in this mission. The lay apostolate is defined as "a participation in the saving mission of the Church itself."[15] As a *priestly* people, the faithful configured to Christ through their baptismal and confirmational characters offer spiritual worship and sacrifices (I *Pet.* 2:5) for the salvation of men and the ultimate glory of God. Their priesthood is exercised by reception of the sacraments, especially the Eucharist, at which they can offer their works, apostolic efforts, and even sufferings.[16] As a *prophetic* people, the faithful are primarily witnesses and heralds of the

---

[11] Cf. F. Hengsbach, "Partnerschaft in der Kirche," *Stimmen der Zeit*, 182 (1968), 90–104. Condensed in *Theology Digest*, 17 (Autumn 1969), 217–221.

[12] *Constitution on the Church*, Art. 32.

[13] *Ibid.*, Art. 11.

[14] *Ibid.*, Art. 17.

[15] *Ibid.*, Art. 33.

[16] *Ibid.*, Art. 34.

saving action of Jesus Christ and a sign that God is a living reality among men. The laity have the mandate to grasp the deep meaning of divine truth and to preach the Gospel daily by their word and example.[17] As a *kingly* people, the faithful have the obligation to spread the kingdom of God: "a kingdom of truth and life, a kingdom of holiness and grace, a kingdom of justice, love, and peace."[18] They must understand the value of the created world and try to relate it to the plan of God. The laity, in fulfilling this mission, should be a leaven of holiness in the world, preach Christ's victory over death and sin, and "illumine the whole of human society with His saving light."[19]

The egalitarian dimension of the People of God is related to another basic principle of social life, that of subsidiarity. Pope Pius XI described this principle as follows: "That which individual men can accomplish by their own initiative and by their own industry cannot be taken from them and assigned to the community; in the same way, that which minor or lesser communities can do should not be assigned to a greater or higher community."[20]

The principle of subsidiarity is basically an affirmation of the personal freedom and dignity which guarantee human rights. The primacy of the person should have priority in every social system, including the Church. The subsidiary function, according to Pope Pius XII, "is valid for social life in all its organizations and also for the life of the Church."[21] The Pope was simply restating the classic concept that society exists for the person and not the reverse. The Church, therefore, is not an end in itself, but rather a vehicle that is directed to the integrity and fulfillment of persons as sons of God. The People of God possess freedom because the Spirit is within them. St. Paul writes: "Now the Lord is the Spirit, and where the Spirit of the Lord is, there is liberty" (II *Cor.* 3:17).

On a practical level, the principle of subsidiarity is a call to

---

[17] *Ibid.*, Art. 35.

[18] *Ibid.*, Art. 36.

[19] *Ibid.*

[20] *Acta Apostolicae Sedis*, 23 (1931), 203.

[21] *Ibid.*, 38 (1946), 145. Cf. W. W. Bassett, "Subsidiarity, Order and Freedom in the Church," in *The Once and Future Church*, ed. J. A. Coriden, (Staten Island: Alba House, 1971), pp. 205–265.

individual and small-group responsibilities in the Church. It is a mandate for pluralism as opposed to uniformity, and decentralization as opposed to institutionalism. Concretely, it means that Rome should grant more authority to episcopal conferences; that episcopal conferences should respect the autonomy of individual bishops; that bishops should recognize the competency of pastors; and that pastors should collaborate closely with the laity.

The laity, as a subsystem in the Church, has been officially emancipated by Vatican II. For the first time in the history of general councils we have a pastoral and authoritative recognition of the layman's role-capacity in the Christian assembly. This is rooted in sacramental egalitarianism through which all believers are radically united without differentiation. The Christian vocation, ratified in baptism, establishes a fundamental spiritual equality and imposes specific responsibilities. The mature Christian is granted a definite autonomy and dignity, but he is expected to contribute, according to his own gifts, to the building up of the system. It is on this basis that certain democratic principles like cooperation, subsidiarity, and shared responsibility can be incorporated into the ecclesial system.

II. *The Hierarchic Aspect*

Equality in the ecclesial system is not absolute. Division of labor necessitates a variety of roles based on diversity of function. Members of the hierarchy, for example, are differentiated from others in the Church by their power, rights, and duties. Christ established the hierarchic structure when he entrusted to the apostolic college and its successors the authority to preach the Gospel, to administer the sacraments, and to rule the community. The present college of bishops, assisted by priests and other ministers, has the pastoral responsibility for the entire Church.[22] Is a divinely established hierarchic structure com-

---

[22] Cf. Trent (Denzinger-Schönmetzer, 1776) and Vatican II (*Constitution on the Church*, Art. 28). On the origin and development of the various hierarchic grades, see K. Rahner, "Reflection on the Concept of 'Ius Divinum' in Catholic Thought," *Theological Investigations* (Baltimore:

patible with ecclesial democracy which emphasizes lay participation in decision-making? A response to this problem requires that two areas be explored: the vesting of ecclesial authority and the structure of ecclesial authority.

A. THE VESTING OF ECCLESIAL AUTHORITY

God is the root source of all authority. Thus, Paul writes: "There is no authority but by the act of God, and the existing authorities are instituted by Him; consequently, anyone who rebels against authority is resisting a divine institution" (*Rom.* 13:1–2). Although Paul is speaking here of civil authority and the responsibility of citizens to pay taxes and to respect officeholders, his words apply even more to ecclesial authority. In the Church and in the state, God is the ultimate source of authority. But what is the immediate source in both these systems? In other words, to whom and in what manner does God transmit authority? We will discuss this vesting of authority in the state and then in the Church.

In a civil society, the citizens are the immediate source of political authority which they transmit to others. This transmission theory, elaborated so well in Jeffersonian philosophy, is the basis of most modern democratic constitutions. It means that a civilly united people (as a people and not as individuals) really possess the ruling power (authority) which they in turn give to specific individuals whom they have designated as their rulers. The first bearer of authority is the people as a whole. They have this power from God and they designate and empower those who will rule in their name. The United States democratic ideal is based on the theory of "power of the people."

Several major theologians have supported this theory. St. Thomas (d. 1274) indirectly referred to it when he stated that the making of law belongs to the whole people (*tota multitudo*)

Helicon, 1966), V, 219–243; K. Rahner in *Commentary on the Documents of Vatican II*, ed. H. Vorgrimler (New York: Herder and Herder, 1967), I, 190–192; A. Grillmeier, *ibid.*, 218–226; H. Küng, *The Church* (New York: Sheed and Ward, 1967), pp. 417–420; P. Huizing, " 'Göttliches Recht' und Kirchenverfassung," *Stimmen der Zeit*, 183 (1969), 162–173; and B. C. Butler, "The Openness of Theology," *The Month*, 1229 (1970), 21–25.

or to a public person who represents the people (*gerens vicem*).[23] Cajetan (d. 1534) developed this idea in his *opusculum* of 1512, "Defense of a Comparison between the Authority of the Pope and that of a Council." Referring to a monarchy, he insisted that "kings are not proximate and immediate ministers of God, but . . . God's ministers by being vice-regents of the people."[24] Robert Bellarmine (d. 1621) in the next century also held the transmission theory,[25] but the most thorough discussion of it is found in Suarez (d. 1617). In his *Defensio Fidei Catholicae* he rejected the notion of the divine right of kings proposed by King James I of England, that the king receives his power immediately from God and not from the people. Suarez agreed with Bellarmine and explained the transmission theory in these terms: "Supreme civil power . . . is given immediately by God to men assembled into a city or perfect political community. . . . It is not placed in one person or in any particular group, but in the whole complete people, or in the body of the community."[26]

The transmission theory applies to every form of legitimate civil government.[27] It easily explains the foundation of direct democracy in which the people rule themselves as well as of indirect democracy in which the people designate representatives to rule them. In both instances, input from the members of the system is regularized as active participation in decision-making. Moreover, the transmission theory helps explain monarchical government. Bellarmine and Suarez lived under monarchies. They wrote of the transmission theory in order to show the principles operative in this legitimate form of political society. In a monarchy, too, power is granted ultimately by

[23] *Summa Theologica*, I–II, q.90, a.3.

[24] *Scripta Theologica*, Vol. I: *De comparatione auctoritatis papae et concilii cum apologia eiusdem tractatus*, ed. V. M. J. Pollet (Rome: Angelicum, 1936), No. 532.

[25] *Controversium de membris ecclesiae*, Lib. 3, C. 6 (Paris: Vivès, 1870), III, 10–12.

[26] *Defensio fidei catholicae et apostolicae adversus anglicanae sectae errores*, Lib. 2, C. 2, 3 (Naples: Ex Typis Fibrenianis, 1872), p. 184.

[27] For further information on the political philosophy of the transmission theory see Y. R. Simon, *Philosophy of Democratic Government* (Chicago: University of Chicago Press, 1951), pp. 158–176, and J. Maritain, *Man and the State* (Chicago: University of Chicago Press, 1951).

the free consent of the people who agree to the kingship of one chosen by lot, by election, or by accident of birth. Continued supportive input from the people is indispensable. Even an absolute monarchy relies on this support, although there is minimal participation by the people in government, since decision-making is almost completely in the hands of the king.

In the ecclesial system, there exists a different concept of the investiture of authority. According to the teaching of the Church, the transmission theory is not applicable. The Christian community is not seen as the first bearer of authority which it then passes on to representatives. Rather it is Christ who gives sacred power and a mandate for exercising it to the hierarchy. Karl Rahner summarizes the traditional view:

> One has to say that office-holders in the Church do not receive their proper authority simply from the people nor are they merely executants of the will and desires of the people; they preach the Gospel, administer the sacraments, and participate in leading the Church in virtue of the mission they have received from Christ.[28]

It is not our intention to examine the complex and difficult problem of the origin and development of papal and episcopal authority.[29] What we will examine here is the official teaching of the Catholic Church reflected primarily in its general councils. Looking at the Church as an open political system, we are more interested in its operative self-understanding than in its theoretical development. At the same time, we recognize that there is a vast literature on every one of the points we will discuss. Contemporary theologians debate the role of Peter in the Roman Church, papal supremacy, and apostolic succession. The debate should continue. The authoritative statements of the Church are not meant to terminate inquiry but to encourage it. Today's ecumenical atmosphere also fosters further investigation of these critical areas.

It is the belief of the Roman Church that Christ made Peter head of the apostles and directly conferred upon him the fullness

---

[28] "Demokratie in der Kirche?" *op cit.*, 7.

[29] A good historical survey can be found in Y. Congar, "The Historical Development of Authority," in *Problems of Authority*, ed. Todd, pp. 119–156.

of power.[30] There is no indication in magisterial pronouncements that it was the community rather than Christ that did the empowering. In the case of Peter, we can properly speak of authority by divine right. Christ both designated *and* empowered Peter as the head of the Church. Vatican I, for example, explicitly rejected any theory which would hold that authority was given by Christ to the whole Church which in turn selected Peter. The Council insisted that Christ gave supreme authority to Peter *directly* and *immediately*. It labeled as a "perverse opinion" the view that this primacy was given "to the Church and through the Church to Peter as an agent of the Church."[31] Vatican II paraphrased the teaching of Vatican I on the Petrine primacy. Thus: "He [Christ] placed blessed Peter over the other apostles, and instituted in him a permanent and visible source and foundation of unity of faith and fellowship."[32]

From whom does the pope receive his authority and in what manner? The Church teaches that the authority comes from Christ and that the primacy of Peter is continued in his successors, the bishops of the Roman See.[33] At his election, the pope

[30] Both Vatican Councils base their statements on the New Testament, especially *Matt.* 16:16–19; *John* 21:15–17; and *Luke* 22:31–32. Cf. M. M. Bourke, "The Petrine Office in the New Testament," in *Proceedings of the Catholic Theological Society of America*, 1970 (Bronx, N. Y.: Manhattan College, 1971), pp. 1–12.

[31] Denzinger-Schönmetzer, 3054.

[32] *Constitution on the Church*, Art. 18. Cf. Denzinger-Schönmetzer, 3051.

[33] On the question of the Petrine office and subsequent papal supremacy consult the following: M. Bévenot, "Primacy and Development," *The Heythrop Journal*, 9 (1968), 400–413; O. Cullmann, *Peter: Disciple, Apostle, Martyr: An Historical and Theological Study* (Philadelphia: Westminster, 1962); C. Ernst, "The Primacy of St. Peter; Theology and Ideology," *New Blackfriars*, 50 (1969), 347–355; 399–404; O. Karrer, *Peter and the Church* (New York: Herder and Herder, 1963); H. Küng, *The Church*, pp. 444–480; H. Küng, ed., *Papal Ministry in the Church*, vol. 64, *Concilium* (New York: Herder and Herder, 1971); J. E. Lynch, "The History of Centralization: Papal Reservations," in *The Once and Future Church*, pp. 57–109; R. A. Markus, "Papal Primacy," *The Month*, 229 (1970), 352–361; R. A. Markus and E. John, *Papacy and Hierarchy* (London: Sheed and Ward, 1969); H. Marot, "The Primacy and the Decentralization of the Early Church," vol. 7, *Concilium* (New York: Paulist Press, 1965), 15–28; and J. F. McCue, "The Roman Primacy in the Second Century and the Problem of the Development of Dogma," *Theological Studies*, 25 (1965), 161–196.

receives the power to govern the Church.[34] A clear rejection of the transmission theory as applied to the pope is found in the condemnation of the Synod of Pistoia by Pope Pius VI in 1794. The decree stated that it is heretical to say "that the Roman Pontiff is ministerial head, if this is to be explained to mean that the Roman Pontiff received the power of his office, not from Christ in the person of St. Peter, but from the Church."[35] There is a difference, however, between Peter and his successors. With Peter, Christ personally designated *and* empowered him with authority. With his successors, Christ directly empowers a person who has been designated by others. At present, the College of Cardinals designates the papal candidate, but this method could be changed. Whatever process is employed, the power "to feed, rule, and govern" the ecclesial community comes directly from Christ and not from the electing body. The Council of Florence, later quoted by Vatican I, affirmed that the Roman Pontiff is the successor of Peter and that "to him alone in the person of St. Peter, was given by our Lord Jesus Christ the full power of feeding, ruling, and governing the whole Church."[36] Vatican II referred to the definitions of Vatican I and proposed them "to be firmly believed by all the faithful."[37]

The bishops, the largest decision-making body in the Church, are successors of the apostles.[38] A special problem exists in regard to their investiture of authority. The controversy centers on a distinction which originated in the twelfth century, between the episcopal power of orders (*potestas ordinis*) and the power of jurisdiction (*potestas jurisdictionis*). Before Vatican II, it was commonly held by theologians that the power of orders alone came from episcopal ordination. Thus, a duly ordained bishop

---

[34] The manualists point out that primacy does not of itself include the power of orders. Thus, a layman elected pope would have jurisdictional power but not the power of orders until he was ordained. Cf. G. Van Noort, *Dogmatic Theology*, trans. J. J. Castelot and W. R. Murphy (Westminster, Md.: Newman, 1951), II, 86, footnote 4.

[35] Denzinger-Schönmetzer, 2603.

[36] Denzinger-Schönmetzer, 1307. Cf. also 3059.

[37] *Constitution on the Church*, Art. 18.

[38] *Ibid.*, Art. 22. The nature of apostolic succession is widely discussed by theologians. For an extensive bibliography see R. Schnackenburg, "Apostolicity—The Present Position of Studies," *One in Christ*, 6 (1970), 243–273.

was a dispenser of divine grace in ordaining priests, performing sacramental rites, and acting as spiritual teacher of the Gospel. He received this power from Christ, but mediately through the ministerial action of those ordaining him. On the other hand, the power of jurisdiction, the authority to teach and to rule, came directly from the pope by means of a canonical mission. This is the position taken by Pope Pius XII in the encyclical *Mystici Corporis*, where he affirmed that the bishops were subordinate to the pope and that they enjoyed the ordinary power of jurisdiction "which they receive directly from the same Roman Pontiff."[39] Charles Journet writes in a similar vein: "When the Supreme Pontiff . . . invests bishops, the proper jurisdiction they receive does not come to them directly from God, it comes directly from the Sovereign Pontiff to whom Christ gives it in a plenary manner."[40]

Vatican II treated this problem from a perspective that stressed the unity of episcopal authority. The Council taught that "episcopal consecration, together with the function of sanctifying, also confers the function of teaching and governing."[41] These functions, however, "can be exercised only in hierarchical communion with the head and members of the college."[42] The *Nota praevia* explains more fully that, "In consecration is given an ontological participation in the sacred functions."[43] The word function (*munus*) is used, rather than power (*potestas*), in

[39] Denzinger-Schönmetzer, 3804.

[40] *The Church of the Word Incarnate* (New York: Sheed and Ward, 1955), I, 405. A similar position is taken in a more recent article by Dino Staffa, "De collegiali episcopatus ratione," *Revue de droit canonique*, 14 (1964), 100–205.

[41] *Constitution on the Church*, Art. 21. Even before Vatican II some theologians were moving in this direction. Thus Wilhelm Bertrams: "The episcopal office of governing is conferred upon a concrete subject through episcopal consecration. To exercise the office of governing in the Church, however, the divinely established and sacramentally conferred power of governing in the Church must be coordinated with the power of governing possessed by the other bishops. This coordination belongs to the Roman Pontiff." *The Papacy, the Episcopacy, and Collegiality* (Westminster, Md.: Newman Press, 1964), p. 54. See also K. Rahner, *Bishops: Their Status and Function* (Baltimore: Helicon, 1963), p. 31.

[42] *Constitution on the Church*, Art. 21.

[43] The *Nota explicativa praevia* is not strictly speaking an official part

order to make clear that consecration does not by itself give "powers . . . ready to go into act" but requires in addition some canonical or juridical determination.[44] Before a bishop is ready to exercise his office, he must have a definite territory given him by a canonical mission. Theologians generally admit that in some way episcopal jurisdiction comes from the pope when he gives this canonical mission. Previously, however, they held that the pope was the immediate cause of jurisdiction. Many now consider the pope to be rather a necessary condition for the validity of jurisdictional acts. The emphasis has shifted from the juridical to the sacramental.

The official Church has explicitly taught that bishops do not receive their authority from the community. Other documents reveal that this applies equally to other divisions of the hierarchy. The Council of Trent, for example, taught that the validity of the ordination of bishops, priests, and other orders does not depend on the "consent, call, or authority, whether of the people or any civil power or magistrate."[45] This proposition was directed against Hus, Wyclif, and Zwingli, who held that the people's consent was necessary, and against Luther, who believed that the approval of the secular power was required for valid orders. In 1917, the Code of Canon Law repeated Trent's statement in Canon 109. Pope Pius XII, in an address to the Roman Rota in 1945, referred to this Canon and added: "In the Church, differently than in the state, the primal subject of power, the supreme judge, the highest court of appeal, is never the community of the faithful." Moreover, the Pope continued: "There does not exist nor can there exist in the Church founded by Christ, a popular tribunal or a judicial power deriving from the people."[46] There is no room, therefore, for a direct application of the transmission theory to the vesting of power in the ecclesial system.

---

of the text of the *Constitution on the Church*. It was prepared by the Theological Commission and distributed to the Fathers before they voted on *Lumen Gentium*.

[44] *Nota praevia,* #2.
[45] Denzinger-Schönmetzer, 1769.
[46] *Acta Apostolicae Sedis*, 37 (1945), 261.

Is ecclesial democratization theologically possible in view of the official teaching of the Church examined above? A distinction must be made between calling the Church a democracy and urging democratization. On a theoretical level, the Church is not a democracy. Since the nonhierarchical members of the Church do not legitimately possess sacred power, they can neither transmit it to others nor divest it from those who do possess it. This is the accepted position of the Church. Thus Pope Paul could write: "The Church is hierarchical and an organic unity; it is not democratic in the sense that the community itself enjoys the priority of faith or authority over those whom the Spirit has placed at the head of the Church."[47] The German Bishops in 1969 and Cardinal Dearden, president of the National Conference of Catholic Bishops in 1970, reaffirmed this truth.[48] On a pragmatic level, however, there is no intrinsic reason why democratic elements cannot be incorporated into the ecclesial system. (1) In the selection of candidates for the hierarchy, God does not personally designate those who shall fill this office. The designation is done by men. The laity and clergy, therefore, should be able to participate in this important decision-making function. One may well argue that this is a right inherent in the faithful because of the common sacramental unity they possess. (2) In the empowering of the members of the hierarchy, God usually does not bestow upon them all the natural talents or even spiritual gifts necessary for the perfect administration of the Church. Hence, institutionalized participation of the laity and clergy in decision-making, in accordance with the principle of subsidiarity, would be a democratic adjunct to hierarchical power; as it is written, "Do all things with counsel and thou shalt not afterwards repent thee of it" (*Eccles.* 32:24).

The juridical questions we have discussed here were unthought of in the early centuries of the Church. Brian Tierney can write: "It seldom occurred to medieval men to ask whether lawful authority came from God *or* the people. They took it for

---

[47] Address to the clergy and religious of Rome, February 2, 1968. (*The Pope Speaks*, 13 [1968], 38.)

[48] *NC News Service* (*Foreign*), Jan. 3, 1969, p. 4, and *NC News Service* (*Domestic*), Nov. 21, 1970, p. 1.

granted that it came from God *and* the people. The popular consent was the normal way in which the divine will would manifest itself to a Christian community."[49] It should be noted, however, that although popular election of Church leaders was the common practice for centuries, the final judgment and sacramental ordination remained in the hands of the bishops. Priests were ordained by bishops and bishops consecrated by other bishops. The community never performed these functions. In the final analysis, regardless of how much members of the Church participate in the designation of the hierarchy or in ecclesial decision-making, the sacred power of the hierarchy comes ultimately from God. This is summed up well by the canonist Sicardus: "In these matters God is the bestower; we are His instruments."[50]

B. THE STRUCTURE OF ECCLESIAL AUTHORITY

The implementation of ecclesial democratization depends upon the openness of governmental structures. The hierarchy is the central information-processing unit and decision-making body in the ecclesial system. Its responsibility is to provide pastoral leadership, an open and free flow of information throughout the system, and a conversion of demands into constructive outputs. In the Church today, these goals are often inadequately fulfilled. One reason for this failure is the confusion over the nature of ecclesial government. The Church continues to seek a better understanding of its structures and their consistency in terms of revealed truth. This is an agonizing process, since two concepts of ecclesial government have been officially proposed over the last hundred years: Vatican I described the Church in terms of a monarchical government, while Vatican II proposed a collegial exercise of hierarchical authority. The precise relationship between these concepts is as yet unresolved. It has become one of the most critical problems facing contemporary ecclesiology and is crucial to any form of ecclesial democratization.

---

[49] "Roots of Western Constitutionalism in the Church's own Tradition," in *We, The People of God*, p. 117.

[50] Quoted by Tierney, *ibid.*, pp. 117–118.

1. THE MONARCHICAL APPROACH

Many theologians in the past taught that of all the forms of government, the Church most closely resembles a monarchy.[51] Yet it is a monarchy *sui generis*. In the Church, as in a monarchy, one person has the fullness of power and is thus in a position of authority above all others. The Church is a monarchy, it is argued, because Christ gave supreme power to Peter and to his successors, the Roman Pontiffs. Vatican I did not use the term "monarchy," but its teaching on papal primacy did, in fact, describe that reality.[52] The pope is the Vicar of Christ, the successor of Peter, and the supreme pastor and judge of all Christians. He enjoys full power, given to him by Christ, to rule in doctrinal and disciplinary matters and to teach infallibly. The pope possesses a primacy of jurisdiction and not simply one of honor. In virtue of this primacy he has ordinary, immediate, and truly episcopal authority over the whole Church and over every single one of its members.

What kind of monarchy is thus described?[53] It is not a hereditary monarchy. The papal office is not passed on from father to son. But can the pope personally designate his successor? The present law of the Church and tradition militate against this. Elevation to the papacy has always been connected with

---

[51] Cf. L. Billot, *De Ecclesia Christi* (Rome: Gregorian University, 1927), pp. 528ff.; M. Nicolau and J. Salaverri, *Sacrae Theologiae Summa* (Madrid: Biblioteca Auctores Cristianos, 1952), I, 546ff.; and G. Van Noort, *Dogmatic Theology*, II, 57ff.

[52] Vatican I, Dogmatic Constitution *Pastor Aeternus*: Denzinger-Schönmetzer, 3050–3075. See also Canon 218 of Code of Canon Law.

[53] Cf. K. Rahner with J. Ratzinger, *The Episcopate and the Primacy* (New York: Herder and Herder, 1962). For scriptural and historical studies on the monarchical episcopate see M. M. Bourke, "Reflections on Church Order in the New Testament," *The Catholic Biblical Quarterly*, 30 (1968), 493–511; P. Burke, "The Monarchical Episcopate at the End of the First Century," *Journal of Ecumenical Studies*, 7 (1970), 499–518; J. Colson, *L'evêque dans les communautés primitives* (Paris: Editions du Cerf, 1951), and *Les fonctions ecclésiales aux deux premiers siècles* (Paris: Desclée de Brouwer, 1956); E. Schwizer, *Church Order in the New Testament* (London: SCM Press, 1960); and H. von Campenhausen, *Ecclesiastical Authority and Spiritual Power in the Church of the First Three Centuries* (Stanford: Stanford University Press, 1969).

some form of election or approbation. There are, however, two instances which have intrigued historians. Pope Felix IV, fearing chaos in the Roman Church after his death, appointed in 530 the archdeacon Boniface as his successor. On the death of Felix, however, the majority of the clergy refused to accept Boniface as the legitimate pope. Later, the Roman synod acknowledged his claim and promised him obedience. The thorny problem remains: did Boniface become pope by the designation of Felix or by the subsequent approval of the synod? The following year, history began to repeat itself. In 531, Boniface, with the support of his clergy and people, appointed his own successor. Before his death, however, he rescinded this arrangement.

The monarchical government of the Church is not absolute but constitutional. There are in the Church certain doctrinal and structural constants over which the pope does not have absolute control. As regards doctrine, the pope cannot deny the content of revelation and its explicitation in dogmatic propositions. He is bound to safeguard and to teach what has been given to the Church. Dogmatic truths must develop, but in consonance with and not in contradiction to what has been previously taught. As regards structure, the pope cannot abolish the episcopate since it belongs to the constitution of the Church and exists by divine right. He may depose an individual bishop for sufficient reason or institute new ways for the episcopate to exercise its authority, but he cannot suppress the episcopal order.

Vatican I concentrated on the papal prerogatives in a juridical framework. Little reference was made to bishops. A schema "*de episcopo*" was prepared for conciliar discussion, but it never reached the floor of the Council. Its contents favored collegiality.[54] The Council, however, stated that "the power of the Supreme Pontiff is far from standing in the way of ordinary and immediate episcopal jurisdiction."[55] This theme was developed five years after the Council in 1875, when the German Catholic

---

[54] Cf. G. Dejaifve, "Primauté et collegialité au premier concile du Vatican," in *L'épiscopat et L'Eglise universelle*, ed. Y. Congar and B.-D. Dupuy (Editions du Cerf, 1962), pp. 639–660, and J. P. Torrell, *La théologie de l'épiscopat au premier concile du Vatican* (Paris: Editions du Cerf, 1961).

[55] Denzinger-Schönmetzer, 3061.

hierarchy issued a declaration on the relation between the episcopate and papal primacy. Several important theological clarifications were made: episcopal jurisdiction is not absorbed into papal jurisdiction; the bishops are not simply functionaries of the pope; and the pope has not in principle taken the place of each bishop. Pope Pius IX praised the German bishops for presenting "the true meaning of the Vatican decrees" in a way that "leaves nothing to be desired."[56]

A monarchical interpretation of Church government obviously impedes the introduction of any democratic elements. An ecclesial system in which the control functions are almost totally in the hands of the hierarchy is not apt to foster consultation and participation. The laity are given a subordinate status and their input, beyond that of support, is discouraged.

2. The Collegial Approach

Vatican II, working from a sacramental, redemptive, and historical perspective, presented a broader view of the Church. A balanced description of the hierarchic structure was given in terms of the doctrine of collegiality. Found in the New Testament,[57] this principle stresses the unity and collaboration that should exist between the papal and episcopal offices. It sees the Church as a *communio ecclesiarum*,[58] a fraternity of local com-

---

[56] The text of the declaration and papal approval can be found in Denzinger-Schönmetzer, 3112–3116; English translation of the declaration in H. Küng, *The Council, Reform and Reunion* (New York: Sheed and Ward, 1961), pp. 193–201. Cf. O. Rousseau, "La vraie valeur de l'épiscopat dans l'Eglise d'après d'importants documents de 1875," in *L'épiscopat et L'Eglise universelle*, 709–736.

[57] The scriptural basis for collegiality is examined in the following: G. Dejaifve, "Les douze Apôtres et leur unité dans la tradition catholique," *Ephemerides theologicae lovanienses*, 39 (1963), 760–778; J. Giblet et al., *Aux origines de l'église* (Paris: Desclée de Brouwer, 1964); J. Lecuyer, *Etudes sur la collegialité épiscopale* (Le Puy and Lyon: Editions Mappus, 1964); M. J. Le Guillou, "Le parallelisme entre le collège apostolique et le collège épiscopale," *Istina* 10 (1964), 103–110; and D. M. Stanley, "The New Testament Basis for the Concept of Collegiality," *Theological Studies* 25 (1964), 197–216.

[58] Several theologians have developed this theme. See: Y. Congar, "Note

munities united in one body by the Spirit. This ancient concept of *communio* preserves both the unity of the universal Church and the individuality of the local Church. The common sharing of the same faith and discipline by various communities under the leadership of their bishop does not prevent the local Church from exercising self-determination and adaptation. The principle of collegiality implies subsidiarity.

The *Constitution of the Church* (*Lumen Gentium*), in Articles 18–29, summarizes the theology of the episcopate. The Council teaches that there exists in the Church a stable and permanent college that is a continuation of the college of the apostles instituted by Christ. One becomes a member of the college by episcopal consecration and can thus, in communion with the head and other members of the college, exercise the threefold function of teaching, sanctifying, and governing. The individual bishop has the duty: to proclaim the Gospel; to promote the unity of faith, love, and discipline; and to celebrate the sacraments. The bishop, however, does not govern the local Church simply as a delegate of the pope, but in the name of Christ. The resident bishop is more than the chief pastor, teacher, liturgist, and administrator in the diocese. He is also entrusted, as a member of the college, with responsibility for the entire Church. This responsibility is not one of jurisdiction but one of service to the whole Christian community.

Article 22 of *Lumen Gentium* presents the core of the doctrine of collegiality. An acute problem of interpretation centers on two sentences in that article: "Together with its head, the Roman Pontiff, and never without this head, the episcopal order is the subject of supreme and full power over the universal Church. But this power can be exercised only with the consent of the Roman Pontiff." Theologians ask the following questions: Who is the subject of supreme power in the Church? and, Is it possible to distinguish the action of the pope as head of the Church from

sur les mots 'Confession,' 'Eglise,' et 'Communion,' " *Irénikon*, 23 (1950), 3–36; M. J. Le Guillou, *Mission et Unité. Les exigences de la communion* (Paris: Editions du Cerf, 1960); J. Hamer, *The Church is a Communion* (New York: Sheed and Ward, 1964); and L. Hertling, "*Communio und Primat*," *Xenia Piana* (*Miscellanea Historiae Pontificate*), 7 (1943), 4–48.

his action as head of the college? All theologians would agree that the college cannot act legitimately without the pope, but they disagree as to whether the pope can act alone without the college. There are two schools of thought.

Some theologians contend that in the Church there are two inadequately distinct subjects of supreme power: the pope as head of the Church and the episcopal college under the leadership of the pope.[59] They argue that from a juridical point of view the title by which the pope has supreme power is personal to him and so independent from the college. To support their position they point to the dogmatic definitions of Vatican I and to the interpretative *Nota praevia* of Vatican II. The *Nota praevia* stated that the pope's fullness of power cannot be jeopardized and that he may exercise it at his own discretion. Thus, the pope can decide the best way to serve the Church, either personally or collegially. Since the pope is the head of the college, "he alone can perform certain acts which in no wise belong to the bishops, for example, the convoking and directing of the college, approving the norms of action, etc."[60]

Other theologians, and they are in the majority, hold that there is only one subject of supreme power in the Church: the college of bishops under the leadership of the pope.[61] This single power is always collegial, because the pope belongs to the episcopal college. Even when he acts alone, the pope is still acting as head of the college. Rahner's assertion is representative: ". . . every primatial action of the pope contains a *de facto*

---

[59] Cf. W. Bertrams, "De subjecto supremae potestatis Ecclesiae," *Periodica de re morali, canonica, liturgica,* 54 (1965), 173–232 and M. Browne, "Il collegio episcopale soggetto di potestà suprema di governo della Chiesa Cattolica e la 'nota explicativa praevia'," *Divinitas,* 9 (1965), 379–384.

[60] *Nota praevia,* #3.

[61] Cf. K. Rahner, *Commentary on the Documents of Vatican II,* I, 202–204; O. Semmelroth, "Die Lehre von der Kollegialen Hirtengewalt über die Gesamtkirche. . . ." *Scholastik,* 40 (1965), 175–177; A. Grillmeier, "Sorgen und Hoffnungen um das Konzil," *Stimmen der Zeit,* 175 (1965), 287–304; C. Duquoc, "Tête et corps dans le collège épiscopale; infallibilté fonctionelle et graduée, l'impossible dilemme," in *L'évêque dans l'Eglise du Christ,* ed. H. Bouëssé and A. Mandouze (Bruges: Desclée de Brouwer, 1963), pp. 81–93; and R. P. McBrien, "Collegiality: State of the Question," in *The Once and Future Church,* pp. 1–24.

reference to the college as a whole."[62] This is even the case when the pope does not act in a strictly collegial way. Rahner argues that his view is in accord with the *Nota praevia:* "To 'act alone' does not mean to act as a 'private person' but as the visible head of the Church, living from its Spirit and from the institution as a whole. If he has to act as visible head of the Church, then he has to act as head of the college."[63]

The theological debate, which was not settled by Vatican II, continues. It can never be properly resolved solely on the juridical level. A more fruitful approach, and one that facilitates democratization, is to see the hierarchic structure as *within* rather than *above* the ecclesial system. Both papacy and episcopacy are essential elements in the Church and both must exercise power for the benefit of all the members. The concept of collegiality should encompass the cooperation of all the subsystems within the Church. There should be a creative interaction not only between the pope and the bishops but also between bishops and their clergy, and between the clergy and the laity. Democratization is one way to realize this goal. By encouraging the active participation of the laity, the Church can utilize the spiritual strengths, talents, and energies of its members. The hierarchic structure can thus function more effectively as a genuine servant of the People of God. Collegiality and a democratized Church are supportive of one another. A fraternal rather than an exclusively paternal hierarchy would guarantee the flow of information throughout the system, increase the number and variety of communication channels, and provide for maintenance and growth of the system.

[62] Rahner, *Commentary on the Documents of Vatican II*, I, p. 203.

[63] *Ibid.*, p. 204. In spite of the fact that most theologians support the theory of one subject of supreme authority in the Church with two modes of action, Rome itself has been reluctant to acknowledge it. During the discussions on collegiality at Vatican II, Pope Paul suggested that the text be amended to read that the pope is "answerable to the Lord alone." The Theological Commission rejected this modification (*Commentary on the Documents of Vatican II*, I, p. 202). Since the Council several documents have been issued by Rome that show little concern for the principle of collegiality: *Regimini universae ecclesiae, Acta Apostolicae Sedis,* 59 (1967), 885–928, and *Sollicitudo omnium ecclesiarum, ibid.,* 61 (1969), 473–484.

III. *The Charismatic Aspect*

The Church is the dwelling "where God lives in the Spirit" (*Eph.* 2:22). The multiplicity and interaction of roles in the ecclesial system is, therefore, intimately linked to the Holy Spirit. The Church, through the Spirit, is a unified fellowship, a charismatic reality. This means that the Holy Spirit freely bestows charisms (spiritual gifts) on the believers for the benefit of the whole Church. Through these gifts every member can contribute positively to the sanctification and growth of the community. The charismatic aspect of the Church provides another element in the theological foundation of ecclesial democracy. Our main concern here is with the charismatic activity of the laity. Two issues will be discussed: the charisms in general and the specific charism of prophecy.

A. THE CHARISMS IN GENERAL

The theology of charisms begins by affirming that the Holy Spirit is a dynamic, abiding presence among the People of God. He gives them life, directs them in truth, and unifies them through love. In the New Testament we find several references to charisms. The Greek word *charisma* appears seventeen times in the New Testament: sixteen times in the Pauline epistles and once in the first Petrine epistle (I *Peter* 4:10). Four meanings emerge: (a) the justifying grace given to man through the redemptive work of Jesus (*Rom.* 5:15,16; 6:23); (b) the unspecified graces, either the gifts that God gave to Israel (*Rom.* 11:29), the graces that Paul could give to others (*Rom.* 1:11), or the favors God gives to believers (II *Cor.* 1:11); (c) the sacramental graces given at ordination (I *Tim.* 4:14; II *Tim.* 1:6); and (d) the specific spiritual gifts given by the Spirit for particular functions (*Rom.* 12:6; I *Cor.* 1:7; 7:7; 12:4,9,28,30,31; I *Peter* 4:10). St. Paul also uses several synonyms for *charisma* in reference to this last category of gifts: *pneumatika* (I *Cor.* 12:1; 14:1,14); *diakoniai* (I *Cor.* 12:5); *energemata* (I *Cor.* 12:6); *charis* (*Eph.* 4:7); and *domata* (*Eph.* 4:8).

St. Paul enumerates specific charisms in four principal lists: *Rom.* 12:6; I *Cor.* 12:8–10; I *Cor.* 12:28–30; and *Eph.* 4:11. The following are found therein: apostleship, prophecy, evangelism, teaching; exhortation; word of wisdom; word of knowledge; faith; speaking in tongues; interpretation; discernment of spirits; healing, miracles; works of assistance; almsgiving; works of mercy; ministering; presiding; pastoring; and governing.

A charism, in the restricted sense used above, is a gift given to an individual by the Holy Spirit (I *Cor.* 12:4,5,11) for the building up of the Church (I *Cor.* 12:7; 14:26). Theologians agree generally on the source and goal of charisms but disagree widely over other aspects. St. Thomas, for example, calls a charism a *gratia gratis data* (gratuitous grace) which is given to a person primarily for the sanctification of others.[64] He contrasts this with *gratia gratum faciens* (sanctifying grace), which is given primarily for the personal sanctification of the person. In reference to the nine charisms listed in I *Cor.* 12:8–10, St. Thomas sees them as graces given to some persons not for themselves but as means for leading others to God by communicating the revealed message.[65] Charisms are beyond the natural powers of man and independent of his merits. Later theologians, if they wrote on charisms at all, followed St. Thomas. For them charisms were extraordinary and preternatural graces different from sanctifying grace, sacramental grace, the virtues, and the gifts of the Holy Spirit.

Contemporary theological reflection presents a somewhat different view. It admits that there are extraordinary charisms—for example, miracles, healing, and speaking in tongues—but insists that most are ordinary rather than exceptional manifestations of grace. Charisms, it is argued, are given to each Christian to enable him to perform a special service in the Church. St. Paul writes: "In each of us the Spirit is manifested in one particular way, for some useful purpose" (I *Cor.* 12:7); and, "Everyone has the gift God has granted to him, one this gift and another that" (I *Cor.* 7:7). For Hans Küng, a charism is simply a gift of grace, that includes every gift of the Spirit, every function in the Church, and everything done in faith. He defines a charism as "the call of God, addressed to an individual, to a particular ministry in the community, which brings with it the ability to

[64] *Summa Theologica*, I–II, q.111, a.1.
[65] *Ibid.*, a.4.

fulfill that ministry."[66] Cardinal Suenens and Karl Rahner propose a similar view.[67]

All theologians would agree that the charisms listed by Paul are not an exhaustive enumeration. The charismatic element in the Church is essential and hence perennial. New forms of charismatic activity, however, will develop to meet new challenges. The action of the Spirit in the Church is continuous, although we cannot predict exactly how it will manifest itself. "The wind blows where it wills; you hear the sound of it, but you do not know where it comes from, or where it is going. So with everyone who is born from spirit" (*John* 3:8).

How does the charismatic dimension of the Church relate to democratization? It shows the Church to be a political system composed of persons playing many roles but all interdependent. Radical unity is achieved through the Spirit who is in all and works through all. No one subsystem in the Church has a monopoly on the charisms of the Spirit. Rather there is a plurality of charisms or ministries with each contributing to the common good. The charisms, as freely given gifts of the Spirit, enable each member of the system to exercise a specific power bestowed

[66] H. Küng, *The Church*, p. 188.

[67] L.-J. Suenens, "The Charismatic Dimension of the Church," in *Council Speeches of Vatican II*, ed. H. Küng, Y. Congar, and D. O'Hanlon (Glen Rock, N.J.: Paulist Press, 1964), pp. 29–34, and K. Rahner, *The Dynamic Element in the Church* (New York: Herder and Herder, 1964) and *The Episcopate and the Primacy*, pp. 11–36. For other studies on the theology of charisms see E. Bettencourt, "Charisms," *Sacramentum Mundi*, I, 283–284; A. Bittlinger, *Gifts and Graces* (Grand Rapids, Mich.: W. B. Eerdmans, 1967); X. Ducros, "Charismes," *Dictionnaire de spiritualité*, II, 1, 503–507; D. L. Gelpi, *Pentecostalism—A Theological Viewpoint* (New York: Paulist Press, 1971); E. Käsemann, *Essays on New Testament Themes* (Naperville, Ill.: A. R. Allenson, 1964), pp. 63–104; A. Lemonnyer, "Charismes," *Dictionnaire de la Bible* (Suppl.), I, 1233–1243; B.-M. Maréchaux, *Les charisme du Saint-Esprit* (Paris: Téqui, 1921); G. Murphy, *Charisms and Church Renewal* (Rome: Catholic Book Agency, 1965); E. D. O'Connor, "The New Theology of Charisms in the Church," *American Ecclesiastical Review*, 161 (1969), 145–159, and *The Pentecostal Movement in the Catholic Church* (Notre Dame, Ind.: Ave Maria Press, 1971); F. Prat, *The Theology of Saint Paul* (Westminster, Md.: Newman, 1952), I, 127–133; 423–428; and J. Wilhelm, "Charismata," *Catholic Encyclopedia*, III, 585–591.

by God. The Church, therefore, through this broad distribution of charisms, has truly been prepared by the Spirit for some kind of participatory democracy.

It is helpful to note that charism may be classed as structural or nonstructural. The hierarchy manifests a structural charism in that it is empowered by the Spirit to shepherd the community (*Acts* 20:28). Nonstructural charisms are actions of the Spirit which are not limited to official Church order. The spontaneous and free work of the Spirit operates among all the faithful in unexpected and novel ways. Yet for all the charisms the goal is the same, the building up of the body of Christ.

The Church, in its official teaching, acknowledges the role of charisms. In the encyclical *Mystici corporis* (1943), Pope Pius XII insisted that the Church is both hierarchic and charismatic. He rejected two extreme positions: that the structure of the Church is composed only of hierarchical elements; and "that it is composed only of those who enjoy charismatic gifts—though members gifted with miraculous powers will never be lacking in the Church."[68] He then mentioned some less extraordinary gifts as possessed by religious, married people, and those who devote themselves to works of mercy.

Vatican II, in several of its documents, developed the theme that the Holy Spirit "distributes special graces among the faithful of every rank."[69] The faithful have the "right and duty" to use these charismatic gifts "in the Church and in the world for the good of mankind and for the upbuilding of the Church."[70] The Council did not discuss in detail the Pauline charisms, with the exception of apostleship and prophecy. It did, however, refer to broad categories of charisms: the "outstanding" and the "simple." What is most significant is the insistence that the laity should use their gifts in order to contribute to the saving mission of the Church to the world,[71] and that priests should foster the development of charisms among the laity.[72]

[68] Denzinger-Schönmetzer, 3801.
[69] *Constitution on the Church,* Art. 12.
[70] *Decree on the Apostolate of the Laity,* Art. 3.
[71] *Constitution on the Church,* Art. 30.
[72] *Decree on the Ministry and Life of Priests,* Art. 9. Other references in Vatican II to the charismatic gifts are: *Constitution on the Church,*

Charisms can be understood as operative elements in an ecclesial system. The various subsystems—hierarchy, clergy, religious, and laity—are charismatic groups endowed with unique graces that benefit the entire system. Inputs (demands and supports) and outputs (authoritative decisions) can be manifestations of the Spirit. The critical question here is how to determine their genuineness. Not every input or output is necessarily charismatic. How does one judge whether the actions of the laity and Church officials are truly the work of the Spirit or simply a human endeavor? This is a delicate question, and no facile set of rules is readily available.[73] Two factors compound the problem: first, the Church is a mystery and the presence of the Spirit may be obscure or may appear in unlikely ways; and second, the Church is incarnational and is thus affected by the sins and defects of its members.

With these qualifications in mind, some criteria for the discerning of charisms may be suggested. First, no charism can be from the Spirit that denies that Jesus is the Lord. St. Paul stated: "No one who says 'A curse on Jesus!' can be speaking under the influence of the Spirit of God. And no one can say 'Jesus is Lord!' except under the influence of the Spirit of God" (I *Cor.* 12:3). St. John also gives the same fundamental rule for discernment of spirits: "Every spirit which acknowledges that Jesus the Christ has come in the flesh is from God" (I *John* 4:2) This criterion would apply to all charisms—teaching charisms as well as others. Any charism that is used to deny the Incarnation, which is a basic tenet of Christianity, cannot be of the Spirit. The charism must be consonant with what has been revealed. In Scholastic terminology this is called the *analogy of faith*. Second, charisms must be used for the profit of the entire Church. Thus, St. Paul insists that the spiritual gifts "must aim at one thing: to build up the Church" (I *Cor.* 14:26). They must lead to unity and not division, encourage a common effort not individual aggran-

---

Arts. 4, 7, 33; *Decree on the Apostolate of the Laity*, Arts. 30, 35; and *Decree on the Missionary Activity of the Church*, Art. 28.

[73] Cf. J. C. Futrell, *Ignatian Discernment* (St. Louis: Institute of Jesuit Sources, 1970) and J. R. Sheets, "Profile of the Spirit: A Theology of Discernment of Spirits," *Review for Religious* 30 (1971), 363–376.

dizement, and develop rather than deform the Body of Christ. Third, the personal life of the charismatic may be another sign of credibility. A virtuous individual is more likely to be the instrument of the Spirit than one who is leading a sinful life. This is not an absolute criterion, since Paul presents the possibility of someone with charismatic gifts but without charity (I *Cor.* 13). Without restricting the power of God, it seems reasonable and fitting to assume that normally He gives His gifts to worthy persons.

These general criteria may help the community discern when a charism is truly from the Spirit. Their application becomes especially difficult when there is a conflict between the charismatic and those in authority. Because of the plurality of gifts, confrontation may be a frequent occurrence. We know that the Spirit transcends rank and works within the laity as well as among the hierarchy. The Spirit can inspire each and every Christian, since all enjoy a fundamental dignity and equality. There should be no opposition between office and charism, since both have their origin in the Spirit: "There are varieties of gifts, but the same Spirit" (I *Cor.* 12:5). Tension, however, frequently does exist. The hierarchy has the responsibility of testing charisms to see that they are of God. At the same time they must not extinguish the Spirit (I *Thess.* 5:19-22). Authorities should recognize that the Spirit works also outside formal structures and appears in unusual ways. Patience, openness, and flexibility should characterize their attitude. The laity, for their part, should remember that charisms are given for the good of the whole community and not for just one part of it, one community or one person. St. Paul advises that charisms be used "decently and in order," since "the God who inspires them is not a God of disorder but of peace" (I *Cor.* 14:40,33). A charismatic laity may well face opposition, ridicule, and rejection. This is especially true when the status quo is challenged. The history of the Church is filled with examples. Many founders of religious orders, reformers, critics of the papacy, and theologians experienced apathy or hostility from authorities. Time, therefore, is perhaps the ultimate test of the authenticity of charisms. If the charism is from God, it will endure. The words of the Pharisee Gamaliel may be recalled when authorities refuse to acknowledge the charisms of the laity. Speaking to the Sanhedrin who wished to put to death Peter and his followers, this teacher of the law proposed a norm that is still valid: "If this idea of theirs or its execution is of human origin, it will collapse; but if it is from God, you will never be able to put them down, and you risk finding yourselves at war with God" (*Acts* 5:38–39).

Vatican II proposes cooperation between the hierarchy and the laity as the way to resolve tension. All members must collaborate in the Church's mission. *Lumen Gentium* endorses the idea of partnership and describes the dialogue that should exist within the Church. The layman is urged to reveal his need to those in authority and to express openly his opinions on those things that concern the good of the whole community. Pastors are exhorted to welcome the suggestions and advice of their flock, to use the talents and experience of the laity, and to grant them freedom in carrying out apostolic work. The goal is that "the whole Church, strengthened by each of its members, can more effectively fulfill its mission for the life of the world."[74]

B. THE CHARISM OF PROPHECY

Prophecy is communication. Prophecy, of all the charisms, has the greatest cybernetic implications. Its focus is on the Church as an information-processing unit. Through prophecy, the Spirit, dwelling within all the members of the Church, can enlighten and guide the whole input-output-feedback cycle. To the extent that the members of the Church are open and docile to divine grace, the life of the system becomes the life of the Spirit. Through the communication exchange fostered by this charism of prophecy, the foundation is laid for an ecclesial democratization in harmony with both the nature of man and the revealed will of God.

1. THE FUNCTION OF PROPHECY

Prophecy can be defined in two ways: strictly and broadly. First, according to the strict definition, prophecy is a direct com-

---

[74] *Constitution on the Church*, Art. 37.

munication of a truth, natural or supernatural, that surpasses the power of human reason and is given to a person through a special enlightenment from God.[75] The gift of prophecy, then, enables a person to know and to communicate to others that which is ordinarily hidden from man's knowledge. The Greek word *prophetes* means one who speaks in the name of another. In this context the person speaks in the name of God. Prophecy may be a foretelling or predicting of the future, but primarily it is an inspired interpretation of the present, which is directed toward the eventual fulfillment of God's will. Secondly, according to the broad definition, prophecy is any communication of God's truth to men. This consists of teaching, witnessing, and any other action or word that manifests the Christian message. This kind of prophecy relies on the teaching of the Church and the deposit of faith. No special or direct communication from God is implied.

Prophecy in the strict sense is found in both the Old and New Testaments. One thing is constant: the prophet is one who speaks with authority in the name of the Lord. The Old Testament prophets knew Yahweh and were impelled to preach His word. They were called and inspired by God to announce to men the meaning of God's design as it applied to their daily lives. God gave them the ability to perceive clearly the will of God amid the complexities of the human situation. By this gift they were able to interpret the present in the light of God's plan.

---

[75] St. Thomas Aquinas, *Summa Theologica*, II–II, qq. 171–174. Although traditional notions of prophecy are based largely on St. Thomas, one should be aware of their limitations. The remarks of Bruce Vawter are appropriate: "Even St. Thomas' tractate *de prophetia*, while qualified by his usual balance and good sense, is seen more and more nowadays to be inadequate to the demands of biblical study. Beginning with Augustine, the Scholastic tradition relied far too heavily on aprioristic theories and prophecy derived from pagan, rabbinical and Muslim concepts, and far too little on what the Bible actually had to say about it or demonstrate about it. The earlier Protestant biblical criticism, however, scarcely offered anything better. . . . If for no other reason, it was inhibited by its philosophical inadequacies from elaborating its ideas systematically and relating them realistically to the historical situation it studied so assiduously" ("Recent Literature on the Prophets," in *The Human Reality of Sacred Scripture*, Vol. 10, *Concilium*, ed. P. Benoit and R. E. Murphy (New York: Paulist Press, 1965), p. 123.

Aside from this common characteristic, they did not possess similar personalities or use similar methods. Amos was a poor shepherd; Hosea, a suffering husband and father; Isaiah, an aristocrat; and Jeremias, a tragic figure and apparent failure. As a group they were unlikely heralds of God's word. They did unexpected and strange things, used harsh and critical words, and disturbed the establishment. Israel's prophets demanded that social evils be corrected and that Israel return to the tradition of its Fathers. In spite of rejection and suffering they persisted in their efforts to arouse men to embrace the truth of God's message.

In the New Testament the charism of prophecy is mentioned frequently. Apparently the office of prophet was a recognized ministry in the early Christian communities. St. Luke mentions Agabus (*Acts* 11:27), Judas, and Silas (*Acts* 15:32) as prophets of the Jerusalem church, and refers to Philip and his four daughters as prophesying in Caesarea (*Acts* 21:8). In the churches founded by Paul, prophets had an honored place. According to Paul, prophecy was the greatest of the charisms (I *Cor.* 14:1), a gift to be sought after (I *Cor.* 14:12,39). Prophecy in the Pauline writings is inspired utterance, a direct communication from God. It is given to some but not to all (I *Cor.* 12:29). Those who do receive it should use it for the improvement, consolation, and encouragement of the brethren (I *Cor.* 14:3) in order to build up the Body of Christ.

Prophecy in the broad sense, as any manifestation of God's word to man, was discussed at Vatican II.[76] The Council taught that all believers, and not just the hierarchy, share in the prophetic mission of Christ. As such they have the obligation of bearing witness to Christ in their lives. Experiencing the Christ-event, they should communicate it to others. In this way, the Christian community becomes a sign of the continuing revelation and presence of Christ in history. The prophet is aware of and sensitive to the flow of history. He is able to read the "signs of the times" and to detect the direction of God's will in a world of limited human achievements and contradictory forces. Each

---

[76] Cf. *Constitution on the Church*, Arts. 11, 12, 31, 35, and *Decree on the Apostolate of the Laity*, Arts. 2, 10.

Christian fulfills his prophetic role differently, but primarily "by means of a life of faith and charity."[77]

An example of the broad coverage of the charism of prophecy is that public opinion in the Church can be a manifestation of prophecy. Vatican II taught that "an individual layman . . . is permitted and sometimes even obliged to express his opinion on things which concern the good of the Church."[78] The free expression of public opinion is guaranteed in civil democracies but has often been restricted in the ecclesial system. Yet it is necessary, if officeholders are to know what is happening within the Church and to learn how effective is their leadership. Public opinion, as an input channel, communicates both demands and supports. A democratized Church must recognize the principle that the Spirit speaks through the laity as well as the hierarchy.

Contemporary theologians insist that prophecy in both senses is needed in the Church today.[79] All Christians should lead a fully committed life in the Spirit, but there are some who are called to do more. These are persons who have the special responsibility to speak in the name of the Lord in condemning abuses and in suggesting patterns for renewal. "Prophecy," as John L. McKenzie notes, "occurs when other channels have become clouded and thinking is obscured."[80] The prophet is one who, guided by the Spirit, courageously speaks out against complacency and challenges Church leaders and members when they deviate from Christian principles. The prophetic input frequently disturbs the status quo. Initial reaction to it is often hostile. In spite of this, the prophet must continue to proclaim his message. If he is really a herald of truth, sooner or later his credibility will be established. False prophets we know are a perennial threat to the Church. Jesus warned his followers to beware of false prophets and gave what has become a rule for discernment:

[77] *Constitution on the Church*, Art. 12.

[78] *Ibid.*, Art. 37. Also see K. Rahner, *Free Speech in the Church* (New York: Sheed and Ward, 1959).

[79] Cf. Y. Congar, *Lay People in the Church*, pp. 258–308; K. Rahner, *Visions and Prophecies* (New York: Herder and Herder, 1964); J. L. McKenzie, *Authority in the Church*, pp. 151–161; and R. Aubert, ed. *Prophets in the Church*, Vol. 37, *Concilium* (New York: Paulist Press, 1968).

[80] McKenzie, *Authority in the Church*, p. 156.

"You will recognize them by the fruits they bear" (*Matt.* 7:15). Prophecies must be proven: "Bring them all to the test and keep what is good in them and avoid the bad of whatever kind" (I *Thess.* 5:21-22).

2. Infallibility and the Faithful

Vatican II described another way in which Christians exercise a prophetic ministry. The entire Church is said to possess an infallible character. In the *Constitution of the Church* we read: "The Holy People of God shares also in Christ's prophetic mission. . . . The body of the faithful as a whole, anointed as they are by the Holy One, cannot err in matters of belief (*in credendo*). Thanks to a supernatural sense of faith (*sensu fidei*) which characterizes the people as a whole, it manifests this unerring quality when 'from the bishops down to the last member of the laity,'[81] it shows universal agreement (*universalem consensum*) in matters of faith and morals."[82]

This text, similar to the position of the Orthodox Church,[83] necessitated a reinterpretation of the traditional distinction between the teaching Church (*ecclesia docens*) and the learning or believing Church (*ecclesia discens*). In the past a rigid dichotomy was often understood. The conclusion was that there are two separate parts of the Church: one, the hierarchy, whose duty it is to teach; and another, the laity, whose duty it is to obey. The former had an active role and the latter a passive one. Vatican II, from a charismatic perspective, proposed a different view. It taught that there is an intimate, reciprocal relationship between the teaching Church and the believing Church because of the presence of the Spirit. The People of God collectively are infallible in believing (*in credendo*).[84] The hierarchy and the laity

---

[81] St. Augustine, *De Praedestinatione Sanctorum*, 14, 27 (PL 44:980).

[82] *Constitution on the Church*, Art. 12.

[83] This idea is very close to the Orthodox notion of *sobornost*. Cf. R. Murray, "Collegiality, Infallibility and Sobornost," *One in Christ*, I (1965), 19–42, and G. Dejaifve, "Sobornost ou papauté," *Nouvelle revue théologique*, 84 (1952), 355–371; 466–484.

[84] Cf. G. Thils, *L'infallibilité du peuple chrétien 'in credendo'* (Paris: Desclée de Brouwer, 1963).

share a common faith. One can say that the teaching Church and the believing Church are united in learning; God alone teaches and men learn.

The college of bishops under the leadership of the pope is, by divine right, the official teacher of that truth revealed to the whole Church. The college of bishops, therefore, besides being infallible *in credendo* is also infallible *in docendo* (in teaching). But even this infallibility is related to the People of God. The teaching of the Church reflects the belief of the entire Church. Vatican I taught that the pope possesses that infallibility "with which the divine Redeemer willed His Church to be endowed."[85] The hierarchy thus teaches infallibly that which the whole Church believes. Rahner insists that "the believing Church can and must be consulted by the magisterium."[86] The judgment of the magisterium is based on tradition, which can only be determined by referring to the faith of the Church. The process of teaching, therefore, involves what Newman called the *"pastorum et fidelium conspiratio,"*[87] the union of the hierarchy and the laity as witnesses to the faith.

The terms *sensus fidelium* et *consensus fidelium* appear in every discussion of the laity's relationship to the teaching Church. We will examine each of these expressions. The *sensus fidelium* (the *sensus fidei* corporately present in the community of believers) is a sensitivity to and a perception of God's revelation. It is the ability of the faithful to discern whether or not a particular teaching is consonant with divine truth.[88] The *sensus fidelium* is neither the private judgment of the laity in opposition to the hierarchy nor an act which validates hierarchic

[85] Denzinger-Schönmetzer, 3074.

[86] K. Rahner and H. Vorgrimler, *Theological Dictionary* (New York: Herder and Herder, 1965), p. 269.

[87] J. H. Newman, *On Consulting the Faithful in Matters of Doctrine*, ed. J. Coulson (New York: Sheed and Ward, 1962). p. 104. Cf. also S. D. Femiano, *Infallibility of the Laity* (New York: Herder and Herder, 1967).

[88] C. Dillenschneider defines the *sensus fidei* as "the intuitive sense of the believer, the fruit of his faith and the gifts of the Holy Spirit, through which he is endowed with a facility in discerning, within the communion of the Church, what is implicit in the revealed truth objectively proposed to him by the magisterium." *Le sens de la progrès dogmatique du mystère marial* (Rome: Academia Mariana Internationalis, 1954), p. 327.

teaching, as some Gallican and Slavophile theologians held.[89] Rather it is an intuition or understanding of the faith. Because of this special gift of the Spirit, the Church as a whole is infallible.[90] The People of God can thus ˈpenetrate more deeply the revealed message, but always, as the Council noted, "under the lead of a sacred teaching authority to which it loyally defers."[91]

The *consensus fidelium* is the unanimous agreement of the faithful concerning their belief in a revealed truth. If it is universal and pertains to the area of faith and morals, the *consensus fidelium* is infallible. In some circles, however, any connection between the faithful and infallibility is still looked upon with suspicion. The source of this uneasiness is the dogmatic definition of papal infallibility at Vatican I. The Council taught that *ex cathedra* pronouncements are irreformable, "*ex sese, non autem ex consensu ecclesiae.*"[92]

The word *consensus* has an interesting history.[93] During the conciliar debates at Vatican I it was frequently used in the patristic and traditional sense of "agreement." The teaching of the magisterium, therefore, is in "agreement" with the belief of the entire Church. Vatican II employs the term once according to that usage.[94] In the definition of infallibility in Vatican I, however, *consensus* was given a very specific meaning of jurid-

---

[89] On this point Cf. *Ibid.*, pp. 266–270, and Congar, *Lay People in the Church*, pp. 265–266.

[90] The *relatio* on this section which was discussed at Vatican II gives an excellent summary: "The Church in which Christ lives on after the completion of His salvific work and which is led by the Holy Spirit to truth, simply cannot deviate from the way of salvation, and, therefore, in this sense is infallible. Although it does not perfectly comprehend the mystery, it is nevertheless preserved from error through the assistance of the Spirit and thus cannot be deceived." (*Schema constitutionis de ecclesia* [Rome: Ex Typis Polyglottis Vaticanis, 1964], pp. 45–46). Translation from G. B. Wilson, "The Gift of Infallibility: Reflections Toward a Systematic Theology," *Theological Studies*, 31 (1970), 629–630.

[91] *Constitution on the Church*, Art. 12.

[92] Denzinger-Schönmetzer, 3074.

[93] Cf. G. Dejaifve, "Ex sese, non autem ex consensu ecclesiae," *Eastern Churches Quarterly*, 14 (1962), 360–378, and T. A. Caffrey, "Consensus and Infallibility: The Mind of Vatican I," *Downside Review*, 88 (1970), 107–131.

[94] *Constitution on the Church*, Art. 12.

ical consent or approval. In order to avoid the Gallican interpretation,[95] the Council taught that there can be no absolute,
strict, legal necessity, no indispensable condition which would
require the pope to have the approval (*consensus*) of the bishops
and the faithful before his teaching is accepted as infallible.
In Vatican I, *consensus* means ratification. Hence the definition
of infallibility means that *ex cathedra* statements are irreformable
of themselves and not from the ratification of the Church.

Many of the Fathers at Vatican I argued that the gift of papal
infallibility does not separate the pope from the rest of the
Church. Archbishop Dechamps, for example, quoting Robert
Bellarmine and Pope Gregory XVI, explained that the pope does
not rashly define dogmas but uses appropriate means to discern
the truth. These means include consultation with wise men,
convocation of councils, and inquiry among the bishops.[96]
Cardinal Guidi likewise held that the pope depends on the
Church in the sense that he must ascertain "whether the truth
to be defined is truly contained in the deposit of tradition."[97]
Bishop Gasser was the leading spokesman for the need of consulting the faithful. "The pope," he stated, "is bound to apply
the means appropriate for properly investigating the truth and
appropriately expressing it."[98] The means differ with the truth
that is to be defined. On some occasions an ecumenical council
may be necessary, on others consultation with learned men.
While Gasser affirmed that "we are not able to separate the
pope from the *consensus* of the Church,"[99] he also made it
clear that the *consensus* was not an absolute condition of infallibility.

Vatican II repeated the definition of infallibility of Vatican I
and used the term *consensus* in the strict sense.[100] It also
taught that since infallible definitions are made with the assist-

[95] Cf. Gallican articles, Denzinger-Schönmetzer, 2281-2284.

[96] Mansi, LII, 67-68. This type of consultation was undertaken before
the definition of the Assumption in 1950. Cf. G. Hentrich and R. G. de
Moos, *Petitiones de Assumptione corporea B. V. Mariae in caelum de-
finienda ad S. Sedem delatae* (Rome: Ex Typis Polyglottis Vaticanis, 1942).

[97] Mansi, LII, 745-746.

[98] *Ibid.*, 1213.

[99] *Ibid.*, 1213-1214.

[100] *Constitution on the Church*, Art. 25.

ance of the Holy Spirit, "they need no approval of others, nor do they allow an appeal to any other judgment."[101] Yet Vatican II urged that the pope and the bishops "strive painstakingly and by appropriate means to inquire properly into that revelation and to give apt expression to its contents."[102] Although no specific means were enumerated, certain ones do suggest themselves. The college of bishops should make use of the input channels that operate within the ecclesial system: national episcopal conferences; theological writings; testimony of experts; lay and clerical organizations; and the work done by research centers. Use of these means can assist the college in determining the genuine *consensus fidelium*.

The prophetic participation of the faithful in the decision-making of the Church should not be divorced from an ecumenical perspective.[103] If the Church is an open system, then it must interact with its environment. An important part of this environment is the non-Catholic Christian world. Vatican II officially acknowledged other churches and ecclesial communities;[104] it recognized an "ecclesial reality" in other denominations. In a genuine theological sense all Christians share a common heritage. If this is true, then we should look to our fellow Christians for insights into the life-giving truth of Christ. Ecumenical input, therefore, is extremely significant. The present dialogue among Christians is a movement of the Spirit and gives us an opportunity to grow in knowledge. The doctrinal formulations of other

[101] *Ibid.* In recent years the question of papal infallibility has again become a controversial issue for theologians. Cf. F. Simons, *Infallibility and the Evidence* (Springfield, Ill.: Templegate, 1968); H. Küng, *Infallible? An Inquiry* (Garden City, N.Y.: Doubleday, 1971); and J. J. Kirvan, ed., *The Infallibility Debate* (New York: Paulist Press, 1971).

[102] *Constitution on the Church*, Art. 25. Cf. also Vatican I, Denzinger-Schönmetzer, 3069.

[103] Cf. O. Rousseau, "Prophecy and Ecumenism," *Prophets in the Church*, 99–112, and J. R. Nelson, "Toward an Ecumenical Ecclesiology," *Theological Studies*, 31 (1970), 644–673.

[104] *Constitution on the Church*, Art. 15, and *Decree on Ecumenism*, chapter 3. On the problem of "ecclesial reality," see R. E. Hunt, "The Separated Christian Churches and Communities in the Mystery of Salvation," in *Proceedings of the Catholic Theological Society of America, 1966* (Yonkers, N.Y.: St. Joseph's Seminary, 1967), pp. 21–32, and J. O. McGovern, *The Church in the Churches* (Washington, Corpus, 1968).

churches and their witness to the Christian ideal deserve our most attentive and prayerful consideration. The ecumenical magisterium is too valuable a source to be neglected. To do so would be to sin against the light.[105]

CONCLUSION

Cybernetically, democracy protects and maximizes human dignity by providing for the greatest input of the supports and demands of its members and the greatest participation by them in the process whereby these inputs are converted into authoritative decisions.

The Church is a unique political organization with a God-given character. For democracy to function in the Church it must be compatible with the Church's nature. History and theology are necessary in order to ascertain this compatibility.

Historically, in the New Testament and in the earlier centuries of the Christian era, the Church encouraged regularized input from its members, even in so important a function as selecting its bishops. This practice, however, declined and finally disappeared as the Church grew larger and became more centralized.

Theologically, power in the Church is held to come directly from God and not from the people. But nothing prevents the designation of the decision-makers by the members of the Church. Moreover, this same type of decision-making could function in other areas, excepting, of course, the special prerogatives of the pope and the college of bishops.

Despite the historical and theological compatibility of democracy and the Church, the actual decision to democratize depends ultimately on the practicalities of democratic rule in the parish, diocese, and universal Church. It is here, however, that ecclesial cybernetics is of special value. In itself, cybernetics is a neutral instrument of analysis. But from this analysis, one may learn whether or not the present structure of the Church is enabling it to fulfill its task of sanctifying man and glorifying God.

[105] The manifestation of the Spirit in non-Christian religions should also be seriously considered. Germinal work in this area has been done by H. R. Schlette, *Towards a Theology of Religions* (New York: Herder and Herder, 1966).

From our analysis of ecclesial cybernetics, we would suggest a greater role for Church members, both clerical and lay, in selecting their decision-makers and even in participating in decision-making itself. Without in any way diminishing the character of the Body of Christ, this fuller sharing of responsibility by all the members must surely foster genuine Christian maturity.

PART FOUR

Future Ecclesial Democracy

THE THESIS OF THIS BOOK is that the Church needs cybernetic reform through democratization. In practice, this means that the faithful should have a more effective voice in the decision-making process, that the authorities should be more open and responsive to input of all kinds, and that the system itself should develop a more refined communications network. These goals are consonant with the divine mission of the Church. In fact, their realization is necessary if that mission is to be fulfilled in today's world.

The need for reform in the Roman Catholic Church is too obvious to demand extensive documentation. Clearly, a critical point has been reached when many bishops withhold complete support from a papal encyclical; when two American bishops resign in protest over Church policy; when priests are so estranged from their bishops that open defiance becomes commonplace; when thousands leave the priesthood and religious life; and finally, when the faithful add their voices to the chorus of clerical dissent. An immense credibility gap exists between officials and members of the Church. The optimism of Vatican II has given way to massive apathy and confusion. Renewal efforts have slowed down and have produced, too frequently, division rather than unity. To talk to any group of Catholics on the merits of the English liturgy, on the new nuns and priests, or on contemporary theology is to sense the sharpness of this division. Nevertheless, liberals and conservatives alike are, for different reasons, dissatisfied with the present state of the Church. Some Catholics are hopeful; others are pessimistic; only the naive are complacent.

The Church today is on the defensive. In cybernetic terms, it is fighting the age-old battle against entropy and social deterioration. The Church faces a problem that is a perennial one for large organizations, namely, the existence of complex structures which no longer adequately meet current needs. When structures begin to lose their vitality, conflicts arise. This is happening in the present Church. There is no assurance that these conflicts will gradually decrease. In the last several years there has been a marked loss of confidence in the Church, and its leaders have not been successful in restoring it.

This bleak picture must, however, be balanced by the fact that the Church is no stranger to conflict. From the beginning it has met and overcome severe opposition. A Church that has survived the fall of the Roman Empire, the end of the Middle Ages, and the challenge of the Industrial Revolution must have a great adaptability. The present crisis will certainly not see the demise of the Church. It has survived and it will survive. Its members affirm the Church's indefectibility. Nevertheless, they acknowledge that no dogma holds that the Church will be immune from spiritual apathy, social deterioration, or governmental weakness. The pages of history attest to this. Such social maladies may not be terminal, but they do impede the Church in its mission of preaching salvation through Christ. It is necessary now that constructive solutions be proposed to assist the Church in extricating itself from the morass of confusion and in restoring once again mutual trust among its members. Democratization of the Church is foundational to any far-reaching and lasting solution to this problem.

The solution, however, lies neither in instant renewal nor in a return to the past. Both must be rejected because they are based on a faulty assessment of the present situation. It is naive to believe that the Church can suddenly regain its vigor by sweeping organizational reforms or vastly improved channels of communication. The present dilemma of the Church is far too complex to be solved immediately. Myriad factors over the centuries have shaped the present Church. They will not be corrected quickly. Development—like its opposite; retrogression—takes time: ideas must germinate and be tested before they can be accepted and implemented. Moreover, it is unrealistic to hope that the Church can solve its problems by returning to its days of former glory. It will not do this because it cannot. Too many radical changes have occurred in the Church and in the secular world for this to happen. New problems and challenges are present. Former responses are inadequate. The old mold has been broken, and it is futile to try to reconstruct it. The Church of the future may be better or worse, but it will never be the same.

The cybernetic solution proposed here attempts to avoid both of the above extremes. It will not effect sudden reform, nor will it attempt to re-create the past. What it will do, we hope, is to set up a system within which continuous self-renewal and growth can occur. Societies, as they age, tend to become paralyzed by rigid customs and fading creativity. Information feedback and co-responsibility can restore youthfulness to the Church, helping it regain flexibility and the increased capacity needed to meet unexpected challenges. By broadening the decision-making process and developing open channels of communication, the Church can become more innovative and adaptive. Both stability and progress can thus be achieved. Changes will always be necessary, but these changes must not destroy continuity nor impede growth. The Church, as in Arnold Toynbee's description of civilization, is, "a movement . . . and not a condition, a voyage and not a harbor."[1] Through a fuller and more creative use of information supplied by all parts of the ecclesial system, the Church will be more apt to move forward toward its own self-awareness as the Body of Christ.

Renewal does not take place automatically. It happens because

---

[1] "The Graeco-Roman Civilization," *Civilization on Trial* and *The World and the West* (New York: World Publishing Co., 1958), p. 50.

people want it to happen and work toward it. No plan for renewal, cybernetic or not, can succeed if there is apathy. As John W. Gardner perceptively writes: "Men who believe in nothing, change nothing for the better. They renew nothing and heal no one, least of all themselves."[2] Commitment, therefore, is an essential ingredient for a self-renewal of the Church. People must care if progress is to be more than notional. Faith in Christ and his Church must be implemented by dedicated action. Renewal in the Church is impossible without the concomitant spiritual revitalization of individual believers. The two complement one another. Unless the Gospel message permeates the life of the faithful, even the best program for reconstruction is destined to failure.

Earlier parts of this book presented three observations of prime significance: first, that a system's adaptability to difficult and changing circumstances is proportioned to its informational input; second, that participatory democracy is an ideal vehicle for this input; and third, that some of the earliest forms of Church government were democratic. It would seem on the basis of these ideas that the Church in this critical period might well renew itself through this time-tested method—greater input through democratization. In this part we will consider: first, the problems of ecclesial democratization; and second, its practical implementation.

[2] *Self-Renewal—The Individual and the Innovative Society* (New York: Harper and Row, 1964), p. xiv.

10

The Problems
of Ecclesial Democracy

IN PRECEDING CHAPTERS, we have purposely omitted any lengthy discussion of the many difficulties that confront ecclesial democracy. The time has come to consider some of these problems. Since the success or failure of renewal depends upon both the hierarchical and nonhierarchical members of the Church, it will be in these two groups that the major obstacles are found.

I. *The Hierarchy*

Leaders in the Church, like their counterparts in civil society, tend to be unreceptive to new ideas involving large-scale changes. In some instances, this caution has been providential. Many self-styled prophets have preached innovations which would have severely compromised the Church. Discerning leaders, sensing potential danger, rejected these teachings. Unfortunately, the Church has also on occasion been equally resistant to truly prophetic ideas. It has often failed to perceive the genuine value of many creative suggestions. Will demands for democratization in the Church be similarly discouraged? If so, the major fault will be found in certain attitudes of the decision-makers. In the hierarchy of the Church today there are three specific problems: immobility, ineffectuality, and isolation.

Immobility is a constant fixture in the corridors of power, rarely because of a dearth of new ideas, but chiefly because of a lack of receptivity. Rigid attitudes can be formidable obstacles to change. Caution characterizes many Church leaders who put in years as underlings before they become bishops. By training and perhaps by temperament, they develop a reluctance to endorse anything that disturbs fixed patterns. Content to maintain an older tradition, they often employ methods which are unsuitable to meet new challenges. Myopic overconfidence in any system makes change difficult. Vested interests, ideological as much as monetary, encapsulate initiative. This proprietary stance encourages the formation of personalities that are inflexible and resistant to change. Innovation for them is seen not as an opportunity but as a threat. Adaptation is something that is grudgingly accepted when it becomes unavoidable—the only way out of a crisis.

The long terms of office of Church leaders also foster immobility. Such lengthy tenure is unusual in big business or government. And for good reasons. The demanding challenges of leadership take a heavy physical and psychological toll. Moreover, if an office-holder is assured that he will remain in his post for several decades, there is a good chance he will become less productive as the years pass. Rome has taken some steps to correct this by asking bishops and pastors to submit their resignations no later than their seventy-fifth year.[1] It has been suggested that specific terms be set for all Church leaders: pope, bishops, and pastors. The Archdiocese of New York was the first diocese in the United States formally to limit pastors to a maximum of twelve years. The new policy also provides for a thorough review of a pastor's work every three years. The New

---

[1] On the retirement of bishops see *Decree on the Bishops' Pastoral Office in the Church*, Art. 21, and *Ecclesiae sanctae*, I, 11. On the retirement of pastors see *ibid.*, Art. 31 and I, 20. The U.S. Bishops' Ad Hoc Committee on Priestly Life and Ministry have recommended that an interdisciplinary committee study the question of limited tenure for bishops. Cf. *Origins (NC Documentary Service)*, October 26, 1972, vol. 2: no. 18, pp. 285, 287, 299, 300.

York rotation plan is expected to lower the age at which younger priests become pastors.

Efforts at further democratization in the Church will meet with resistance from some immobile Church officials. It is inevitable that pleas for shared responsibility, consensual decision-making, and elective procedures will face strong opposition. Some will deplore the change as contrary to tradition. Others will see it as dangerous, or at least inopportune. In the past, the prestige of Church authorities and the power they wielded was sufficient to discourage innovators. This is no longer true. Ideas must now be judged on their merits not according to an aprioristic mind-set.

Ineffectuality of Church leadership also weakens renewal efforts. Indecisive and uninformed bishops can hardly be expected to read the "signs of the times" accurately and to make appropriate adaptations. A bishop, in the words of Vatican II, is "the principal dispenser of the mysteries of God"[2] and "the high priest of his flock."[3] His ultimate goal is "that all men walk 'in all goodness and justice and truth' " (*Eph.* 5:9).[4] A deep spirituality, then, is required of those who are special ministers of the divine Word. Moreover, as decision-makers and servants of the people, bishops need to be well-informed, open to advice and criticism, and, above all, sensitive to the concerns of their fellow Christians. To the extent that defensiveness and closed-mindedness increase, effectiveness decreases. Outstanding bishops are desperately needed now to guide the Church through this troubled transitional period. Conflict and unrest in the Church create a heavy episcopal burden. St. Augustine's comments on the office of bishop are applicable today:

> What I am for you terrifies me; what I am with you consoles me. For you I am a bishop, but with you I am a Christian. The first is a duty accepted, the second a grace received. The former is a danger, the latter salvation. Since it is a far greater joy to me to be redeemed with you than to be placed over you, I shall, as the Lord commanded, be more completely your servant.[5]

---

[2] *Decree on the Bishops' Pastoral Office in the Church*, Art. 15.
[3] *Constitution on the Sacred Liturgy*, Art. 41.
[4] *Decree on the Bishops' Pastoral Office in the Church*, Art. 11.
[5] St. Augustine, *Sermo* 340 (PL 38:1483).

There are several reasons why so many Church leaders are labeled ineffectual. First, their selection process is inadequate. In the final analysis they are chosen by their peers, rather than by a representative group of clergy and laity. This procedure encourages inbreeding, patronage, and promotion based more on unquestioning loyalty than on merit.

Second, the "upward mobility" syndrome of bishops, especially in the United States, is undesirable. Young bishops, once admitted to the episcopal fraternity, must be careful not to harm their chances for advancement. Bishops must impress the Holy See with their ability and reliability, since transfers to more prestigious dioceses and elevation to the rank of archbishop or cardinal may be open to them. There was once a solid patristic and canonical tradition that forbade a bishop to leave his diocese and take up another. The analogy frequently used was that the bishop was indissolubly wedded to his flock and became a "spiritual adulterer" if he moved to another diocese.[6] In the Eastern Churches this idea is still accepted. Such a rule effectively limits episcopal ambition and its unfortunate by-products.

A third reason for ineffectuality among ecclesiastics is incompetence—which is no respecter of rank or persons. The Peter Principle is applicable here: "In a hierarchy every employee tends to rise to his level of incompetence."[7] By hierarchy is meant any organization—government, business, academic, or religious—in which the members are arranged according to rank or class. The nature of organization, Peter argues, allows members to rise in the hierarchy until they no longer perform satisfactorily enough to merit further promotion, until they achieve incompetence or final placement. It is only a question of time until every post in the hierarchy is filled with people incompetent to carry out their duties. Who, then, does the work? "The

---

[6] This term is used by Pope Callistus, St. Jerome, Pope Siricius, and others cited in W. W. Bassett, "Subsidiarity, Order and Freedom in the Church," in *The Once and Future Church*, ed. J. A. Coriden (Staten Island, N.Y.: Alba House, 1971), p. 224. Bassett adds: "The Latin practice of recent centuries is a scandal, for it supposes the bishop to be primarily an appointed administrator, not the chosen leader of a Christian people."

[7] L. J. Peter and R. Hull, *The Peter Principle* (New York: William Morrow, 1969), p. 25.

work is accomplished," according to Professor Peter, "by those employees who have not yet reached their level of incompetence."[8]

The satirical and pseudoscientific tone of the Peter Principle does not invalidate its main thrust. Incompetence is rampant in every organization. The sacramental power of episcopal consecration carries with it no immunity against incompetence. Many persons who are qualified for subordinate positions show themselves to be incompetent when promoted. An old monastic axiom warned against this possibility: the prior should never become abbot (*Prior numquam abbas*). Nor do successful fund-raisers, famed preachers, or distinguished scholars necessarily make good bishops. Many priests, elevated to the episcopal rank, find the task beyond their intellectual, psychological, and spiritual competence. Unable to handle their new responsibilities successfully, they may resort to various stratagems to counterbalance their inadequacies. Procrastination, misguided confrontation, or insipid compromise may become part of their *modus operandi*.

Prudent risk-taking should be a working technique for Church leaders. Unless the courage to fail is present, renewal is inconceivable. "Men will always be making mistakes," Goethe said, "as long as they are striving after something."[9] This does not mean the abandonment of prudence or the wholehearted acceptance of any and every idea. It does mean the recognition of pluralism within the Church and the acceptance of the possibility that other and better ways may be found to solve critical situations. Heavy-handed suppression of dissent may have short-term success, but in the end it is productive only of further and more hostile opposition. A circulation of fresh talent in the hierarchy is needed badly at this time. Young, energetic, and informed bishops would give great impetus to renewal efforts. There is evidence that a few younger American bishops are beginning to move away from the conservative patterns of their elders. Perhaps they will be the leaven of a "new breed" of episcopal leadership.

[8] *Ibid.*, p. 27.
[9] Quoted in W. L. B. Beveridge, *The Art of Scientific Investigation* (New York: W. W. Norton, 1957), p. 60.

The *isolation* of Church authorities is the third major obstacle that can impede the implementation of ecclesial democratization. Open communication and free exchange of information cannot function when leaders isolate themselves from their constituency. Feedback has no value when bishops become "chancery prisoners," who hear only what their trusted advisors want them to hear. When acceptable input is restricted to supportive accolades, a deadening complacency results. Removed from the real world of conflict, such bishops are out of touch with the genuine needs of their flock. In large urban dioceses this can easily happen. Administrative details can occupy most of the bishop's time, leaving him little energy for valuable spiritual leadership. It is tragic when unilateral decisions, with little or no consultation, become the norm rather than the exception. In such an alien environment cybernetic progress, with its emphasis on openness and flexibility, has no chance of survival. Preoccupation with the smooth running of administrative machinery can close the doors to creative communication. The faithful are expected to be docile, to obey, and to make adequate financial contributions. Frequently, little thought is given to their unique witness or to the vast potential of energy and wisdom within their ranks. Leaders who are remote from their members neglect this rich source of help.

The unsuitable use of language is another reason for the communicative isolation of many Church authorities. Clarity and credibility, the hallmarks of effective communication, are often absent in Church pronouncements. Obfuscation rather than illumination seems to be the effect of many papal and episcopal statements. A Victorian and platitudinous style still persists. Saint Hilary's prayer should not be forgotten: "Grant us precision in language, light of understanding, grace of style, and loyalty to truth."[10]

How does the ordinary Catholic react to official Church documents? If he reads them at all, he probably finds them unconvincing. They are usually too pious, abstract, or polemical to make any impact. Often they are like typical United States Government documents, which Harold Orlans described as "baked, blanched, steamed, starched, and utterly devoid of

---

[10] St. Hilary, *On the Trinity*, I, 38 (PL 10:49).

human emotion."[11] People used to the crisp style of *Time* or *Newsweek* and the incisive comments of television reporters find Church pronouncements painfully dull. Church officials desperately need someone to advise them on what to say and what not to say, how to say it, and when to say it. Too often, in the past, the medium of ecclesiastical statements became the message.

Roman documents present a special problem. What language should the Church use to speak officially to its some 500 million members? How can it speak with one voice to diverse peoples? For more than seventeen hundred years, Latin has been the official language of the Church. This choice has obvious advantages. Latin is a precise, inflected language with a stable vocabulary, grammar, and syntax. Ancient documents are as easily read as recent ones. Latin, as it transcends the varieties and changes of the other world languages, symbolizes ecclesial unity and continuity. On the other hand, Latin has disadvantages, too. It is a dead language in a modern world. Few people study it, and even those who do feel unequal to the task of translating a Roman document. This hesitancy is true also of priests and religious, especially since the vernacular liturgy and divine office have made the knowledge of Latin less necessary even for them. Moreover, today significant Vatican documents are translated in many modern languages. These translations, however, often contain serious discrepancies, at times of a substantial nature. This frequently happens because the document was not originally written in Latin. The encyclical *Pacem in terris*, for example, was first written in Italian, and *Populorum progressio* in French. These were then translated into Latin, which became the official, authoritative text. In both of these encyclicals, serious debate and misunderstanding resulted because the vernacular texts and the Latin text did not agree. One can support the proposal made by the editors of *America*, who suggested that a document should be issued in the language in which it was originally written. That version should be official, and all other versions, Latin included, should be considered as derivative.[12]

Secrecy is another pillar of hierarchical isolation. Needless

---

[11] "The Apoplectic Years," *Saturday Review*, January 10, 1970, p. 33.
[12] *America*, April 22, 1967, p. 577.

secrecy is a violation of the faithful's right to know. It creates an atmosphere of distrust and gives rise to rumor and half-truths. In democratic societies, the norm is as much openness as possible in matters that concern the common good. The Church, unfortunately, has often acted according to another norm: What the faithful do not know will not disturb them. Ignorance, then, becomes the best guarantee of security. In the past, the Church has exercised excessive caution in the matter of secrecy and thereby weakened its credibility. Issues that involve the whole Church are too frequently discussed behind closed doors.

Secret documents, however, have a way of reaching the public. The partial report of the Birth Control Commission, for example, appeared in *Le Monde* and in the *National Catholic Reporter* without any official approbation. This has happened with several other "top secret" Vatican documents. Increased suspicion and lack of confidence in the Church has resulted. Unofficial disclosure also raises a knotty ethical problem. Those who leak secret materials remain anonymous. They are apparently motivated by what they consider to be the cause of justice and truth. At the same time, their action smacks of professional disloyalty and betrayal of trust.

The total abolition of secrecy in the Church is, of course, unwarranted. Limited secrecy and confidentiality have a legitimate justification. This is especially true when the reputation and private life of an individual is at stake. The Church, for example, may take disciplinary measures against a person without publicly revealing the full circumstances. This is done to protect him from embarrassment. The recent *Pastoral Instruction on the Means of Social Communication* wisely limits the use of secrecy: "Secrecy should therefore be restricted to matters that involve the good name of individuals or that touch upon the rights of people whether singly or collectively."[13] Secret meetings at times are necessary. Even in the most open of democratic governments a certain amount of high-level confidential discussion is normal. There should be no objection to similar procedures in the Church. What is reprehensible is applying secrecy to those matters that rightfully concern the whole Church.

[13] Washington: United States Catholic Conference, 1971, Art. 121.

Encouraging signs are appearing. The National Conference of Catholic Bishops at its November 1971 meeting voted to open most of its meetings to newsmen and other observers. Many dioceses in the United States have made public their financial statements. The veil of secrecy is gradually being lifted. It can only have a good effect in restoring good will and mutual trust.

Ecclesial democratization, then, to be successful must have the support of Church authorities. If they are convinced of its value, the task of implementing it becomes much easier. Statistically, there are not many members of the hierarchy who are enthusiastic about a democratized Church. European and Canadian bishops are much more open to the idea than their American colleagues. Many in the American Catholic hierarchy, however, still evidence some immobility, ineffectualism, and isolationism. There are, of course, other bishops who are genuine spiritual leaders, gifted with remarkable flexibility, competence, and awareness. The majority of bishops, however, fear a decentralized Church, since they see it not only as a threat to episcopal and papal power but as a serious danger to the unity of faith. These doubts are not unreasonable, as history has shown. Yet we feel that in the Church of today, the advantages of a greater openness outweigh its disadvantages. Progress has been made. The approval of parish councils and priests' senates is significant. There are also some grounds for hope that a new generation of Church leaders will emerge who will be more attuned to contemporary needs and more willing to experiment. As yet they are not in positions of power, but that time may come. In the meantime, demands for broader decision-making will continue to accelerate.

II. *The Clergy and the Laity*

Decision-making in the Catholic Church is highly concentrated: Some 3,000 bishops rule some 500,000,000 clergy and laity. Although the lower clergy do have some supervisory power, Church authority is fundamentally the prerogative of the hierarchy. It would, therefore, be a radical change to allow participation by millions of Catholics in the authority of the power elite of 3,000 bishops. Problems would inevitably arise, as we see from a consideration of the two types of new participants.

A. THE CLERGY

The co-responsibility of bishops and clergy has not been a major problem in the Church, because the clergy have generally deferred to hierarchical wishes. This subordination, however, has not been entirely voluntary, though it has certainly been taken for granted. One should realize that the power of a bishop over his priests is protected by moral and canonical laws as well as by economic dependencies. The current agitation for due process in ecclesial litigation, primarily in disputes between priest and bishop, suggests the hitherto almost unchallengeable power of the local bishop. A priest who insisted too persistently on his rights found himself at the mercy of his adversary. He did not litigate from a position of strength, for he was locked into the ecclesial system. To leave the priesthood was socially shameful and economically unfeasible. He was usually not prepared for a nonpastoral job, he had no savings, and he would be ostracized by the Christian community. Moreover, an ex-priest was rarely given permission to marry. The result of all these controls was a dependent and docile clergy.

Two things have changed the attitude of the clergy. The first is Vatican II's emphasis on liberty, equality, and collegiality. These were revolutionary ideas for the traditionally submissive clergy. They accepted wholeheartedly this authoritative output of the ecumenical council of bishops and pope. These words fell on fertile ground, for the second factor in changing the attitude of the clergy was the emphasis in secular society on human rights, minority power, and participatory democracy. Priests were involved in protests and demonstrations in areas such as poverty, war, discrimination, welfare, and housing. Then they began to turn their efforts to Church reform. They applied these secular principles canonized by Vatican II to their relationship to their pastor, their bishop, and their pope.

The result has been a steady stream of demands from the clergy to the system, including such diverse items as due process, optional celibacy, laicization with dignity, salary parity, retirement and health benefits, election rights, collegial parishes, job selection, priests' senates, disclosures of church finances, and socially active and outspoken bishops. In the past, the clergy's input consisted primarily of supports. Now demands are in the preponderance. These demands, however, are not simply individual communications. The clergy has organized within dioceses and on regional, national, and international lines. Both activists and intellectuals have united for what is ultimately a greater share in ecclesial power.

Increased power for priests, although essentially a good thing, will undoubtedly give rise to problems. After their release from political bondage, the clergy may experience that inebriation from sudden liberation that sometimes borders on excess. But it will be a tame exuberance moderated by the disciplined sacerdotal way of life. Of course, there will be problems. Here are some possible ones: (1) the rebel spirit of the successful revolutionary may tempt some priests to an attitude of contumaciousness; (2) the tendency may develop to consider doctrinal truth the product of a majority vote; (3) the order in the Church may be weakened by a move toward ecclesial anarchy; (4) the clergy may form an opposition party to the hierarchy or may split into factions; and (5) factions among the clergy may develop deep and even schismatic parallels among the laity.

Nevertheless an abundance of problems is no sound argument against fuller participation by the clergy in ecclesial power. The problems are not purely counterindications: they are signs of a dynamic and vital clergy honestly confronting the critical issues of life in the modern Church. The problems are the prolegomena to a future synthesis. If the Church is to grow, it will do so by confronting squarely its inner flaws. In today's world, conflict resolution is achieved not solely on the level of ideas but in the practical arena of politics. This is the age in which the whole system becomes aware of itself, so that ultimately, in the words of St. Augustine, the Church can truly be "one Christ knowing and loving Himself."

B. THE LAITY

The laity, through most of the Church's history, have not been in a position of power. It is true, their participation was greatest in the early days of the Church; but their potentialities may be greatest in the Church today. This new development is as it should be; for, after all, the laity make up most of the Church. The priests, the bishops, and the pope are the servants of the servants of God. Christ died to save all men, and most men are laymen. The Church is the congregation of the faithful, and most of the faithful are laymen. Whether they have power or not, laymen determine the health and holiness of the Church. As John Henry Newman phrased it, "In all times, the laity have been the measure of the Catholic spirit: they saved the Irish Church three centuries ago and they betrayed the Church to England."[14]

Formally speaking, the laity's role has been passive. Their faith and their fidelity have directly influenced the course of ecclesial history: their part in decision-making has been small. To give them a larger role in these questions which so intimately concern them is to run the risk of creating new problems, perhaps serious ones. Two areas are of special concern: the competence of the laity for ecclesial democratization; and the extent of the control that they will be given or they may take.

First, the degree of *competence* required for participation in decision-making is a problem that faces both civil and ecclesiastical societies. The communication of support and demands presents no difficulty. All members ought to be able to communicate their input in a reasonable way. The function of transforming the multitude of conflicting inputs into sound and consistent outputs, however, is a highly specialized task. Not every member of a system has the ability or the will to fill the role of a decision-maker, although many aspire to the prestige that goes with the office. Fundamental, then, to the issue of democratization in the Church is the question: Are there any levels of competence required for lay participation in ecclesial decision-making?

One of the myths of contemporary theology is the glorification of twentieth-century man. In the world come of age, to use Bonhoeffer's phrase, human nature is often pictured as having reached an elevated state of perfection without moral or intel-

---

[14] *Lectures on the Present Position of Catholics in England* (New York: Longmans, Green, and Co., 1903), p. 390.

lectual limitations. In the last decade, the image of the layman has changed from that of a passive and dependent subject to that of a skilled political thinker. The truth is someplace in the middle. Democratization, however, is not helped by wishful thinking. Even the councils of the intellectual and political elites manifest the limitations that have ever characterized human endeavors. Grass-roots participation is not a shortcut to social perfection.

Since man is not perfect, but perfectible, education is necessary if he is to have the information, intellectual skills, and set of values necessary for successful and civilized living. A culturalization process operates in both the Church and the state so that diverse members can be incorporated into their respective political systems. Education, in the broad sense, is a major instrument for this social adaptability.

The Catholic layman shares in the beliefs, ethical standards, and liturgical activities of the Church, as well as in its history, traditions, myths, and even prejudices. The essence of incorporation into the Body of Christ is faith and the sacraments. It is the commitment of a man of good will formalized by the congregation of believers.

The clergy and the hierarchy have, in addition to this common heritage and dedication, a highly specialized and protracted course of religious studies. In the United States, four years of college is followed by four years of theological training. Thus, the pool from which decision-makers are drawn is made up of men who have not only been trained in religious matters but have lived a life dedicated to things of the spirit. Their clothing, their way of life, their celibate status, all distinguish them from the other members of the Church. This does not mean that the priests, religious, and bishops are holier than the laymen, but it does mean that they have concentrated their life and efforts on affairs of the Church to a degree unequaled by most laymen. As we judge the various levels of competence for decision-making, we must take into consideration these differences.

It should be recalled that, historically, participation in Church elections ceased when the laity were no longer well-educated. Today, at least in the United States, most Catholics are literate and at least high school graduates. They may not, however, have received anything more than a very sketchy education in their religion. In other parts of the world, even secular education may be very limited. When we speak of democratization in the Church, we must realize that the world is not religiously or politically homogeneous. The United States is just beginning to admit that democracy will not work in every nation of the world despite the initial impetus of free elections and the trappings of participation. As for ecclesial democratization, its success depends largely on the secular background, both cultural and political, of the Church members; for grace builds on nature, it does not destroy it. Cardinal Newman gives some of the qualities the laity should possess. If we consider the requirements of a democratized Church, his remarks have special value:

> I want a laity, not arrogant, not rash in speech, not disputatious, but men who know their religion, who enter into it, who know just where they stand, who know what they hold, and what they do not, who know their creed well, that they can give an account of it, who know so much of history that they can defend it. I want an intelligent, well-instructed laity.[15]

Despite the problems of lay competence, there is a fundamental advantage which outweighs innumerable dangers. It is the safeguard to human dignity that democracy provides. To share in political power is to have some control over one's role in the system. Participatory democracy is cumbersome and inefficient, but it protects the individual from the arbitrary use of power. When those who are subject to the law have a share in making the law, there is at least a greater chance that their own interests will be taken into consideration. Above all, they will be functioning with freedom and accountability in the restoring of all things in Christ.

Second, the degree of *control* over decision-making obtained by the laity is, like lay competence, a basic problem in ecclesial democratization. The allocation of power is critical in a Church that has so long depended on an exclusively hierarchical regime. Moreover, the Church has experienced serious attempts by laymen to take over large segments of ecclesial jurisdiction. Two

[15] *Ibid.*

examples will illustrate the danger still feared by the Church. The nearest one, in time and space, is the problem of trusteeism in nineteenth-century America, whereby laymen took charge of individual parishes. The second, and earlier, example is the eleventh-century controversy in Europe over lay investiture. There the stakes were higher: the secular powers asserted control on a diocesan level. Feudal lords claimed the right to confer upon the bishop not only temporalities but even ecclesiastical jurisdiction. These two examples differ in that one is on the parish level, the other on the diocesan, but they are similar in that they both concern the permissible degree of lay participation in ecclesial power.

Trusteeism was a controversial issue in the Catholic Church in the United States for almost a hundred years.[16] Thus Guilday wrote: "The serpentine trail of trusteeism winds its vicious way along the highlands of canonical legislation from 1791 to 1884."[17] It reached its peak in the early 1800s, but traces of it appeared even in the twentieth century. The legal situation was this. A board of lay parishioners would become trustees of a parish by incorporating it according to the laws of the state. Consequently, the board claimed to have administrative power over the parish, including property and monetary rights, as well as possessing the right to select and dismiss a pastor. This practice spread to parishes in some twenty states and became a painful matter for the hierarchy. The most dramatic instances, which always involved open dissent and at times ended in schism, occurred in the parishes of St. Mary's in New York City, Holy Trinity in Philadelphia, St. Louis Cathedral in New Orleans, and St. Mary's in Charleston, South Carolina.

The rise of trusteeism can be attributed to several factors. First, many Catholic immigrants were familiar with lay parish boards in their native lands. In France, for example, the *marguilliers* or churchwardens were common, and in parts of Germany

[16] Cf. P. J. Dignan, *A History of the Legal Incorporation of Catholic Church Property in the United States, 1784–1932* (Washington: Catholic University of America, 1933), and R. F. McNamara, "Trusteeism in the Atlantic States, 1785–1863," *Catholic Historical Review*, 30 (1944), 135–154.

[17] P. Guilday, *A History of the Councils of Baltimore* (New York: Macmillan, 1932), p. 88.

there were lay committees in the parishes. Yet in both of these countries the boards were under the control of the bishop. Second, some Catholics were influenced by the American Protestant tradition in which trustees were an accepted structure in parish governance. Third, some Catholics, finding themselves in American democracy, wished to apply its philosophy of independence to their churches. As a result, trusteeism spread rapidly.

Despite its growth, trusteeism produced many excesses. The lay trustees, complaining that the bishops were interfering with their rights, often refused to release funds unless their demands were met. At other times, they mercilessly extracted church dues from the poorer members of the parish. Furthermore, some of the most radical of the lay trustees were lapsed Catholics, who were often supported by malcontent priests. The First Provincial Council of Baltimore (1829) thus condemned those Catholics who "claimed imaginary rights from the misapprehension of facts and laws with which they were badly, if at all, acquainted; they have sometimes been abetted by ignorant or unprincipled priests."[18] Even stronger words came from the Third Provincial Council of Baltimore (1837), which asserted that the most troublesome trustees "were notorious for their total neglect of religious practices and were found most ready to abuse any power they were able to obtain."[19]

Hierarchic response to the trustee controversy was predictable. Two popes in the 1820s wrote documents concerning trusteeism in which they insisted that Church property be under control of the hierarchy.[20] Moreover, the provincial and plenary councils

---

[18] H. J. Nolan, ed., *Pastoral Letters of the American Hierarchy, 1792–1970* (Huntington, Ind.: Our Sunday Visitor, 1971), p. 30.

[19] *Ibid.*, p. 78.

[20] *Non sine magna* (August 24, 1822) of Pius VII and *Quo longius* (August 28, 1828) of Leo XII. The emergence of the parish council as an important element of shared responsibility in the diocese could, if a power struggle develops, cause problems similar to those of lay trusteeism. Recently, in the Virginia diocese of Richmond, the pastor of St. Mark's parish in Vienna was transferred to another parish because he permitted communion in the hand, a practice not yet allowed in this country. The parish council opposed his removal and sought unsuccessfully to obtain a restraining order to prevent it (*Washington Post*, October 31, 1972, p. A-15). Both sides have agreed to submit the dispute to the diocesan

of Baltimore issued a series of warnings and regulations that denied the right of lay trustees to appoint or dismiss a pastor and that gradually strengthened canonical and legal control over the parishes.

One bishop, John England of Charleston, South Carolina, successfully neutralized trustee agitation by introducing a remarkable diocesan constitution which had many democratic features.[21] The diocese was divided into districts or parishes, and in each a Vestry was formed, which was made up of priests and a number of elected laymen. Only the bishops could remove a priest from his parochial duties, but provision was made for the congregation to petition the bishop for removal. There was also a board of General Trustees, composed of seven clergymen (including the bishop) and twelve elected laymen, who administered the general fund of the diocese. Another interesting provision was the annual diocesan convention attended by the clergy and lay delegates. The jurisdiction of the convention was carefully limited to the administration of church temporalities, and it had no power over doctrine, the sacraments, and the appointment of pastors.

The Charleston Constitution remained in effect from 1823 to 1842, when Bishop England died. It is not clear whether Rome gave official approbation of the constitution. Propaganda Fidei (the Congregation for the Propagation of the Faith), however, was well aware of its existence, and on one occasion they apologized to Bishop England for an earlier admonition that had been based on faulty information.[22] Apparently Rome found nothing in the constitution that was incompatible with Catholic principles.

Even this brief view of lay trusteeism in the United States helps us understand why both Roman and American Church authorities would be reluctant to expand lay control over ecclesial matters. This danger of misuse of power is present wherever

---

Board of Administrative Review for an impartial review according to the procedures of due process.

[21] The complete text of the Constitution may be found in I. A. Reynolds, ed., *The Works of Right Rev. John England* (Baltimore: John Murphy, 1848), V, 91–108.

[22] Cf. P. Guilday, *The Life and Times of John England* (New York: America Press, 1927), I, 364.

power operates. What one can learn from the trustee experience is that in a democratized Church, the specific rights and obligations of each group—hierarchical, clerical, and lay—must be clearly delineated, so that they can all function together without excesses on the part of any one group.

The controversy over lay investiture was much more serious than that over trusteeism, although both involved control by laymen over the Church. Lay investiture, however, was control on the grand scale involving popes and emperors, bishops and feudal lords. Here were two systems, the ecclesial and the civil, in conflict over power and temporal possessions.

In the Middle Ages bishoprics, abbeys, and great churches had lands, revenues, and men. These things the nobles needed in their secular power struggle. Control of the appointment of bishops and abbots gave them control over the resources of the Church and even over the Church itself. These feudal lords claimed to confer not only the temporalities but the jurisdiction as well. Although all the persons involved were at least nominally Catholic, there were two systems interacting, with the secular usurping the decision-making power of the sacred.

The phenomenon of state interference in Church affairs is a perennial one. Lay investiture was practiced by Clovis in the fifth century. But by the eleventh and twelfth centuries this practice had been institutionalized on a widespread scale. Despite efforts of popes like Gregory VII and reformers like the Cluniac monks, it was not until 1122 and the Diet of Worms that the Holy Roman Emperor, Henry V, finally acquiesced to ecclesial pressures and agreed that secular princes should no longer, through the power of episcopal investiture, control the Church. Since the bishop was a temporal lord as well as a spiritual one, the Emperor would continue to grant the scepter, the symbol of the temporal office, but he would not grant the ring and crozier, symbols of the ecclesiastical jurisdiction.

CONCLUSION

All systems face problems. History shows that the Church is no exception, and even that history repeats itself. Persecutions, caesaro-papism, worldliness, poverty, ignorance, heresies, schisms, and apostacies appear again and again throughout the Christian era.

Each age, however, has its peculiar difficulties: Persecution in the first century, corruption in the eleventh century, and rationalism in the nineteenth century. The Church crisis today is one of liberty. It is an internal crisis and it, too, is a product of its age. The Church is in transition between authoritarianism and co-responsibility, between paternalism and Christian maturity. The Church, by confronting the implications of "the perfect law of liberty," is coming of age, is facing up to what it means to say that the People of God are the offspring not of the slave but of the freewoman.

11

The Techniques
of Ecclesial Democracy

IN THE PRECEDING CHAPTER we confronted some of the problems that face a democratized Church. Now we examine the techniques of reform. Reform is a frustrating undertaking which, at best, succeeds only temporarily, for the Church will always be reformable, an *Ecclesia semper reformanda*. This was true of the primitive Jerusalem community, and it will be true of future communities, because the Church is an incarnational reality. In spite of its divine foundation, the continuing presence of the Holy Spirit, and the promise of indefectibility, the Church is still an assembly of fallible men. The Church will always, to some degree, be victimized by weak members, poor leaders, and oppressive enemies. Charles Frankel's description of the United States government may be applied, with appropriate changes, to the Church. "The government," he says, "may be decrepit, disjointed, or myth-ridden—but even after we have finished reforming it, it will still be an institution created by an animal whose balance with its environment is always precarious."[1] Renewal,

---

[1] "Out of Touch in Washington," *Saturday Review*, November 1, 1969, p. 54.

therefore, is a perennial challenge. No ecclesial system, whether it be democratic or monarchic, can provide an absolute guarantee of success. We believe, however, that today greater participation by the members of a cybernetically sophisticated Church gives the greatest hope for that success.

The Church, however, is a complex social system. It is, in cybernetic terminology, a nonlinear, multiple-loop-feedback system with variable elements. Because of this complexity, efforts to improve things through change may only make matters worse. In technological circles, this is called Forrester's Law. Dr. Jay W. Forrester, Professor of Management at the Massachusetts Institute of Technology, argues that "in complex systems the short-term response to a policy change is apt to be in the opposite direction from the long-term effect."[2] Complex systems tend to delude us because they are counterintuitive—that is, they behave in ways that are contrary to what we expect. Our experience with simple systems, where cause-effect relationships can be easily predicted, does not apply to more sophisticated patterns. In the latter, there is never *one* cause for system breakdown. "The 'cause' is in the structure," warns Forrester, "and in the interactions of components interrelated in complex ways."[3] We often attack symptoms and overlook the deeper roots of the problem. As a result, we naively make changes and are amazed that we have failed to revitalize the system. What is needed, Forrester insists, is not acceptance of the status quo but a thorough exploration of alternatives.

The caveat contained in Forrester's Law is a sobering one in the discussion of Church reform. It is easy to dismiss the cultural and traditional practices of millions of Catholics and blithely suggest a utopian vision. But no lasting reform takes place easily or quickly. Renewal must be planned; and even when this is done, it may take years before it becomes fully realized. An initial period of confusion must often be endured before the long-term effects emerge. Serious and unexpected problems occur, however, when *ad hoc* decisions are implemented without taking

[2] "Systems Analysis as a Tool for Urban Planning," *IEEE Spectrum*, January 1971, p. 54.

[3] "A Deeper Knowledge of Social Systems," *Technology Review*, April 1969, p. 26.

into account how other areas will be affected. To overlook the linkage between the various elements in the total Christian environment is to invite future failures.

The techniques listed below are suggestions, tentatively proposed, which could be implemented without causing major disruption. They range from broad recommendations to more specific proposals. In no way do they pretend to be definitive. There are many unexpected variables that will arise and necessitate further adaptation. The techniques that follow are practical conclusions based on the theory of information feedback. They can help make the Church more responsive to the challenges of renewal by enabling it to react positively to existing problems, rather than to remain inactive, simply guarding the memories of past glories.

I. *Commitment to Community*

This is the most critical element in any renewal effort. Unless people are convinced that the goals of the Church are worthwhile, they will not work together in trying to achieve them. Commitment is the opposite of selfishness, laziness, or inconstancy. It involves a wholehearted dedication and cooperation rooted in allegiance to a value system. Christians affirm a value system that is based on the Christ-event. They are convinced that this life has its fullest meaning because of the redemptive word and works of Christ Jesus. At the same time, their final goal is union with the Triune God in heaven. Until that takes place, Christians are a pilgrim people or, in the words of Vatican II, a Church "that strains toward the consummation of the kingdom with all her strength."[4] The People of God are united by a hope in the future which gives meaning to the present.

How is commitment fostered among the members of the Church? Obviously, it cannot be imposed by mandate. No papal or episcopal directive can of itself guarantee greater commitment. The values of the Christian life have to be internalized, not simply as abstract formulas but as concrete demands and

---

[4] *Constitution on the Church*, Art. 5.

clear-cut attitudes. A committed Christian believes that Christ is truly God and loves him personally. Consequently, he dedicates his life and work to Christ and to his fellow man. Exhortation, teaching, and one's own personal witness can help convince others of the Christian truth. But in the final analysis each person, with the grace of God, must make the decision to integrate the Gospel into his own life.

Vatican II attempted to instill a lively sense of God among Christians. Yet, as James Hitchcock notes, "the bitterest failure of the years of reform in the Church has been the evident failure of spiritual regeneration."[5] There is some truth in this observation. Signs of hope, however, also abound. Many Catholics find deep sources of spirituality in the renewed liturgy and in Bible study and prayer groups. Religious are experimenting with various forms of communal life. Several noncanonical Christian communities are beginning to emerge. One of the most interesting examples of the quest for spiritual rejuvenation is the Catholic Charismatic Renewal Movement.[6] By conservative estimates, some seventy-five thousand American Catholics are involved in the movement. Catholic charismatics stress the acceptance of Jesus as a personal Saviour and believe in the abiding presence of the Holy Spirit. At the same time they view the Church, the sacraments, and the hierarchy as essential components of the total Christian covenant.

Intense commitment becomes increasingly difficult in proportion to the size of the community. Anonymity and impersonalism tend to increase in large social groups, with the resultant loss of identification and cooperation. This is true also in the Church, where parishes of several thousand people are quite common. To call such assemblies "communities" is perhaps to overextend the use of the word. Many observers feel that the time has come for the Church to move in the direction of small communities.[7]

[5] *The Decline and Fall of Radical Catholicism* (New York: Herder and Herder, 1971), p. 180.

[6] Cf. E. D. O'Connor, *The Pentecostal Movement in the Catholic Church* (Notre Dame, Ind.: Ave Maria Press, 1971) and D. Gelpi, *Pentecostalism, A Theological Viewpoint* (New York: Paulist Press, 1971).

[7] Cf. K. Rahner, *The Christian of the Future* (New York: Herder and Herder, 1967); M. Delespesse, *The Church Community: Leaven and Life-*

Today most parishes are territorial ones, but in the future they may well be smaller groups of worshipping Christians, freely formed communities in which people who know each other are joined together not because of merely sociological reasons but by a deep attachment to Christ. Already there are several extra-territorial parishes in the United States; for example, the Community of John XXIII in Oklahoma City, Oklahoma, and the charismatic Community of the Holy Spirit in St. Charles, Illinois. Karl Rahner foresees the time when there will be small groups of Christians all over the world. The Christians in these groups "will know they are like brothers and sisters to one another" and that they have "by their own deliberate decision staked their own heart and life on Jesus the Christ."[8]

In a democratized Church, small, semi-autonomous communities would be a natural development. These communities would not be parallel structures, formed in opposition to the institutional Church and separate from any connection with the bishop. Rather, they would be integral parts of the wider diocesan structure and united to it by a common faith and discipline. Moreover, the small parishes would have the right of self-determination by selecting their own pastors and by deciding issues which concern them. This kind of functioning co-responsibility would involve all the mature members in the life of the parish and foster a greater personal commitment to the Christian tradition.

II. *Minority Power*

The presence of a "creative minority" can act as a powerful force for change in any society. It has been demonstrated repeatedly through the centuries that the initiative and determination of a few can alter the course of history. For example, Buddha, Mahomet, Luther, Marx, and Hitler were all persons who began with a small following, but in spite of initial rejection and ridicule, eventually attracted millions.

Style (Ottawa: Catholic Centre of St. Paul University, 1969); G. Moran, *The New Community* (New York: Herder and Herder, 1970); and R. Currier, *The Future Parish* (Huntington, Ind.: Our Sunday Visitor, 1971).

[8] Rahner, *The Christian of the Future*, p. 80.

In the Church, the power of the minority is often misunderstood. For centuries Catholics have looked to the hierarchy alone for leadership and have criticized them when this was not forthcoming. Since the Church is not to be identified with her leaders and the Holy Spirit "breathes where it will," Catholics should expect that God will speak to men in a variety of ways. He may speak through the hierarchy, through the faithful, and as well through other Christians and non-Christians. The Spirit transcends structures, and we cannot restrict his activity.

Minority groups have exerted power in the Church from the beginning. The earliest example was the controversy between the Judaizers and the Hellenists over the Mosaic Law. In every period of Church history there have been individuals who have objected to Church policies. At times disputes centered on a single word, such as the debate in the fourth century over the choice between *homoousios* and *homoiousios* to refer to the comparison of the Logos with the Father. On occasion, heated dispute arose even over the translation of an unimportant, nontheological word. St. Augustine, for example, writes about one of his brother bishops whose congregation became enraged when he read them a passage from St. Jerome's translation of the Book of Jonah. Jerome's version, Augustine explains, was different from that "enshrined in the memory and hearing of all." The problem was whether it was an ivy- or gourd-plant that covered the head of Jonah. The disturbance reached such major proportions that, as Augustine tells us, the bishop "was forced to correct an apparently wrong statement, not wishing to run the great risk of remaining without a flock."[9] In those days, it seems, an organized laity, even on an *ad hoc* basis, had great strength.

A more recent example of the value of minority input is seen in the writings of several theologians prior to Vatican II on ecumenism, religious liberty, and the supernatural. Men like Yves Congar, John Courtney Murray, and Henri de Lubac wrote on these subjects in the 1950s and were looked upon as *novatores*, dangerous innovators, by some officials in the Vatican. Yet they persisted in their scholarly work and the documents of Vatican II reflect many of their ideas.

[9] St. Augustine, *Ep.* 71 (PL 33:243).

The Canon Law Society of America illustrates what can be done in communicating intellectual input. The Society over the last seven years has sponsored several major symposia with an international participation of canon lawyers, theologians, historians, and sociologists. These seminars have discussed, among other things, the nature of law in the Church, the bond of marriage, priestly celibacy, co-responsibility, and collegiality. The papers presented at these meetings were serious and carefully documented studies. Their recommendations were reasonably formulated and soundly researched. It is regrettable that they did not receive wider publicity. The Canon Law Society is to be commended for its positive and persistent efforts at developing a realistic program for reform in the Church. By avoiding sensationalism, ready-made solutions, and extravagant demands, it has gained a deserved respectability in academic circles and among the more progressive members of the hierarchy.

Another style of input in the post-Conciliar Church has been the emergence of many pressure and protest groups. In North America and Europe especially, both liberals and conservatives have mounted extensive campaigns on issues from optional celibacy for priests to the retention of the Latin Tridentine Mass. A deluge of petitions, position papers, and recommendations have been transmitted to Church leaders. Furthermore, through national meetings, press conferences, and extensive publicity, many have attempted to elicit popular support and to force the hierarchy to act in their favor.

At the 1971 Synod of Bishops unofficial pressure groups were much in evidence. The largest was Operation Synod, an international organization of liberal priests and lay groups that claimed to have offices in thirty-nine countries and representation in sixty. At the synod, it established a press service with daily briefings for newsmen and critiques of synod documents. Two lobbies came from the United States: the National Federation of Priests' Councils, which advocated optional celibacy, due process for priests, and a greater voice for priests in selection of bishops; and the National Office of Black Catholics, which demanded a black bishop in Washington, D. C., and a separate rite for black Catholics. In Rome, there was also a lobby of Latin American Priests, Priests for the Third World, and an alliance of nineteen traditionalists groups called Pro Ecclesia Romana Catholica. The latter was vehemently opposed to the synod and saw it as a threat to the primacy of the pope.

How successful are protests and pressure groups? Immediate results from this type of input are rare for two reasons. First, the style of protest may be counterproductive. Abrasive rhetoric and unreasonable demands strain rather than open the lines of communication with decision-makers. As a result, a backlash among leaders may develop which makes them more resolute in their determination not to concede. Second, members of the hierarchy are not as vulnerable as authorities in civil society. The bishops, since they are not elected by the people, have no direct accountability to them. Adverse publicity, therefore, does not threaten their job security. Consequently they can ignore protest and refuse to take any action.

It should be noted, however, that protests and pressure groups are valuable in the ecclesial community. Through their efforts, they bring to light sensitive issues and stimulate discussion about them. Important matters can move from a theoretical level to a practical one in a short time. Feedback, if adequately publicized, can at least force those in authority to listen. Well-organized and reasonably conducted protest has the best chances of success.[10]

A democratized Church affirms the principle of pluralism. If freedom is the presence of alternatives, then in the Church there should be a freedom to disagree on matters which do not contradict revealed doctrine. We cannot expect the Church to be above criticism in every aspect of its corporate life. In fact, the existence of different approaches helps the Church avoid stagnation. But creativity and freedom need protection if they are to con-

---

[10] In March 1972, thirty-four Catholic theologians from Europe and North America issued a statement outlining five steps to end the present stagnation in the Church. Catholics facing inflexible Church officials were advised: "Do not remain silent," "Do something yourself," "Act together," "Seek provisional solutions," and "Don't give up." The text of the statement can be found in the *National Catholic Reporter*, March 31, 1972, pp. 3, 17. Cardinal Garrone, head of the Congregation for Catholic Education, criticized the statement as "not in the spirit of the faith and in the tradition of the Church" and called it "aggression by criticism" (*New York Times*, March 29, 1972, p. 17).

tribute to the Church's continuing self-renewal. Suppression of every kind of dissent and severe restriction of academic freedom should, therefore, be alien to a Church that holds human freedom in such high esteem. Groups of intellectuals, social activists, and holy men and women can, if they act with prudence and faith, direct valuable informational input into the decision-making process.

III. *Communications Media*

The Church, as an international information-processing unit, needs a highly developed system of communication. This is especially true of a democratized Church in which local communities are given greater autonomy and flexibility. The move toward decentralization, however, should not affect the fundamental oneness of the Church in creed, code, and cult. For the unity and catholicity of the ecclesial system are reflected anew in the bonds of electronic communication, which bring together the many believing communities. For example, with the help of communication satellites, the face of the Vatican is no farther away from the parishes of the world than the nearest television set. Using Aristotle's conclusion that the size of a political community is determined by the range of one man's voice, we find that electronically, the whole world is practically a single community. As a result, the Catholic Church, always one Body, benefits tremendously from the communicative intimacy that modern technology provides.

The official Church is aware of the exciting possibilities of social communication. These are admirably outlined in the 23,000-word pastoral instruction on communications issued in 1971 by the Pontifical Commission for the Means of Social Communication. Six years in the making, the new instruction is a detailed examination of the media. It takes a global approach by insisting in its opening sentence that the chief aims of social communication are "the unity and advancement of men living in a society."[11] The common brotherhood of man, mutual understanding, and the assessment and comparison of differing views

---

[11] *Pastoral Instruction on the Means of Social Communication*, Art. 1,

are listed as some of the positive benefits of communication. The Church, therefore, should guarantee open public opinion, freedom of speech, and the rights to know and to inform. "Since the Church is a living body," the document says, "she needs public opinion in order to sustain a giving and taking between her members."[12] Arguing against suppression of information, the instruction insists that secrecy should be used sparingly. Reference is also made to developments in satellite transmissions and the immense opportunities they present for effective religious instruction. A theme repeated throughout the document is that social communications are vehicles to "multiply contacts within society and to deepen social consciousness."[13]

Will the guidelines in the pastoral instruction be implemented? If they are, the Catholic Church can develop a communications system that would be a powerful agent of preaching the saving Word. Yet much work has to be done. At present both the Catholic press and television-radio are badly in need of revitalization. In most countries, the diocesan newspapers are, with some exceptions, chancery organs, dull and uninspiring. Few Catholic newspapers fulfill the admonition in the Instruction to "comment on the news and, without boring the reader, interpret it in a way that makes him think for himself."[14] Moreover, Catholic magazines face severe financial problems and a shrinking constituency. Many journals, like the century-old *Ave Maria* and the *Messenger of the Sacred Heart*, tried to modernize according to the vision of Vatican II. They soon discovered that their older readers were displeased and new readers were not attracted. Both periodicals eventually ceased publication. A more recent demise was the Catholic weekly *Publik*, published in Germany. In November 1971, the West German bishops stopped their annual subsidy for the reason that it was no longer feasible economically. Critics of the decision argued that the real reason was that the paper had become too controversial. Karl Rahner lamented the bishops' move as "retreat into a Church ghetto" and "a step toward a Church that resigns from having a meaning in the public life of the German nation."[15]

[12] *Ibid.*, Art. 115.
[13] *Ibid.*, Art. 8.
[14] *Ibid.*, Art. 136.
[15] *New York Times*, November 21, 1971, p. 28.

Catholic radio broadcasting has had only limited success. Programs are aired usually on public service time at very early or very late hours. The only Catholic religious network in the world is Radio Vaticana, a multi-million-dollar operation whose transmission capacity equals any network in the world. Unfortunately, it is also perhaps the most underused of any radio system. The programs are heavy with excerpts from papal speeches, notices of unimportant papal appointments, and one-sided editorials. Its best features are interviews and panel discussions on topical matters. A low pay scale, a lack of professional and imaginative personnel, insufficient funds, and poor organization hamper the effectiveness of Radio Vaticana.

There are three areas in which the Church should concentrate its efforts concerning the media. First, sound professional training should be mandatory. The Vatican's pastoral instruction mentions national centers, seminary courses, and university departments that would provide thorough scientific programs in the media. This will help reduce mediocrity. Secondly, the Catholic press should broaden its horizons "by bringing a knowledge of the Church to the world and a knowledge of the world to the Church."[16] Liberated from purely regional concerns, the Catholic media should increase their dialogue with the world and reveal the Christian message to others. Thirdly, considerable support from Catholics and institutional support from bishops are needed if the above goals are to be realized.

IV. *Study Commissions*

The information explosion and the complexities of life in the Church today make it impossible for decision-makers to assimilate the vast amount of diversified input coming into the ecclesial system. Consequently, Church leaders need help from others in analyzing controversial and difficult problems. The study commission provides this assistance. It is a collaborative effort of specialists, preferably with interdisciplinary backgrounds, who gather, process, and refine information concerning a particular

---

[16] *Pastoral Instruction on the Means of Social Communication*, Art. 137.

issue. The study commission can be a valuable research tool for decision-makers, supplying them with the theoretical data and practical recommendations required for the ongoing work of renewal.

The idea of study commissions, of course, is not something new in the Church. Experts have always been called in to help decision-makers. The need for them today, however, is most urgent because of the increase in the number of Catholics throughout the world, the complexity of the theological and social problems, and finally, the polarities that exist within the Church. For these reasons independent organizations and national churches are making wide use of this input-processing vehicle. Also in the Roman Curia there are several permanent commissions, and others have been established—for example, the Birth Control Commission—to study specific problems.

The success of commissions depends, in part at least, on the initial selection of members. If all the members are of the same persuasion, the results will be predictable and perhaps of little value. What is needed is a diversity of opinion so that opposing views can be thoroughly debated and their merits tested. One of the main criticisms of the several permanent pontifical commissions is that they fail to represent a wide spectrum of opinion. Most of the members selected, however outstanding their credentials may be, are more or less committed to similar positions. Without the challenge of dissent and the stimulus of reassessment, stagnation is inevitable. The Vatican's Birth Control Commission was a notable exception. From the outset there were differences. Two fundamentally opposed approaches finally emerged. It is true that this prevented an ultimate reconciliation, but it did encourage a direct confrontation over the issues. From that point of view, the Commission was a success.

On occasion, commissions can be misused. They can become a bureaucratic ploy, a dilatory tactic to avoid or to shift responsibility. By foisting a difficult problem on a commission, those in authority can buy time and postpone, sometimes indefinitely, any decisive action, all the while giving the impression that they are facing the issues. Furthermore, some commissions go over matters that have previously been thoroughly examined. Other commissions are formed simply to discredit earlier studies. No doubt commissions honestly strive for unanimity, but even this goal can easily result in a weak compromise position. As Senator Ribicoff of Connecticut has noted, this formulation "leads to a watering down of strong ideas and strong views. It would be much better for commissions to issue minority and majority opinions."[17]

Secrecy can also threaten commission effectiveness. Commission findings should be made public and not relegated to archival limbo. This apparently was to be the fate of the report of the Birth Control Commission, had it not been partially "leaked" to the press. Even today the Vatican has never published any part of the report; this fact, too, has served to weaken confidence in the Church.

Public opinion polls are used by many study commissions and research organizations as a means of determining public sentiment on critical issues.[18] This technique, based on random selection and the law of probability, is a controversial one. Should the Church, then, use public opinion polls? Yes, but with caution. There is some evidence that polls create as well as reflect public opinion and thus become a kind of self-fulfilling prophecy. In administrative matters, in which preferences are sought, polls could be most useful. In doctrinal and moral issues, however, their value is less clear and more open to misinterpretation. Any use of polls, however, must take into account the presence of variables both in the interviewing procedures and in the interviewees. Polls should not be taken as an infallible index of public sentiment, but as one of many ways for the Church to determine more accurately the *consensus fidelium.* Consequently, they can be used profitably in the Church, since the laity may be more sensitive at times to the needs of the Church than those in positions of power.

Study commissions are not meant to supplant ecclesial authority but to assist it. The presupposition is that if the hierarchy are well-informed, they are more likely to govern wisely. There is, however, always the possibility that decision-makers will ignore critical recommendations, shelve them for further investi-

17 *Washington Post,* June 28, 1970, p. A7.
18 Cf. L. Bogart, *Silent Politics: Polls and the Awareness of Public Opinion* (New York: Wiley-Interscience, 1972, and C. W. Roll and A. H. Cantril, *Can the Polls Be Trusted?* (New York: Basic Books, 1972).

gation, or implement them only after major surgery. Political interference or intrigue may also adversely affect commission findings. If, however, study commissions are used honestly and critically by Church leaders, they can become both a valuable source of information and an example of functioning co-responsibility in the decision-making process.

V. Selection of Bishops

The selection of bishops should be a community decision, because the Church is an assembly of believers and not just a hierarchy. Episcopal authority, if it is to regain its credibility, should emerge from the community and not be unilaterally imposed upon it. Since bishops are not selected by the people, accountability, a fundamental aspect of representative government, is lacking. What is needed, therefore, is a broad participation by all segments of the community: bishops, priests, religious, and laity. The historical and theological basis for this kind of democratic procedure was analyzed in Part Three. Now we can discuss the problem on a more practical level, one that is most relevant, since the 1972 norms from the Vatican on the selection of bishops give only minimal recognition of any genuine democratic procedure.

The two generally suggested methods for selecting bishops in the Church are by a general plebiscite and by an elected committee. After examining the merits of each of these procedures, we will deal with some details of the voting process.

A. SELECTION BY GENERAL PLEBISCITE

According to this method, every adult member of a diocese would participate in an open election of episcopal candidates. Through a popular election the will of the community would be made manifest and the bishop elected would have the mandate of the majority. The model to be followed would be the electoral procedures of the democratic system. Proponents of this method argue that it would guarantee the direct involvement of all levels of Church membership and thus promote interest and cooperation.

Now, while popular election should not be rejected on principle, it does present certain problems. It implies the real possibility of campaigning. A glance at the contemporary American experience of political campaigns reveals some of the difficulties the Church might expect. Two specific areas are worthy of note: electioneering and finances.

Electioneering, or campaign hucksterism, has always been a feature of the American political system. With the advent of television and its audience of millions, the selling of the candidate has become an art in itself. Slick commercials can boost an unknown candidate to the level of a real contender. The gullibility of the voter is taken for granted. Thus Harry Treleaven, a member of Richard Nixon's media team in the 1968 campaign, notes: "Probably more people vote for irrational, emotional reasons than professional politicians suspect."[19] There is a whole industry today whose sole job is to get candidates elected. These professionals market candidates to the electorate. The candidate may be told to lose weight, get a better tailor, change his hair style, or take diction lessons. He has to be a credible and appealing person or he won't be elected. To achieve this goal a variety of emotional, ideological, and symbolic techniques are employed. Robert Goodman, a first-rank political advertiser, describes his tactics this way: "If he's got it, we project it. If he hasn't, we try to fudge it. But we never strain the credibility of the viewer."[20] Besides television, the usual campaign includes direct mail advertising, press conferences, fund-raising dinners, speaking engagements, and perhaps an occasional walking tour.

The financial burden of waging a successful campaign in the United States is immense. The Federal Communications Commission reported that in 1968, all presidential, gubernatorial, and senatorial candidates spent $58.9 million for media time—mainly television. This was a 70 percent increase over the 1964 campaign. If one adds to that the cost of producing the film and tapes, the total would be close to $90 million. It has been estimated that it costs a minimum of $10 million for a presidential candidate to reach the Convention, and then an additional $30

[19] *Newsweek*, October 19, 1970, p. 38.
[20] *Ibid.*, p. 37.

million to run his campaign. Running for the Senate in the larger states costs at least a half a million dollars, and some candidates have spent as much as four million. All this has led Senator Charles McC. Mathias, Jr. of Maryland to state: "If you have to be rich or have rich friends and backers to reach high office, then democracy is a fraud. This is the most undemocratic flaw in our system, and yet nothing is done about it."[21]

In February 1972, President Nixon signed the first major reform of campaign spending laws since 1925. It set a ceiling, ten cents per voter, on advertising expenses for candidates for federal offices. The new law should help correct some of the more egregious abuses of the past. It is doubtful, however, that it will completely satisfy those critics who claim, with some justification, that elected officials do not represent the people who vote for them, but the people who pay their bills.

The experience of modern democratic governments indicates some of the drawbacks of general citizen participation in a popular election. This does not mean that such abuses would inevitably occur in the Church on the same scale, but it does indicate the dangers in such a method. There are two further reasons why the general plebiscite would not be a feasible election procedure in the Church today. First, it could easily encourage the formation of the party system and partisan politics. At a time where there is already a serious polarity among Catholics, this would be an unwelcome addition. Furthermore, history has shown that one of the reasons for the decline of election *per clerum et populum* was that it created factionalism. Secondly, the complexity of the modern diocese makes a popular election unsuitable. Unlike the diocese of the early centuries of the Church, the modern diocese is larger, more diversified; but it lacks the strong sense of community involvement. Members of a large diocese do not live close together in one section, and the local church is not the center of their community life. In the first centuries of the Church, the diocese was relatively small and its members perhaps knew each other personally. In such an atmosphere the general election was a reasonable development. Today,

---

[21] Quoted by R. Harris in "Annals of Politics—A Fundamental Hoax," *New Yorker*, August 7, 1971, p. 38.

however, it would prove unwieldy. Therefore, the election of bishops by general plebiscite does seem, on balance, to have so many disadvantages as to be prohibitive.

B. SELECTION BY ELECTED COMMITTEE

This method of selecting bishops involves the whole community, but only indirectly. Instead of a diocese-wide plebiscite, a small committee handles the selection procedure. Yet representation is preserved.

A detailed plan of this method was proposed, after two years of preparation, by the Canon Law Society of America (CLSA) at their annual meeting in Atlanta, Georgia, in October 1971.[22] The Society advocated that a permanent eleven-member committee for nominating bishops be established in each diocese. The committee would consist of ten members *chosen* by the diocesan pastoral council from its own membership and one member appointed by the bishop. Of the ten members there would be two from each of the following groups: diocesan priests, religious women, religious men, lay women, lay men. Although the majority of dioceses in the United States have pastoral councils, in those dioceses that do not, the CLSA plan suggests that the priests' senate establish a committee according to the above norms.

The function of the nominating committee, in a process that is begun anew every three years, is: first, to determine the needs of the diocese; second, to specify the qualification required of the next bishop; and third, to draw up a list of nominees. To do this the committee asks for recommendations from the diocesan pastoral council, the priests' senate, the parish councils, and from other organizations, lay or clerical, within the diocese. Individuals may also make recommendations. The committee then, "according to its own rules of procedure," prepares a list of nominees which it gives to the priests' senate, which narrows the list to no more than ten names and presents it to the Ordinary of the diocese.

The CLSA report seems to end rather abruptly, remaining

---

[22] The CLSA plan is reprinted in Appendix A with the permission of the Society.

solely on the diocesan level. The original draft of the report, however, indicated, in accord with the existing legislation, that at the annual meeting of the provincial bishops the list of nominees would be discussed, together with the other names added by the bishops. A secret vote would determine the final list that is sent to the National Conference of Catholic Bishops and then to the Holy See. The Holy Father would make the final choice of appointing a bishop.

At the CLSA meeting, many objected to this addition, especially in regard to the secretive manner in which the bishops were to act. It was argued that to include this in the report would seem to give endorsement to it. Therefore the Society agreed that the report should confine itself to procedures within the diocese.

The word *election*, it should be noted, appears only twice in the CLSA plan, in connection with the formation of the nominating committee. Yet election is not obligatory, since members may also be appointed. In the actual selection of nominees no definite procedure is mentioned. The plan obviously wishes to provide for the greatest possible procedural flexibility. Election, however, would be an appropriate method throughout the process.[23]

The CLSA proposal has several advantages which make it

[23] Most recently, as the proofs of this book were being corrected, it was learned that the CLSA had made some additions to its earlier plan (Cf. *New York Times*, October 29, 1972, p. 17). The latest recommendations, which continue to insist on broad consultation on the diocesan level, attempt to adapt the 1972 Vatican norms to the American Church. The major features of the plan are that it limits the role of the Apostolic Delegate and increases the responsibility of the national episcopal conference. Two procedural methods are recommended: (1) The Ordinary of the diocese, after evaluating the list of ten names received from the Priests' Senate, would submit his choices to the meeting of the regional bishops. They, in turn, would present the names of the endorsed candidates to a special committee of the National Conference of Catholic Bishops (NCCB). The committee's report would then be taken to Rome personally by the President of the NCCB. (2) When a diocese becomes vacant, the bishop on the committee who represents the region in which the vacancy occurs, would personally consult with those in the diocese who had drawn up the list of candidates. He would then report his findings to the committee which, after discussion, would send to the pope a list of three to five names from which the new bishop would be chosen.

preferable to the 1972 Vatican norms. First, it uses structures (the priests' senate and the diocesan pastoral council) established by Vatican II, and hence it could be implemented immediately; second, it guarantees a participation of the various categories of members in the community; third, it provides for accountability, since the diocese is continually apprised of the progress of the committee; and fourth, because of the public nature of the process and the large number of candidates, it reduces the possibility of electioneering.

C. VOTING RIGHTS

If we opt for the selection of bishops by a representative committee, then at several junctures in the process there will be some kind of voting. This will be true at the level of the local parish council, the diocesan pastoral council, the priests' senate, and other lay and clerical organizations. The question then arises: Who in the Christian community should enjoy voting rights? What are the requirements for voting eligibility?

In the American democratic system, voting is a means of obtaining the consent of the governed. Generally, the more people that vote the better, but in practice this ideal has encountered some opposition in the United States, primarily in determining voter eligibility. Citizenship, of course, is a basic requirement. Other suffrage requirements have dealt with property, residency, sex, age, and race.

In future Church elections, what should be the voting requirements? At the outset we can dismiss any restrictions based on property ownership, sex, or race. It would seem reasonable to grant the right to vote to eighteen-year-olds. Perhaps some residency in a diocese would be a prudent demand, since it would give the new parishioner an opportunity to assess the parish and diocese and to understand its needs. The most vexing problem would be the determination of membership. Many parishioners are Catholics in name only. Although baptized and listed as parish members, these "statistical Catholics" contribute almost nothing to the spiritual or material maintenance of the Church. They do not attend Mass or receive the sacraments, nor do they take any interest in parish life. Should such individuals, therefore, have the right to vote in the election of Church leaders and to share in forming major decisions? Or would such persons, if allowed to participate, introduce anti-ecclesial elements?

It is not easy to resolve these problems satisfactorily. Voting privileges should be denied those Catholics who have left the Church, joined another denomination, or been excommunicated. Besides that general rule, it is difficult to set any further criteria that could be practically implemented. It would be unwise to set up a system to verify weekly church attendance. Fulfillment of the Easter duty, since it pertains to the internal forum, cannot be a criterion. Perhaps some form of voter registration, already employed in some parish council elections, could be used as a screening method and as an index of parish interest. In the final analysis one must recognize that there will always be certain individuals who are spiritually weak, immature, and apathetic. It is unlikely that they will present any serious threat to the viability of elective procedures.

CONCLUSION

Ecclesial cybernetics is the science of communication and control in the Church. For us it has been a means of analyzing that sacred structure of roles for the purpose of facilitating its work of self-renewal. Moreover, ecclesial cybernetics has a dual inspiration: it is related both to traditional ecclesiology and to modern communications theory. In it, faith and reason work together toward a fuller implementation of the prophetic and pastoral mission of the Church. Four points should be mentioned.

First, ecclesial cybernetics strengthens Church unity. It enables the Church to assimilate intelligently the growing feedback from the faithful, avoiding the danger that Paul VI warned against, the forming of "two parallel hierarchies, as it were two organizations side by side,"[24] but realizing the Vatican II goal, "diversity of service but unity of purpose."[25]

[24] Paul VI in an Address to the Third World Congress of the Lay Apostolate, October 15, 1967 (*American Ecclesiastical Review*, 158 [1968]. 273).

[25] *Decree on the Apostolate of the Laity*, Art. 2.

Second, ecclesial cybernetics provides valuable insights into the most profound theological problem that we face today: doctrinal development. Assessment of trends, accurate information concerning the belief and practice of the entire Church, and an effective teaching authority are significant factors in doctrinal development which for their perfection require a sound communication system enabling the Church to be more sensitive to the growing edge of truth.

For ecclesial cybernetics enables a pilgrim Church in a changing world to buttress its wisdom with information, its eternal truths with concrete facts for the perfecting of that unique system which is the Body of Christ.

Third, ecclesial cybernetics presents the need and the justification for further democratization, so that through participation in decision-making the members may share actively in responsibility for the Church. As co-heirs with Christ, they are fittingly co-workers in His vineyard.

Finally, ecclesial cybernetics presents graphically the obligation of each person to assume a role in building up the Kingdom. The structure of the Church consists in the ordering of the role activities of all the members. It is their input, output, and feedback that enables the congregation of the faithful to function as a living organism. The Holy Spirit as the vivifying principle of the Church operates through its members. Their role activities inspired by grace brings them into an organized sacramental system.

Our task has been to analyze the mystery of the Church with help from the science of cybernetics. Indeed it is fitting that communications theory be put to the service of theology for the better understanding of the truth that sets men free. Ecclesial cybernetics, then, helps us to grasp that unique communication whereby the Son of God became man so that man might share eternal life in His Body which is the Church.

Appendixes

APPENDIX A

Canon Law Society of America
Plan for Choosing Bishops for the United States

1971

A. PRELIMINARY REMARKS

In 1969 the Canon Law Society of America established a special committee to research the problem of selecting bishops. The decision, which was made at the annual convention, came as a result of the intense interest shown by many in the question of ecclesiastical leadership. The committee brought together experts in the ecclesiastical sciences with others whose competence was in sociology and psychology. Meeting for the first time in the spring of 1970, the committee approached its task in two stages.

The first consideration was the feasibility and legitimacy of broadening participation in the selection of bishops. Data was gathered from canon lawyers, church historians, and theologians; the findings of the committee were published in the spring of 1971 in the book entitled *The Choosing of Bishops*. As these studies made clear, there are no theological, canonical, or historical obstacles to a broad participation of clergy, religious, and laity in the selection of bishops. On the contrary, there are many indications that such participation is desirable.

The present paper represents the second stage of the committee's work: a plan whereby this wider participation can be achieved. For many reasons the time seems opportune for the presentation of this plan. On September 1, 1970, the Holy See issued norms for selecting bishops which clearly call for the involvement of all segments of the People of God. Throughout the world national conferences of bishops have been invited to submit their observations. Certain areas of agreement and disagreement have developed, and the final document has not yet appeared. Obviously, procedures should differ from country to country, and in offering this plan, the committee has in mind the Church in the United States.

The plan is relatively simple and can be easily adapted to any diocese. It involves the structures that the Vatican Council created: priests' senates, diocesan pastoral councils, and local parish councils. It anticipates divergent points of view and allows for healthy dialogue among these various bodies. It also provides for participation by other groups and individuals who wish to have a voice in the process. The plan is offered as an initial way of involving the People of God in the choice of bishops. In the on-going development of the structures of the Church, continual modifications of this plan should be encouraged.

(1) *Reasons for Revising the Process*

It is widely recognized today that all authority has taken on new scope and depth: new scope due to the varieties of continuing change; new depth due to an increased awareness of interpersonal relationships and the meaning of loving service.

The selection of bishops forms an integral element in the Church's whole self-renewal process. The times call for bishops of bold vision, men of creative concern and visible love who will lead others to the abundant life envisioned by God. The needs of men and bishops capable of serving those needs must be discovered within the Church in a vital and orderly manner. Moreover, participation in the choosing of a bishop can help people to realize the dignity of their Christian membership as they define and search for church leadership. Thus the gifts given by the Holy Spirit to the entire Church can be accepted and appreciated by everyone.

Furthermore, when the manner of selecting church leadership in a country is inconsistent with the social and political experience of its people, anguish results. At present many American Catholics find their exclusion from the process of choosing bishops frustrating and insensitive to their hopes and heritage. Bishops too experience anguish because they often find themselves standing apart from the people they wish to serve rather than in their midst.

The plan proposed in this paper will allow the Church to respond to contemporary man's view of authority and will strengthen authority by widening consent.

(2) *Need for a Continuing Process on a Diocesan Level*

Each diocese is unique. Social, cultural, economic, political, and religious factors give each diocese a recognizable profile. As a result, different qualifications are to be looked for in the bishops who will serve different dioceses.

Moreover, within the same diocese there can be significant changes within a relatively short span of time. The arrival of Cuban refugees in Florida, the movement of millions of black immigrants to the cities, and the geographical mobility of industry can and do rapidly change the characteristics of a diocese. Therefore, continuing research is important in the assessment of the needs of a specific diocese at a given time.

(3) *Basic Qualifications of a Bishop Today*

A bishop is first of all a servant of the Church, personifying both a far-reaching concern for all that is human and a deep involvement in the mission of the Church. More than other individuals, a bishop must be able to enter into the minds and hearts of his people, to listen to them, to speak with them, to them and for them. As builder of a Christian community, he must share both the memories and the hopes of other faithful men. Out of these memories and hopes will come the collegial action which is the bishop's primary responsibility.

Traditionally the Church has looked for profound spirituality and a sense of dedication in the men chosen to be bishops. Personal integrity is no less necessary today, and in this time of accelerated transition moral courage and a communicable vision of the future take on new importance. A bishop must be a man whose transparent character, interests and reactions project Christian values and ideals. Such a person will be able to invite willing and competent participation in the life of the Church and the tasks of the world. Thus he will stir up the faith of the People of God and the hope of all men.

In selecting a bishop the Church should consider carefully a man's previous experience. Sound and deep theological learning are indispensable. But theological wisdom and awareness, administrative skill, and secular knowledge are only developed through varied experience. Such competence should be demonstrated before a man is chosen to be a bishop, but skills and experience are not the full measure of a bishop. He must visibly share the basic concerns of his people if he is to share with them his own insight into the Christian message. Therefore, he will need to be straightforward in his motivation, spontaneous in his way of speaking to and responding to men's real concerns, and tireless in his wish to know and heal human weakness. Such personal dynamism, rooted in the priesthood of Jesus Christ, is a guarantee that the authority conferred in the episcopacy will grow into trustworthy leadership.

B. THE PLAN FOR CHOOSING BISHOPS

(1) *The Committee for Nominating Bishops*

1. In every diocese, the task of inaugurating a new process for choosing bishops, whether it be the Ordinary, a Coadjutor, or an Auxiliary, will be fundamentally the same—namely, (1) to determine the current needs of the diocese; (2) to ascertain the specific, in contrast to the general, qualifications required of the bishop; and (3) to arrive at a list of nominees to be submitted to the Priests' Senate.

2. To pursue this threefold task, a Committee for Nominating Bishops shall be established in each diocese. The Committee shall be composed of eleven persons, one of whom is appointed by the bishop. The remaining members shall be chosen, either by election or appointment, by the Diocesan Pastoral Council from its own membership, two from each of the following categories: diocesan priests, religious women, religious men, laywomen, laymen. If no such Council exists, the Priests' Senate shall choose the Committee, either by election or appointment, from the priests, religious and laity of the diocese. The precise proportion of representation on the Committee as herein described may vary, should the circumstances of a particular diocese warrant it.

3. With the exception of the bishop's appointee, the Committee members shall serve for a period of four years. For the sake of continuity, however, the original Committee shall designate by lot one-half of its members to serve a term of only two years. Replacements are to be made from the same categories as those whose terms have expired.

(2) *Functions of the Committee for Nominating Bishops*

1. The Committee for Nominating Bishops shall keep itself informed of the developing needs of the diocese and through appropriate instruments shall inquire from the total membership of the diocese what its felt needs are.

2. Through the same or similar instruments, the Committee shall invite the broadest participation of the whole People of God in determining the special qualifications sought for in the next bishop, and in proposing names of persons who possess those qualifications.

3. The Committee shall arrive at its list of nominees by seeking recommendations from the Diocesan Pastoral Council, the Priests'

Senate, local parish councils, organizations of religious men and religious women, organizations and movements of laity, and from any other groups who wish in the name of their members to present nominations. Moreover, any individual—cleric, religious or lay—may submit names to the Committee. Nominees may be chosen from outside as well as within the local Church.

4. This process shall be initiated at least every three years. However, when a See becomes vacant or upon the determination of the need of a Coadjutor or Auxiliary Bishop, the results of the last triennial process shall be restudied and a new process, if necessary, shall be initiated immediately.

5. With the initiation of the aforementioned process, all previous lists of episcopal nominees are automatically cancelled. The names thereon, however, must be reconsidered with a view to possible renomination.

6. The Committee shall consider each of the names submitted and shall determine according to its own rules of procedure whether or not the name should appear on the final list to be forwarded to the Priests' Senate.

7. In the order of preference, the Committee shall propose its list of nominees with their respective qualifications, as well as the Committee's determination of the needs of the diocese, to the Priests' Senate. At the same time, the Committee shall make available this same information to all those who have participated in the process.

8. The Priests' Senate shall narrow the list to not more than ten names, having obtained beforehand the consent of each nominee.

9. In the order of preference, the Priests' Senate shall draw up its list of nominees with their respective qualifications, as well as the statement of the needs of the diocese, for the Ordinary of the diocese to present at the annual meeting of the Provincial Bishops. At the same time, the Senate shall make the list known to the Committee for Nominating Bishops.

APPENDIX B

Vatican Norms for Selecting Bishops

1 9 7 2

The choice of bishops is to be made in such a way as to insure that the Church will be entrusted to pastors who will be "examples to the flock" (1 *Peter* 5:3). Thus in the past the Apostolic See has provided for the selection of bishops by issuing particular rules for various countries.

The decisions of the Second Vatican Ecumenical Council however must also be applied in this field. Hence, Pope Paul VI, accepting the wishes of many of his brothers in the episcopate, and having sought the views of the competent departments of the Roman Curia, proceeded to give effect to what was laid down in the motu proprio *Ecclesiae Sanctae*, 10: "The episcopal conference shall each year, in accordance with the norms made or to be made by the Apostolic See, prudently discuss in private the ecclesiastics to be called to the office of bishop in their territory and propose the names of candidates to the Apostolic See." He accordingly gave instructions that a document on this subject be very carefully drawn up and placed before the episcopal conferences for their examination.

This having been done, the Pope has approved the annexed norms on the promotion to the episcopacy of ecclesiastics of the Latin rite. The norms do not affect the laws proper to the Eastern Churches. They are to come into force on 21 May 1972, on which date the particular decrees mentioned above will be abrogated.

All things to the contrary notwithstanding.

From the Vatican, 25 March 1972

J. Cardinal Villot
Prefect of the Council for the Public Affairs of the Church

ARTICLE I

1. Bishops have the faculty and the duty of making known to the Apostolic See the names of priests whom they consider worthy of the episcopal office and suited for it, whether these priests belong to the diocesan clergy, or are religious performing their sacred ministry in the diocese, or are priests of another jurisdiction who are well known to them.

2. Every diocesan bishop and other local ordinaries, with the exception of vicars general, shall take care to obtain all the information needed for carrying out this important and difficult duty. They shall do so either by personal investigation, or by appropriately consulting, within the limits of their jurisdiction, although not collectively, priests of the cathedral chapter or diocesan consultors, or members of the council of priests, or other members of the clergy, diocesan or regular, or members of the laity.

3. With regard to ecclesiastical territories entrusted to missionary

institutes, it is recognized that the superiors general concerned have the faculty, in accordance with the present practice of the Sacred Congregation for the Evangelization of Peoples, to propose candidates from their institutes, while the Apostolic See always retains the right to make other provisions, if it considers it opportune to do so.

ARTICLE II

1. The names of candidates for the office of bishop shall as a general rule be examined and proposed by the bishops during their meetings. But every bishop and every other ordinary as above (article I,2) can propose candidates directly to the Apostolic See.

2. The meetings or conferences in question shall usually be on a provincial level; in other words they shall be composed of the bishops and other ordinaries as above belonging to the same ecclesiastical province, unless special circumstances suggest interprovincial, regional or even national meetings. In these last cases prior notice shall be given to the Apostolic See.

ARTICLE III

1. All the bishops of the province or of the region or nation who according to the respective statutes belong to the same episcopal conference and have a deliberative vote take part in the meeting with equal rights.

2. In the case of a provincial meeting, the metropolitan is to prepare the agenda and preside over the meeting; in his absence this is to be done by the senior suffragan. In the case of a regional or national meeting the task is to be carried out by the president of the respective Conference.

ARTICLE IV

1. The meetings are to be held at fixed intervals, in accordance with the rule laid down in the motu proprio *Ecclesiae Sanctae*, 10. It is fitting that they should be held during the usual assemblies of the bishops.

2. The periodical meetings are convened in order that the bishops may propose candidates, or, if appropriate, supply further information concerning candidates previously proposed. It may also happen that some candidate previously put forward should no longer be

kept on the list, because of age, ill health or some other reason making him unfit for the episcopal office.

ARTICLE V

At a suitable time before the meeting, the names of the candidates to be proposed shall be sent to the president by those who have the right and duty to be present at the assembly. The president, with proper precautions, shall take care to communicate to them the complete list of names.

They shall examine the names of the candidates and consider what they know about each one.

ARTICLE VI

1. At the meeting the bishops shall share their information and observations on each candidate, indicating whether they are speaking from first-hand knowledge or expressing what they have heard from others.

2. The candidates are to be examined in such a way that it may be seen whether they are endowed with the qualities necessary for a good pastor of souls and teacher of the faith: whether they enjoy a good reputation; whether they are of irreproachable morality; whether they are endowed with right judgment and prudence; whether they are even-tempered and of stable character; whether they firmly hold the orthodox faith; whether they are devoted to the Apostolic See and faithful to the magisterium of the Church; whether they have a thorough knowledge of dogmatic and moral theology and canon law; whether they are outstanding for their piety, their spirit of sacrifice and their pastoral zeal; whether they have an aptitude for governing. Consideration must also be given to intellectual qualities, studies completed, social sense, spirit of dialogue and cooperation, openness to the signs of the times, praiseworthy impartiality, family background, health, age and inherited characteristics.

ARTICLE VII

1. When the discussion has been completed, votes, or abstentions, concerning each candidate are to be expressed in writing or in some other suitable manner.

2. Votes are to be cast in secret, to preserve the complete freedom

of each one in voting. It is fitting that, apart from the vote itself, a clear indication should be given of the nature of the diocese or office for which each candidate appears more suitable.

3. After the votes have been cast for each candidate, they are to be exactly counted.

4. If it seems advantageous, the president may invite the bishops to hold a further discussion on one or more candidates, and have another vote taken, so that the particular characteristics of each candidate may be clarified.

ARTICLE VIII

1. Before the close of the meeting a list is to be drawn up of those who, being worthy of and suitable for the episcopal office, are to be proposed to the Apostolic See.

2. Likewise, before the meeting closes everything from which it might be possible to discover how each has voted is to be destroyed. However, the minutes of the meeting are to be drawn up according to the norms of the law.

3. It is very desirable that the bishops should not depart before they have read, approved and signed the minutes.

ARTICLE IX

The president of the meeting will send to the Apostolic See through the Pontifical Representative a complete copy of the minutes and of the list of candidates.

ARTICLE X

1. In the case of nations where there is more than one ecclesiastical province, if at least two-thirds of those with a deliberative vote in the national episcopal conference judge it opportune, the list drawn up by a provincial or regional meeting shall be sent for information to the president of the national episcopal conference. He can add comments and information, keeping in mind the needs and circumstances of the Church in the whole country.

2. Likewise, if the majority, specified in the preceding paragraph, of the members of the national episcopal conference consider it opportune, it may be arranged that either a permanent committee of the conference, or a special commission, of restricted size, may add com-

ments and information as in paragraph 1 above. The members of this special commission will be elected for a fixed term by the plenary meeting of the conference; the president of the national conference will preside over the commission.

ARTICLE XI

1. When candidates for a particular episcopal office are to be proposed to the Apostolic See, the lists drawn up by the provincial meetings, or by regional or national meetings in the cases described in article II, 2, are to be taken into account.

2. These lists however do not detract from the liberty of the Roman pontiff, who in virtue of his office is always free to choose and appoint men who do not appear on the lists.

ARTICLE XII

1. Before any candidate is appointed bishop, the Apostolic See conducts a careful and wide-ranging inquiry about him. It consults individually people who know him very well and who are able to provide the fullest possible information and to make before God a prudent and considered judgment about him.

2. This inquiry is entrusted to the pontifical representative. He submits the questions drawn up for this purpose to ecclesiastics; bishops, priests and religious. Prudent and genuinely reliable lay people who possess useful information about the candidate can also be consulted in the same way.

ARTICLE XIII

1. When there is a question of appointing someone to a diocese or of naming a coadjutor with right of succession, the pontifical representative will ask the vicar capitular or apostolic administrator or the ordinary himself for a full and careful report on the condition and needs of the diocese. The clergy and laity, especially through their canonically established representative bodies, may also be consulted, as well as religious.

2. Apart from cases legitimately exempted by a particular law or custom or for some other reason, before proposing the "ternae" to the Apostolic See, the pontifical representative has the task of requesting, individually, the suggestions of the metropolitan and suffragans of the

province to which the vacant diocese belongs, or whose meeting it attends, as well as those of the president of the national episcopal conference. These suggestions, together with his own recommendation, he will then transmit to the Apostolic See. The pontifical representative moreover will, as may be opportune, hear the opinions of some members of the cathedral chapter, or of the diocesan consultors, and of other members of the clergy, both secular and religious, especially members of the priests' council in existence while the diocese is still filled.

3. With the necessary adjustments, a similar method of procedure is to be followed by those who have the task of proposing candidates for nomination as auxiliary bishops.

ARTICLE XIV

In all these matters, the prescribed "papal secret" is to be strictly observed by the bishops, the pontifical representative, the priests and the laity in any way involved. This is demanded by the very nature of the matter and by the respect due to the persons being considered.

ARTICLE XV

Maintaining unaltered the desire expressed by the Second Vatican Ecumenical Council in the Decree *Christus Dominus*, 20, concerning the free election of bishops, the preceding norms neither abrogate nor replace the privileges or rights that have been lawfully acquired, or special procedures approved by the Apostolic See by agreement or in some other way.

INDICES

Index of Scriptural References

General Index